I & II CHRONICLES, EZRA, NEHEMIAH

Introduction and Commentary

by

P E T E R R. A C K R O Y D

Samuel Davidson Professor of Old Testament Studies
University of London, King's College

SCM PRESS LTD
BLOOMSBURY STREET LONDON

334 00235 4 *(paper)*
334 00233 8 *(cased)*

First published 1973

© *SCM Press Ltd 1973*

Printed in Great Britain by
Northumberland Press Limited
Gateshead

CONTENTS

INTRODUCTION

COMMENTARY

THE TRUE PEOPLE OF GOD

DAVID

5

C. FROM REFORM TO DISASTER
II Chronicles 28-36

THE BOOKS OF EZRA & NEHEMIAH
THE BOOK OF EZRA
THE FIRST PERIOD OF RESTORATION

PREFACE

The introduction to this commentary makes some reference to the problems of writing a short book on so substantial an Old Testament work as 'The Work of the Chronicler', the four books of I and II Chronicles, Ezra and Nehemiah. Inevitably many questions are not handled or are touched on only very briefly. For the historical background, for geographical questions, and for many of the details concerning the life and thought, the institutions and religious practices and beliefs of the people of the Old Testament, the reader must turn to the general books on these and other topics and to the larger commentaries, some of which are noted on pp 13-15. The translation on which the commentary is based is that of the Revised Standard Version; other versions, particularly the New English Bible and the Jerusalem Bible, may usefully be consulted for different interpretations and suggestions. I must express my particular thanks to my secretary, Miss Jean Kemble, and to others who have assisted with the typing of the manuscript; and to Miss Enid Mellor for help with the reading of the proofs. And to the Press which has waited a very long time for the completion of this commentary, I must present my apologies for the delay.

PETER R. ACKROYD

ABBREVIATIONS

ANEP   *The Ancient Near East in Pictures Relating to the Old Testament*, 2nd edition with supplement, ed. J. B. Pritchard, Princeton University Press 1969

ANET   *Ancient Near Eastern Texts Relating to the Old Testament*, 3rd edition with supplement, ed. J. B. Pritchard, Princeton University Press 1969

DOTT   *Documents from Old Testament Times*, ed. D. Winton Thomas, Nelson, London 1958; Harper, New York (paperback) 1961

Heb.   Hebrew text

LXX   Septuagint, the Greek version of the Old Testament

MS(S)   Manuscript(s)

NEB   New English Bible

RSV, RSVmg   Revised Standard Version (margin)

RV   Revised Version

SELECT BIBLIOGRAPHY

Commentaries

BATTEN, L. W., *Ezra and Nehemiah* (International Critical Commentary), T. and T. Clark, Edinburgh 1913 (1949)

BROCKINGTON, L. H., *Ezra, Nehemiah and Esther* (The Century Bible, New Series), Nelson, London 1969 – the series now published by Oliphants, London

CURTIS, E. L. and MADSEN, A. A., *The Books of Chronicles* (International Critical Commentary), T. and T. Clark, Edinburgh 1910 (1952)

GALLING, K., *Die Bücher der Chronik, Esra, Nehemia* (Das Alte Testament Deutsch), Vandenhoeck und Ruprecht, Göttingen 1954 (1958)

MICHAELI, F., *Les Livres des Chroniques, d'Esdras et de Néhémie* (Commentaire de l'Ancien Testament), Delachaux et Niestlé, Neuchâtel 1967

MYERS, J. M., *I Chronicles, II Chronicles, Ezra, Nehemiah* (3 vols., The Anchor Bible), Doubleday, New York 1965

RUDOLPH, W., *Chronikbücher* (Handbuch zum Alten Testament), J. C. B. Mohr, Tübingen 1955

RUDOLPH, W., *Esra und Nehemia* (Handbuch zum Alten Testament), J. C. B. Mohr, Tübingen 1949

Short commentaries

ELMSLIE, W. A. L., BOWMAN, R., in *The Interpreter's Bible*, Vol. III, Abingdon Press, Nashville 1954

NORTH, R., in *The Jerome Biblical Commentary*, Geoffrey Chapman, London 1968

BROWNE, L. E., in *New Peake's Commentary on the Bible*, Nelson, London 1962

13

FRITSCH, C. T., in *The Interpreter's One-volume Commentary on the Bible*, Abingdon Press, Nashville 1971

MULCAHY, F., SIMSON, P., in *A New Catholic Commentary on Holy Scripture*, Nelson, London 1969

ACKROYD, PETER R., *1 and 2 Chronicles, Ezra, Nehemiah, etc.* (Mowbrays Mini-Commentary), A. R. Mowbray, London 1970

General works

ACKROYD, PETER R., *Israel Under Babylon and Persia* (New Clarendon Bible), Oxford 1970

ANDERSON, G. W., *A Critical Introduction to the Old Testament*, Duckworth, London 1959

BRIGHT, JOHN, *A History of Israel*, rev. ed., SCM Press, London 1972

EISSFELDT, O., *The Old Testament: an Introduction*, Blackwell, Oxford 1965

FOHRER, G., *Introduction to the Old Testament*, SPCK, London 1970

NOTH, M., *The History of Israel*, rev. ed., A. and C. Black, London 1960

DE VAUX, R., *Ancient Israel. Its Life and Institutions*, Darton, Longman and Todd, London 1961

Special studies

ACKROYD, PETER R., *The Age of the Chronicler* (Supplement to *Colloquium – The Australian and New Zealand Theological Review*, 1970)

ACKROYD, PETER R., 'History and Theology in the Writings of the Chronicler', *Concordia Theological Monthly* 38, 1967, pp. 501-15

POHLMANN, K.-F., *Studien zum dritten Esra. Ein Beitrag zur Frage nach dem ursprünglichen Schluss des chronistischen Werkes*, Vandenhoeck und Ruprecht, Göttingen 1970

VON RAD, G., 'The Levitical Sermon in I and II Chronicles', in *The Problem of the Hexateuch and other essays*, Oliver and Boyd, Edinburgh 1966, pp. 267-80
(Most of these works contain bibliographical references to the literature on the subject)

A good biblical atlas should also be consulted, e.g. H. G. May, *Oxford Bible Atlas*, Oxford University Press 1962

BC

1000	David *c.* 1000-961
	Solomon *c.* 961-922
	Division of kingdoms
900	Jehoshaphat *c.* 873-849
800	Uzziah *c.* 783-742
	721 Fall of Samaria
700	Hezekiah *c.* 715-687
600	Josiah *c.* 640-609
	597 1st Fall of Jerusalem
	587 2nd Fall of Jerusalem
	538 Cyrus' conquest of Babylon
	515 Rebuilt temple
500	
	445-433 Nehemiah
	432-? Nehemiah – second term
400	
	398* Ezra
300	
	*Cf. the discussion on pp 24-26

LOGICAL TABLE

			BC
			1000
			900
		—	800
	Amos	Period	
	Hosea	of	
	Isaiah	Assyrian	700
	Micah	Power	
	Jeremiah	—	
		Period of	600
	Ezekiel	Neo-Babylonian	
	Second Isaiah	Power	
Cyrus 550-530		—	
Cambyses 530-522	Haggai		
Darius I 522-486	Zechariah		500
		Period	
Xerxes I 486-465		of	
		Persian	
Artaxerxes I 465-424		Power	
Darius II 423-404			400
Artaxerxes II 404-358			
Darius III 336-331		Alexander the Great	
		Greek Rule	300

(For fuller detail, cf. New Clarendon Bible volumes and John Bright, History of Israel, *rev. ed., SCM Press, London 1972)*

INTRODUCTION

A LINE OF APPROACH

Producing a short commentary on the writings of the Chronicler presents certain problems. A quite substantial proportion of the material included in his work is also to be found, often in a virtually identical form, in the books of Samuel and Kings and in Pentateuchal lists of names and genealogies. Whereas in a full-scale commentary it would be proper to discuss much that would by necessity also belong in a commentary on the earlier works, if the present volume is to be kept to a manageable size the reader will have to be asked to turn for a discussion of many of the details to the commentaries on these other books. This is not an ideal situation, but it is appropriate to the present purpose.

Yet it is not possible or desirable to carry through a completely consistent policy in this matter. Some comment is often needed on the small differences between the two forms of the text, though the precise relationship is not easy to determine in every case and we certainly cannot simply assume that every difference is due to the Chronicler's own viewpoint, his modification or editing of the earlier material. The additions and omissions are likely to shed light on his purpose, but so too is the placing of the material. Even where in a particular passage the two texts are virtually identical, or where we may be able to detect little that points to the Chronicler's own modifications of an existing text, we have to consider whether the selection and ordering may not themselves reveal something of what the author is doing.

The reader must therefore be prepared to do two things. He must be willing to find that many points are not explained and must look for information elsewhere. He must also strike

a balance between looking only for signs of how the Chronicler
modified his sources and endeavouring to see how a particular section fits into the overall impression which he may
gain of what type of theological interpretation is being offered.

Here again there are sources of difficulty. While in this
commentary relatively little space will be devoted to the very
difficult literary problems (the questions of earlier and later
material, the additions made subsequently to the main structure of the work), we must nevertheless be aware that we are
ultimately dealing with a work which is not all of one piece,
and that conclusions regarding the viewpoint of the author(s)
are in large measure dependent on the degree to which we
are able to detect the literary processes. As a general principle
of working here, it seems best to make an assumption – and
to abandon it only where the evidence is clearly opposed to
it. This assumption is that the modifications and additions
made to the work after its main stage of composition are not
to be regarded as totally contrary to its purpose. This may be
seen in the Nehemiah narratives, which are here treated as a
later addition to the main work; they are not so different in
outlook for us to be forced to assume that whoever inserted
them was quite unsympathetic to the main purpose of the
work. Similarly some extensions of the David material may
be held to point towards a greater degree of political concern
in the restoration of the Davidic monarchy, where the
Chronicler appears rather to have seen the Davidic 'idea' as
a fruitful one for re-thinking and representing the history of
his people. Such a difference of emphasis, if sharpened, could
be regarded as offering a correction of a view of life that was
too detached from politics, too quietistic; but there can be a
wide variety of intermediate positions between the political
activist and the quietist. We need not divide quite so sharply
as to find polemic where there is perhaps only a difference
of emphasis and a concern for the meaning of the material
for a particular situation. What the Chronicler saw to be
theologically valid in the fourth century BC is not necessarily
going to be the same for a writer of the second century BC.
The Chronicler with his more quietistic thinking is one with

the activists of the later period in the intensity of his religious loyalty; he could well have stood close to the writer of the book of Daniel, himself perhaps more of a quietist than an activist.

Again, our basis for detecting the Chronicler's viewpoint must be in part our consideration of the ways in which he modifies his source material. Our knowledge of the history of the text – particularly in the light of the Qumran discoveries and of the text of the Greek translations – suggests that there was more than one text-form at any given moment. If it is likely that the Chronicler used a text of Samuel–Kings very close to that which we know, there is much to suggest that his text was not identical with ours. Only a detailed examination of every verse can determine with some degree of probability whether the differences between the texts are due to deliberate modifications, or to the many chances and changes which affect all texts which are copied and re-copied over a period of many years.

It is here that the reader must be urged to read the work as a whole. There are long sections which he will look at only briefly, though their place in the whole must be appreciated. But it just will not do to read the Chronicler's work solely to pick up the bits and pieces of information which are not found in the earlier works, or merely in order to consider which version of a narrative has greater historical verisimilitude. The great advantage for us in having two major presentations of the course of Israel's history from Exodus to Exile (and beyond) is that we are able the better to appreciate that these are theological works, offering interpretations of stories which were for the most part well known. The fact that the books from Joshua to II Kings are a major source for the history of Israel, and shed light too on the life of the ancient Near East, must not blind us to the fact that their real concern is much more than a historical one. The possibility – a real one, though much exaggerated in recent years – that the work of the Chronicler preserves some otherwise unknown but reliable historical material does not alter the fact that the whole presentation offered here is, as we can see, a theology couched in the form of narrative and sermon, prayer and comment, list and genealogy. The almost obsessive concern with history which has become so much a part of our theological make-up has meant that the work of the Chronicler has been used most often to fill supposed gaps; this is a misunderstanding which can be traced as far back as the title given to the books of Chronicles in the Greek translation: *ta paraleipomena*, the things omitted. It is almost as if someone, observing that Calvin does not deal with a particular theological question, were to interpolate passages from Karl Barth in a reading of Calvin's *Institutes*. Yet this is what happens when, as often in the artificially contrived lectionaries commonly in use in Christian churches of various persuasions, long sections from Samuel and Kings are inter-rupted with single passages or narratives from Chronicles, without the reader or hearer being reminded that two hundred years or so separates these works and that the Chronicler's overall viewpoint is by no means identical with that of his predecessors, however much he may owe to the influence of their profound assessment of their people's life and condi-tion.

LITERARY PROBLEMS

The treatment of the four books – as they appear in the English Bible – within one commentary rests on the assump-tion that they really do form parts of one substantial work. The view is not universally held, and some considerable dif-ferences have been traced between the language and style in the books of Chronicles and that in the books of Ezra and Nehemiah. A recent very strong statement in support of dividing the work has been put forward by S. Japhet in an article entitled 'The Supposed Common Authorship of Chron. and Ezra-Neh. Investigated Anew', *Vetus Testamentum* 18, 1968, pp.330-71. Other scholars have supposed that a first stage in the development of the work is to be found in a rework-ing of the earlier history of Samuel–Kings shortly after the exile, with a selection of the material concerned with Jerusalem and the temple, and that it is upon this that the later work rests. Others have suggested the existence of a much expanded version of Samuel–Kings – the so-called 'Midrash' mentioned in II Chron. 13.22; 24.27 (translated in RSV as 'story' and 'Commentary') – and supposed the Chronicler to be using this. Such views are not in fact entirely mutually exclusive, for we must remember that every copy of an ancient work may be in some degree a new edition, though we need also to consider, with a degree of controlled imagination, for what particular situation a copy was being made.

Discussion of the literary problems is made very difficult by uncertainties about the degree to which the work in its present form represents an expansion of an earlier one. It will be noted at various points in the commentary that some at least of the archival material – some scholars would argue for much of it, e.g. the whole of I Chronicles 1-9 – has been added later to the text. Some have proposed a thoroughgoing 'two-edition' theory, but the additions, where they are sufficiently agreed, do not appear to have the kind of consistency which would point to a single revision. It is more probable that this writing at first had a less authoritative status than the books of Samuel and Kings (and other books which had already acquired something approaching a canonical position), and so additions could be made to it more readily. The difficulties of decision in these matters are heightened by the evidence we can see in the text of quite substantial differences in the handling of sources. Sometimes, as we can see from a comparison of the text of Chronicles with Samuel–Kings, there is a very close correspondence. Then suddenly there is a marked departure. When we come to the second part of the work in Ezra and Nehemiah the problem is made more difficult, since we do not have an earlier form with which to make a comparison. How far did the Chronicler rewrite here? How far did he simply take over the existing material? Some of what appear to be differences between the books of Chronicles and the books of Ezra and Nehemiah may be due to changes of method.

There is one important point, however, at which there is a growing, though not unanimous, conviction that the work has received a substantial addition. This is in regard to the account of Nehemiah's activity. The view that the Nehemiah account was an independent work, incorporated at a later stage in the last section of the Chronicler's work, has much to commend it. This does not resolve all the problems, because when the combining took place there was still room for a considerable measure of harmonization. But at this point the literary problems tie up with a major historical one.

THE HISTORICAL PROBLEM OF EZRA AND NEHEMIAH

A close examination of the narratives from Ezra 7 to Nehemiah 13 reveals a great many curious chronological and other problems. Ostensibly, if the narratives are read as they stand, Ezra came first, to be followed thirteen years later by Nehemiah, and only then did Ezra undertake the commission on which he had been sent. Furthermore, although at a few points both names appear together, there is no overlap of their work, nor real relationship between them. A close study of the detail strongly suggests that Nehemiah came first and that Ezra followed at a later date. The arguments for this lie in matters of relationship to external historical evidence, particularly that of the Aramaic documents from Elephantine (some of which will be found in DOTT and ANET), from which the date of Nehemiah in the twentieth year of Artaxerxes I may be regarded as sufficiently established. If Ezra came later, then the date in Ezra 7 must either be in error – a figure missing (this view of the matter is presented very fully in John Bright's *History of Israel*) – or the date must refer to a different ruler of the same name, i.e. Artaxerxes II. This latter date has been assumed in the present commentary because it appears to me to fit the evidence best. A short exposition of the matter may be found in my *Israel under Babylon and Persia*, pp.191-6; fuller discussions may be found in L. H. Brockington, *Ezra, Nehemiah and Esther*, pp.29ff.; H. H. Rowley, 'The Chronological Order of Ezra and Nehemiah', in *The Servant of the Lord*, Lutterworth Press, London 1952, 2nd ed. Blackwell, Oxford 1965; and J. A. Emerton, 'Did Ezra go to Jerusalem in 428 BC?', *Journal of Theological Studies* 17, 1966, pp.1ff., this being a critical discussion of Bright's views and those of others who take a similar position.

To the points of detail – some of which will be seen by the reader in the text itself – some general ones may be added. First we may note that Josephus in his *Antiquities of the Jews*, XI, 5, treats the two men separately and not as partly contemporary, as in the present biblical text. Josephus' account of the whole post-exilic period presents many problems for historical interpretation, and not too much weight should be laid on it. But the separation is confirmed by the discovery that in the praise of the forefathers in Ecclesiasticus (the Wisdom of Jesus ben Sira) 49, Nehemiah is named but not Ezra; in II Maccabees *1*, enormous weight is given to Nehemiah's work, so that he becomes the builder of the temple. In I Esdras in the Apocrypha, a part only of the Chronicler's work is given, extending from the reform of Josiah to the law-reading by Ezra, with no place for the Nehemiah material; and in II Esdras we may observe the further glorification of Ezra. It looks very much as though traditions concerning these two great men were handed down separately, and that when they are combined – as in the biblical text and in Josephus' placing of them side by side – there is no clear knowledge of how they are related to one another.

The question then arises: when did the Chronicler write? For this may help to clarify the problem. So long as it was supposed that he had dovetailed the work of the two men, it had to be thought that if the order was wrong, either he was very muddled – and so were his readers – or that he wrote a very long time after the date of Ezra. On the other hand, the lack of any indication that Persian rule has come to an end, and the very evident high place given to Ezra, strongly suggests that he wrote not very long after Ezra but before the conquest of Persia by Alexander the Great, perhaps in the middle of the fourth century BC. If the Nehemiah material was not part of the original work, then the disorder was not the Chronicler's responsibility, but rests upon a quite understandable confusion in the minds of those who, at a later date, believed that the dates must refer to the same ruler.

The resolving of these questions remains a problem on which there is no full agreement. The working hypothesis adopted in this commentary is that Nehemiah came first, and that the account of his work developed independently of the Chronicler's writing. This would also account for differences of style. Ezra came later, and it was to him that the Chronicler looked as he endeavoured to assess the position of his community in the mid-fourth century BC.

The complexity of the relationship is made greater by two further factors. A study of the later traditions concerning both men reveals that similar things are being said about both of them – for example, they are both credited with involvement in the formation of the canon of scripture, and both credited with substantial involvement in the rehabilitation of worship. Overlap within the biblical books themselves – particularly evident in the last part of the Nehemiah account – suggests that these heroes of post-exilic life have been in some degree 'paired' and that the traditions concerning the one have influenced the development of the traditions concerning the other, in addition to some measure of harmonizing once the two were brought together. Such cross-influence from one great figure to another may be detected elsewhere in the Old Testament, for example in the figures of Moses and Aaron, and Elijah and Elisha. A fuller discussion may be found in the second chapter of my *The Age of the Chronicler*, where some of the consequences for interpretation are drawn out; these have been used in the comments on individual passages.

THE PURPOSE OF THE WORK

It is clear that a statement of a general kind can only be made satisfactorily in regard to the main moment in the development of this complex writing. And our assessment of it depends first on a decision about the date – already suggested as *c.* 350 BC – and then on any knowledge we may have of the situation at that time to which the work may have been directed. On this second point, we draw largely a blank, since our knowledge of the fourth century BC is minimal. The work of the Chronicler itself provides us with a major source of information, but here we have to beware of arguing in a circle – from what we deduce from this work as to the conditions to which it is directed and from those conditions back to the interpretation of the work. At a more general level, however, we may see that there must be relevance in what is being said to a position of political dependence; and from this see that a re-presentation of the ancient history, from creation onwards, but particularly from David onwards, must be designed to show the meaning of that past to the contemporary situation. It is here that we may stress the strongly homiletical aspects of the work, and see the Chronicler 'preaching' his people's history. His themes of preaching are consistent and limited, but they are profound. It has often been supposed that he presents merely a rather rigid view of divine retribution, and applies this doctrine blindly to his material. What seems much clearer is that he sees a great overall pattern in experience, and that this is presented in terms of failure and judgment, grace and restoration. It is not for nothing that the exile at the end of II Chronicles marks a decisive break; indeed the convention of dividing the history of Israel at 587 BC may be said to derive ultimately from the Chronicler's view, though in this he rested heavily on his predecessors, the Deuteronomic writers of Joshua to II Kings. He sees his contemporaries in the middle of the great new era of restoration, though he is fully aware of the problems which being a subject people presents for the recognition of that ideal. He traces through the earlier history a pattern of unbelief and disaster, of faith and restoration, which provides a theological unity for the whole.

Within this, he presents the work of David as determinative, for here the full establishment of the people as a worshipping community, resting upon older Mosaic prescription, is set out. The contemporary restoration represents the re-expression of that Davidic ideal, separated from its political aspects. He is concerned, through narrative and through genealogy, to show the reality of a continuing community, the true people of God. If he is concerned with its purity, as especially in Ezra's work, he is also aware of its potential breadth, for acceptance of the law is the mark of belonging. There is a degree of appeal for uniformity of belief, the establishment of an orthodox position, and also some measure of ecumenism, the call to all who will separate themselves from alien influences to join the true community. To his work, the narrative of Nehemiah added a comparable but not identical note of protection and security, and perhaps at some points a sharper tone of division from the outside world. If, as some have thought, the Nehemiah narrative in its present form reflects in some degree the second-century situation, with its acute religious and political divisions, it is perhaps not surprising that this severer tone appears.

What did the Chronicler achieve? What did Nehemiah and Ezra achieve? The attempt is often made in commentaries at summing up the life and work of the great heroes; but this is best done at the end, by the reader, after he has worked through the material. What may be said may perhaps be put in more general terms. It arises out of the reflection that of all the peoples of the ancient world some are known better historically or from the details of their day-to-day life; but none is so well known as the Old Testament community in its religious life and thought. Where the religion of other peoples – great and small alike – may in some degree be reconstructed out of documentary and other evidence, the Old Testament religion alone is attested by the continuity of its life in the Jewish and Christian communities and in some

measure also in Islam. The Chronicler – and with him
Nehemiah and Ezra, to whom his writings, as they now stand,
bear the fullest witness – is one of the theologians to whom
we may attribute that survival. He is one of those through
whom the great wealth of earlier thought came to be re-applied
and re-assessed, so that it was meaningful not only for his
generation but for those that followed.

THE TRUE PEOPLE OF GOD

I Chronicles 1-9

These opening chapters do not provide exciting reading: they consist almost entirely of lists of names with relatively few historical notes or narrative fragments. To a large extent, though not by any means entirely, they are related to other biblical lists, and it is therefore convenient to examine them with a text in which cross-references are given in the margin, as in full editions of RV, RSV and the Jerusalem Bible. There are many detailed problems of text, small deviations from other forms of the lists, inconsistencies within the existing form of the material, which makes the full study of the chapters a matter of great complexity. Where parallel texts exist, there are questions of relationship to be considered. Where no such parallels are available, we may still most naturally suppose that the element of chance in the survival of material has left us with deficient information.

The study of these chapters is, however, important to the understanding of the work as a whole. Whatever the precise literary history (cf. 22ff.), we are now confronted with a form of the Chronicler's work which includes this material, and, however much we may be tempted to look for earlier and less complex forms of the work, such earlier forms are inevitably purely hypothetical; this is essentially the only form we know. We cannot ignore the whole first part of a book without missing something of the author's intention.

That the lists provide important genealogical information, topographical material, pointers to historical situations, is clear, though the full elucidation of this is very delicate and its results are always open to debate. For our purpose, it is the theological intention which matters, for here, as we shall see as we look at the content of the individual chapters, we are led into an understanding of the nature of the people of God and of the relationship between divine purpose and human failure. The community of the post-exilic period to which the Chronicler belonged and for which he wrote is seen to be the descendant of that totality of Israel which lay within the creative and redemptive purpose of God. The writer points us through from the very creation of the first man to the tribes of the one Israel, to the true community within those tribes which was itself to fall under judgment; he portrays in these opening chapters, complex and sometimes overloaded as they are, an understanding of divine grace, through promise and failure and restoration, which is to be a major component of his theological interpretation of the contemporary situation of his own people. As we turn the pages of these lists we must not allow the detail to obscure this basic concern.

FROM ADAM TO ISRAEL

1.1-54

1-54. The Chronicler covers the period from Adam to Israel, the primary ancestor of his people, in a list of names. Sometimes a longer form is given, as in v. 34: ABRAHAM WAS THE FATHER OF ISAAC; but for the most part, only the names appear. Here and there an odd detail is preserved, as in the description of NIMROD in v.10 as A MIGHTY ONE; but whereas Gen. 10.9 explains this as meaning 'a hunter', here the meaning is left open. Does it mean 'warrior' or 'tyrant'? More probably, as often in these books, we should assume that the author expects his readers to be able to supply the detail from their knowledge of the traditions.

At each stage the subsidiary lines of descent are disposed of first (though we may note that the line of Cain is entirely excluded): JAPHETH and HAM (vv.5-16) before the first-born SHEM (vv.17-27); THE SONS OF SHEM other than the line leading to ABRAHAM (vv.17-23), before that line (vv.24-27). Primary interest clearly centres on the line of ISRAEL – who is referred to here only by this name and not as Jacob. The principle of divine election is being made plain at the outset. Yet the other lines are not omitted, as we might have expected. Concerned as the Chronicler is with the true line of Israel, we may wonder whether he does not here – as for example by his lengthy survey of the KINGS OF EDOM (vv.43-54) – remind his readers, as does Paul (Rom. 9-11), that physical descent is not everything, and also that their neighbours are not unrelated to them.

For him the time of David is central, and to this the lists lead; it was then that the neighbouring lands acknowledged the rule of Israel. Did he perhaps dream of a new age when such a widespread recognition of Israel's place should again be made? Such a thought is reflected in Zech. 9 – perhaps from the fourth or third century BC – as well as in other Old Testament passages, and in the second century BC the Hasmonean rulers endeavoured to give practical expression to it in bringing their neighbours forcibly within the pale of the Jewish community. Their method was disastrous, but we should not necessarily attribute to them motives only of national aggrandizement. The idea of a new Davidic age meant more than that. The elucidation of the Davidic theme is to prove a major concern of the Chronicler.

FROM ISRAEL TO THE CLANS OF JUDAH

2.1-55

1-2. Sons of Israel These verses are preparatory, and form a heading for the whole section to the end of ch.8, for here are the ancestors of the twelve tribes. But before this theme is developed, as it is in chs.4-8, there is a section dealing with JUDAH. Thus the order is different from that in ch.1, where the subsidiary lines are taken first. For here Judah, which emerges as the primary line, is taken first, and the lists show considerable signs of elaboration, particularly to emphasize the family of David, to whom the whole of ch.3 is devoted.

3-4. Judah A summary of the fortunes of the family, set out more fully in Gen. 38. The story of Judah and TAMAR is alluded to but not related; it is assumed that the reader will know the details. The true line of Judah derives strangely enough from Tamar; the point is picked up in the New Testament in the genealogy in Matt. 1.3.

5-6. Perez, Zerah From here to v.55 we have the various lines from the two sons of Judah from whom the later community derived its descent.

7. Achar This reminds us of the story of Achan (Josh. 7), but here the name is spelt differently, thus permitting a word-play, for the root means 'to trouble', and so Achar is THE TROUBLER OF ISRAEL; it is the phrase used also between Ahab and Elijah (I Kings 18.17f.). Such allusive use of phrases which appear in quite other contexts in the Old Testament is characteristic. In it, the Chronicler anticipates later Jewish and Christian exegetical method, inviting his readers to reflect at this point on the fact that Achan, like Ahab, had nearly brought total disaster on his people.

13-17. David These verses give extended space to his family (cf. ch.3): I Sam. 16 makes David the eighth son of Jesse, whereas here he is the seventh.

20. Bezalel His appearance provides a link to the making of the tabernacle (cf. Exod. 31.2-11; 35-39), which in its turn points forward to the building of the temple, so important a theme for the Chronicler.

In the verses which follow, there are many allusions to local and clan traditions, some of which can be filled in from elsewhere; but much remains obscure, as for example the allusions of vv.34-35.

42-50a. Caleb Continued in 50b-55. The lists give important indications of the areas claimed by tribal groups closely linked with Judah.

55. This verse contains an occupational note.

THE FAMILY OF DAVID

3.1-24

1-9. A list of the sons and daughters born to David, including, as do the source passages in II Sam. 3 and 5, some brief references to the actual period of reign of the king. The variant form BATHSHUA appears for the name Bathsheba in v.5. The story of David and Bathsheba (II Sam. 11-12) is not included in this book, but the reader will pick up the allusion. The special reference to David's daughter TAMAR (v.9) recalls the story of Absalom (II Sam. 13ff.), also not included in I Chron.

10-16. A list of the kings of Judah, omitting the non-Davidic usurper Athaliah. The information is found in detail in the full accounts in I and II Kings and II Chron., though one or two additional names appear here.

17-24. The line of David is continued from JECONIAH, THE CAPTIVE (cf. II Chron. 36.9) through the post-exilic period, though only some of the descendants are given, and these not at every stage in the line through the eldest son. This takes the family down to the seven sons of ELIOENAI (v.24). PEDAIAH (v.18) was the third son of the captive king of Judah, JECONIAH (Jehoiachin), who was eighteen years old in 598-597 BC; the last group of descendants mentioned belongs to the sixth or eleventh generation later (depending on the reading of v.21; cf. RSV text and mg). We may suppose that the list was compiled at a time when these last individuals were still young. It is difficult to determine the length of such a period, but it is unlikely to be much less than 150 or 275 years (allowing twenty-five years for each generation), so that we are here brought to about the middle of the fifth or towards the end of the fourth century BC.

This does not really help us with deciding the date of the Chronicler, since it is likely that the whole of this chapter is a later addition to the work. Had it been original, it would have been expected after 2.17; part of its material appears also in 14.3-7. Yet it elaborates the Chronicler's own interest in David by supplying in summary form information which we do not possess elsewhere. It does not, however, coincide with the genealogy of the Davidic family given in Matt. 1, and in addition it curiously gives Pedaiah as the father of Zerubbabel and not Shealtiel, as other texts indicate (cf. Ezra 3.2; Hag. 1.1). The list suggests that the Davidic family continued to be of importance in the post-exilic period. But the Chronicler nowhere seems to lay special stress on this. For him the Davidic *idea* appears to be more important than Davidic *descent*.

THE DESCENDANTS OF THE TRIBES

4.1-8.40

These five chapters deal with the twelve patriarchs, the sons of Israel, in turn. For the most part, there are lists of names, but there are also pieces of traditional material and historical notes. Fuller space is given to the family of Levi (ch.6), and this is to be expected in view of the particular interests of the Chronicler's work.

4.1-23. Judah This to some extent overlaps with ch. 2. At many points it is likely that this list and that of Simeon which follows reflects the inter-relationship of various clan groups in the southern part of Palestine.

9-10. Jabez A curious tradition. The name is noted in 2.55 as a place name associated with scribal families. A play on JABEZ and the word for PAIN (*ya'bēṣ,'ōṣeb* – the words have the same basic letters but not in the same order), perhaps a piece of popular etymology, introduces the assurance that God answers prayer and gives blessing.

11-15. These verses deal with various descendants of CALEB; it appears that they are smiths, like the Kenites. RSVmg has 'valley of craftsmen' for GE-HARASHIM (v.14), a translation of the proper name; for IR-NAHASH (v.12) we may perhaps understand 'city of bronze', suggesting a further link with metal-working.

17. RSV places the last clause of v.18 here, and this provides a clearer order. It is interesting to note that in these verses there is reference to a Jewish wife and also to a wife THE DAUGHTER OF PHARAOH. We may observe that these genealogies do not exclude the descendants of foreign marriages.

21–23. A further piece of tradition indicates various craft groups – linen workers and royal potters. Jars with royal pottery marks from a number of sites in the Judaean area are well known to archaeologists.

24–43. Simeon It is clear that here the absorption of Simeon into Judah is reflected (cf. the comment on the smaller numbers of Simeon in v.27 and the indications of the Simeonite cities until the reign of David in vv.28-31). Comparison may be made with other, probably earlier, Simeon lists in Josh. 19.2-7 and 15.26-32, 42. Verses 39-43 indicate the fortunes of Simeonite groups which moved to other areas. If 'Gerar' is read with the LXX in v.39 for GEDOR, one movement is indicated as to the coastal area of rich pastures, and the second is eastward to the Amalekite territory in the region of Mount Seir. The first of these movements is attributed to the reign of Hezekiah. The phrase TO THIS DAY (vv.41, 43) may simply mean 'in perpetuity'.

5.1-26 The tribes of Transjordan.

1–3. Reuben The oldest son of Israel is introduced with a reminiscence of the shameful act (Gen. 35.22) which led to his disinheritance. The birthright passed to the sons of Joseph (cf. Gen. 48.8-22), though Judah took pre-eminence (v.2).

4–10. Joel This family, evidently a line of Reubenite chieftains, is traced to the time of Assyrian conquest in the mid-eighth century (v.6). Certain historical details are included here linking them with settlement in areas which belonged to Moab (v.8) and extending east to the Euphrates. In the time

of Saul they are said to have defeated THE HAGRITES (Arabian
tribes) and to have lived EAST OF GILEAD (vv.9-10).

11-17. Gad This is a tribal group living also beyond Jordan,
in GILEAD and BASHAN (v.16). The information here is associated with the period of JOTHAM of Judah and JEROBOAM (II)
of Israel, i.e. about the middle of the eighth century BC (v.17).
All these groups were evidently cattle-breeders, wandering
in the pastoral lands of the eastern area as the changing
seasons required; they did not fully occupy such a large
territory, but presumably claimed it as their area within which
they could by right pasture their flocks and herds.

18-22. A different kind of list is introduced here, a kind of
military census. It also indicates warfare against THE HAG-
RITES (cf. v.10), and introduces a favourite conception of the
Chronicler, namely that those who cry to God in battle, who
put their trust in him, find deliverance; the help referred to
is, of course, divine help. The text of v.20 is not completely
clear; a possible alternative rendering is: 'they overpowered
them and the Hagrites ... were given into their hands'. The
war (v.22) is indeed described as a holy war, one to which
the people's God has sent them and in which he himself is
the giver of victory. The Chronicler's battles are often in
fact almost liturgical demonstrations of the power of God,
and not military combat at all. The settlement of these groups
in this area is indicated as lasting until their exile, presumably
at the hands of TILGATH-PILNESER (erroneously for Tiglath-
pileser, also PUL, as here in v.26). It is not completely clear
from the text whether the Chronicler knew that the two
names indicated one Assyrian ruler, or whether he thought
there were two rulers involved.

23-25. The half-tribe of Manasseh Its apostasy led to disaster, and it was carried away into exile by the Assyrians.

26. This verse takes up v.25 in interpreting the history of all
these tribes in theological terms, closely linked to Deuteronomic and prophetic thought.

In the main narrative of II Chron. the fortunes of the
northern kingdom are rarely alluded to; for the Chronicler,
their history is one of apostasy, and he concentrates his
attention on Judah. But these lists fill in the picture in some
measure, and they serve also as a pointer to an important
element in the Chronicler's thought – his belief that those
who are willing, even from the apostate north, can be re-
united with the true people of God.

6.1–81.* Levi A much fuller treatment of a family which
was clearly of central importance to the Chronicler, whose
concern with the temple and its institutions is so great. Some
of the themes adumbrated here are much more fully developed in the subsequent narratives. The present form of the
material shows signs of different stages of compilation, for
there are some clear overlaps.

1-15. These verses begin with a brief statement of the SONS
OF LEVI, leading to the naming of the four sons of AARON
(v.3). For the purposes of the present material, the interest
rests in the line of high priests to the exile, listed as descendants of ELEAZAR. The wider aspects of the priesthood are
picked up again at I Chron. 24. The list, partly repeated in
vv.50-53, is perhaps intended to have a balanced structure –
twelve names to the time of Solomon, twelve names (perhaps
with the addition of Jehoiada, accidentally omitted – cf. II
Chron. 22-24) to the fall of Jerusalem, though the numbers
are not completely clear. (A comparable artificial arrangement is to be seen in the genealogy in Matt. 1.) The list is
picked up again in Neh. 12 for the post-exilic period. Such
a tracing of priestly genealogy is important for the establishment of legitimacy of priestly activity (cf. Ezra 2.59-63 for
the problem created by priests without confirmed ancestry).
For the continuity of worship after the exile a clear link with
the earlier priesthood was vital, and we may note that the

* Heb. 5.27-41; 6.1-66. Verses 1-15 correspond to Heb. 5.27-41.
For ch.6, the Heb. verse numbers are in each case 15 less than the
English.

Samaritans equally claimed such a reliable ancestry for their priesthood.

16-47. The Levites came gradually to be regarded as a group especially set aside for technical religious duties. They are described here, as elsewhere, as belonging to a particular tribe, one which lost its normal position among the tribes of Israel, but acquired a special place for its religious duties and a special inheritance, 'the LORD himself' (Deut. 10.9). After a listing of families, vv.31ff. stress the place of the levitical singers whose position and responsibility were ordained by David. This is a theme to which much attention is devoted subsequently (cf. I Chron. 15-16), and one which was clearly central to the Chronicler's interests. The ordering of the three groups – those of HEMAN, ASAPH and ETHAN – places Heman first, though elsewhere we find Asaph in this position and there are other important names which appear, notably that of Korah. Perhaps there are here reflections of changes in the levitical orders over some period of time. An odd feature in these lists is the appearance of the name of SAMUEL (vv.28, 33). According to the story in the opening chapters of I Sam., he was not of a levitical family but belonged to the tribe of Ephraim. It would appear likely that his priestly and prophetic activities have led to the assumption that he must in reality have belonged to the proper family. He is also (v.33) ancestor of an important family of musicians.

48-53. The same point appears when we consider the further description of Levites and priests, where there is first a distinction made between the Levites who perform the whole range of duties and the Aaronite line which alone is permitted to engage in sacrificial practice. Then we have yet again the list of the priests in the line from ELEAZAR (cf. vv.4-9), culminating here in ZADOK and AHIMAAZ. The real ancestry of Zadok is unknown; most often it is supposed from his sudden and unexplained appearance in the David narratives and his prominence under Solomon that he belonged to the pre-Israelite, Jebusite priesthood of Jerusalem. His incorporation into the family of Aaron is then to be regarded as a pious fiction, designed to stress the legitimacy of the Jerusalem priesthood over against all others.

54-81. The remainder of the chapter lists the lands which are allocated to the levitical families for their support. The material is closely based on Josh. 21, itself perhaps derived from a list of the cities in which there were ancient sanctuaries. These had also been places of refuge for those who had committed manslaughter. The centralizing policy of Josiah necessitated a secularizing of this practice, as we may see in Deuteronomy. The connection of the Levites with the sanctuaries is then preserved by the territorial link with them. We may perhaps wonder at the attention to geographical detail which goes into such lists as these. They may be seen to express the conviction that the land belongs to God. The placing of Levites throughout the territories of all the tribes makes plain the claim which, as the servants of God in a special sense, they make upon land and people. There is here a concern with the whole relationship between God and people, and this chapter, with its levitical and priestly names and places, prepares for the central place of worship in the Chronicler's writing.

7.1-40. This chapter completes the survey of the tribes, but problems immediately appear. We note that Benjamin (vv. 6-12) reappears in ch.8 in a much longer list of names; Dan and Zebulun are missing. Furthermore, it is clear that these lists are not all of one kind, and in marked ways they differ from those of the preceding chapters. The compiler has made use of a great wealth of traditional material; he has preserved within it scraps of story about particular tribes and individuals. In particular, he has here made use of census lists and military lists unlike those of chs.4-5.

7.1-5 Issachar We note here the stress on the period of David; this is a pointer to the share which all the tribes are to have in placing David on the throne of Israel (cf. 11.1-3).

6-12. Benjamin In reality v.12 stands outside the section, and it seems very probable that the second half of that verse conceals a fragmentary reference to Dan: 'Son of Dan: Hushim, a single son' (cf. Gen. 46.23; Num. 26.42).

13. Naphtali and
14-19. Manasseh Here we may observe some curious pieces of tradition, and in particular an emphasis on the mothers of various of the persons mentioned. The reference to the DAUGHTERS of ZELOPHEHAD (v.15) is a pointer to an important piece of legal narrative in Num. 27 and 36.

20-29. Ephraim Some narrative material is built into the lists in vv.21-24. Neither the Manasseh nor the Ephraim verses contain census numbers as do the other main lists in this chapter.

30-40. Asher

8.1-40. Benjamin A much fuller list is given here (cf. 7.6-12). It would appear that this, like the Judah elaborations in earlier sections, expresses the view, clearly held by the Chronicler and already being developed in the earlier Deuteronomic history, that the true people of God was to be found in the two tribes of Judah and Benjamin (cf. I Kings 11.36; ten tribes are allocated to the northern kingdom, one, i.e. Benjamin, to the southern, which must of course contain Judah). This is a theme which will become apparent in the succeeding narrative, though it allows also for the possibility of both rebellion and apostasy by Judah (and Benjamin), and also faithfulness by a select few from the other tribes.

Benjamin is significant also because it is within the area of this tribe that Jerusalem lies. This point too is already anticipated in I Kings 11.36. It is emphasized in the lists of this chapter in two passages (vv.28 and 32) which underline the presence of Benjaminites in Jerusalem itself.

We appear to have several groups of names of the Benjaminite families, linking them with different parts of the land. GEBA is named in v.6 with a reference to exile at an unidentified place; this is possibly exile in the sixth century BC, but may belong to some other occasion. A tradition of Benjaminite settlement in Moabite areas is found in v.8. Places in the centre and west appear in vv.12ff. with an allusion to an occupation of GATH, possibly the Philistine city. Other place names appear, but the most significant is Jerusalem in vv.28 and 32.

The appearance of the name of KISH in v.30 (and perhaps 'Ner' should also occur here) may have provided the occasion for linking the identical name in the family tree of Saul. This material, with the Saul family names in particular, reappears in 9.35-44, where it provides an introduction to the brief narrative of Saul in ch.10. The details of Saul's family do not entirely correspond to the information given in I Sam.; there were evidently deviant traditions. The list is carried through for twelve generations after Saul, and this shows that the continued existence of the family was known. The biblical narratives of the monarchy concentrate so entirely on the Davidic line and its legitimacy that they largely conceal the existence of support for Saul and his descendants. Perhaps behind the preservation of such a family list as this there lie traditions assigning a greater importance to that line. It is also interesting to note the preservation here of the more original forms of the names of Saul's son and grandson – ESHBAAL and MERIBBAAL. In the Samuel narratives, these names have been modified to avoid the use of the divine title 'Baal' (*ba'al*), originally quite properly used in its meaning of 'lord' to describe Israel's God, but subsequently thought to be so alien as to need replacement by the word *bōsheth*, meaning 'a shameful thing', giving the names Ishbosheth and Mephibosheth (both names further modified). The text of the books of Samuel was perhaps more fully revised to eliminate undesirable elements than the text of Chronicles, which was probably less used in public worship. Even to mention the title of an alien deity was felt to be dangerous, a point made plainly by Hosea (2.16).

39-40. The last element in this chapter, while linked to the

Saul family tree, introduces a theme of MIGHTY WARRIORS comparable to that which is associated with David (cf. 11.10-47), and perhaps to be linked with the Benjaminite traditions of ch.12.

With this the survey of the tribes comes to an end, and the significance of these chapters is immediately picked up by the opening of ch.9. The first verse of that chapter can indeed be regarded as a kind of colophon to the previous chapters, a resumé of their purpose.

THE RESTORED COMMUNITY

9.1-44

The main part of this chapter (vv.2-34) sets out a picture of the restored Jerusalem and its leading inhabitants. The lists of names run very closely parallel to those found in Neh. 11, where the same basic material has been used to provide a picture of the Jerusalem to which Nehemiah brought a fuller population after his restoring of the city walls. The differences suggest that two forms of the same original list have been used in the two places; we may compare this double use with that of Ezra 2 and Neh. 7, where the same list has been used equally for two quite distinct purposes. Both these double usages are a pointer to the original independence of the Nehemiah material from the main work of the Chronicler (cf. pp. 24ff). To understand the Chronicler's intention, we need to look at the use made of the material at this point.

The main content of the chapter is prefaced by v.1 and has an appendix in vv.35-44.

1. This, as we have seen, might very properly be regarded as the colophon to the preceding chapters, a resumé of the tribes of ALL ISRAEL – an important concept to the author – and with it a note of the recording of that whole community IN THE BOOK OF THE KINGS OF ISRAEL. What book is here referred to is not known; it would hardly seem to be the same

as those works to which reference is made both in Kings
and Chronicles, works of an annalistic kind. We should suppose rather a census document. It is perhaps on such an
analogy that we have the concept of a 'book of life' (cf. Exod.
32.32f. and Mal. 3.16), one in which God himself records
those who are part of his accepted community. Such an
analogy would here point to the author's belief that the true
Israel ultimately ought to consist of the whole of the tribes.
But this ideal concept is immediately contrasted with the sad
picture of JUDAH ... TAKEN INTO EXILE IN BABYLON BECAUSE
OF THEIR UNFAITHFULNESS. The name JUDAH here should
probably be seen as a shorthand term for the true (southern)
community; even that community has failed totally.

2. It is in this context that the list of the restored community
is set out, and the list serves a purpose here not altogether
unlike its purpose in Neh. 11; a restored land and city demands a restored people. The interpretation of v.2 is not
entirely certain, and it has been supposed that we really have
here a list of the former (pre-exilic) inhabitants of Jerusalem:
THE FIRST TO DWELL AGAIN is a free translation of the text.
If this view were correct, then vv.2-34 would be a list introduced to amplify the references to Jerusalem in ch.8. But
it is more satisfactory to follow the RSV's interpretation,
especially since the term rendered POSSESSIONS most naturally
denotes 'ancestral properties'. Here is the community pictured
as re-entering its family property, just as the prophetic symbol
enacted in Jer. 32 indicated it would. The post-exilic community is in continuity with the pre-exilic.
    The community is classified into Israelites – literally ISRAEL
(the context indicates that this means 'ordinary population'
as distinct from cult officials) – PRIESTS, LEVITES and TEMPLE
SERVANTS, three orders which are set out in what follows. The
TEMPLE SERVANTS or 'Nethinim' (so termed only here and in
Ezra-Nehemiah) may be compared with officials known in
the Canaanite documents of Ras Shamra as *ytnm*. The origin
and precise meaning of the term is not known; but it would
seem probable that it suggests 'those given' or 'dedicated' to

the service of God, perhaps originally temple slaves who then came to form a particular series of family groups. (A similar group may be detected in the descendants of the Gibeonites, who, according to Josh. 9.23, are to be in perpetuity slaves 'for the house of my God'. On this, cf. J. Blenkinsopp, *Gibeon and Israel*, Cambridge University Press 1972.)

3-9. The 'laity', the heads of the families, are listed here, divided into groups and including some from EPHRAIM and MANASSEH in addition to those from JUDAH and BENJAMIN – though the actual lists do not name the two former groups. If the reference to SHILONITES in v.5 is correct, it could be an indication that members of the earlier important sanctuary city of Shiloh had come to be associated with Jerusalem. (The long existence of that sanctuary and its importance are suggested by the references to it in Judg. 18.31; Jer. 7.12-14; 26.9.)

10-13. The priestly lists here need to be compared with other lists such as those in I Chron. 24, and indeed much of I Chron. 23-26 provides fuller material for the cult-officials than is given here. The opening list of the leading house of ZADOK is at some points confused (cf. 6.4ff.). The phrase VERY ABLE MEN (v.13) perhaps indicates rather 'men of standing'.

14-16. The Levites In fact the precise relationship between these and the lists of minor officials following is not clear. THE VILLAGES OF THE NETOPHATHITES (v.16) were probably near Jerusalem; this would point to a procedure for which other evidence is available (cf. for a later time the narrative of Luke 1), by which cult-officials lived on their own property and were present at the sanctuary only for their term of duty.

17-34. The attention devoted to a variety of minor officials here has suggested that the compiler of the list was specially concerned with their status. It is not necessary to suppose that the Chronicler himself was a gatekeeper any more than that he was a levitical singer or preacher, though his interest in all three is very evident. That he was concerned with the

proper ordering of the cult-officials is, however, clear, and
here we may see an expression of that concern in relation to
the guarding of the entrances to the house of God. The
psalmist who asks 'Who shall sojourn in thy tent? ...' (Ps.
15.1) is expressing a comparable concern. That the shrine
should not be contaminated by those in an unfit condition
is a central object of much cultic legislation. For the ideal
future land of Ezekiel 40-48, it was a prime necessity to
preserve the purity of the shrine. If the life of the people is
to be preserved and the divine blessing mediated, such care
at the centre may be seen as a proper expression of an ideal.
Here we are given a description of this guardianship, expressed in terms of the antiquity of the office; for it is claimed
that it goes back ultimately to the guardianship of THE EN-
TRANCE TO THE CAMP in the wilderness period (v.19). A similar,
but not identical picture is provided in Num. 2, and the
special position of PHINEHAS is indicated in Num. 25 and
Ps. 106.30. The earlier origin is then described as confirmed
in the Davidic age, by DAVID AND SAMUEL THE SEER (v.22).
Such an interpretation of the office as originating in the
Exodus-wilderness period and as renewed or organized in the
Davidic age runs through much of the Chronicler's material.
The phrase AT THE THRESHOLDS (v.22) is probably an error
for a word meaning 'in number'.

28-32. Fuller details of the various duties are given here. The
temple vessels must be carefully accounted for, since they
acquire a sacred and hence a dangerous quality (v.28). The
supervision of stores and the preparation of SPICES and
CAKES, including the 'bread of the presence' (v.32), must also
be assigned to the proper officers.

33-34. the singers Much attention will subsequently be given
to these (cf. I Chron. 15-16). We note here a contrast between
those whose duty demanded their continuous presence in the
temple, and those (cf. v.16) who could live outside. Both here
and in vv.26 and 31, the precise position of these minor
officials in relation to the Levites is not clear. Perhaps we
should suppose a stage of separation, as a minor order, fol-

lowed by one of more elevated status, inclusion in the levitical order. So much of the history of the priesthood and of the other cult-officials is obscure that we can only surmise what happened.

35-44. The appendix is an almost exact copy of 8.29-38. The GIBEON material (vv.35-38) is perhaps to be seen as a preparation for the particular place given to this city in the tradition as a sanctuary (cf. I Chron. 21.29 and II Chron. 1). Again we have the impression that a tradition which accorded great significance to Gibeon has been so overlaid with later interpretation that we can no longer trace its real position. The absolute claim for Jerusalem as sole sanctuary has imposed limitations on those narratives which point to other holy places, though relics of such narratives may be detected. The Saul material in this position provides an introduction to the Saul narrative of ch.10, and its repetition at this point is therefore intelligible. But the precise literary history of these chapters remains obscure.

These last verses form a transition from the picture of the ideal Israel, created, enumerated, apostate and restored, to the tracing of the establishment of the ideal Israel in the Davidic age which is a central theme.

DAVID

I Chronicles **10-29**

More space is devoted to the Davidic period in the work of the Chronicler than to any other single section. The whole of the remainder of I Chron. centres on David, his position as king and his ordering of worship and preparations for the building of the temple. The original material of the Chronicler has been elaborated at certain points, notably in chs.15-16 and 23-27, but though these additions have complicated the picture and have laid more stress still on the detailed organization of personnel, they represent an extension of the Chronicler's original concern rather than a departure from it. The complexity of the lists suggests that there are in fact several different additions rather than a single reworking by one editor. The additions, like the original, are ultimately concerned with one basic point: the contemporary worship and organization, that of the Chronicler's own time and that of his successors, are to be understood as in continuity with the ancient establishment of worship at Jerusalem in the time of David. There is in this both an appeal for right understanding of the contemporary situation and a warning against departure from the true line of faith and practice.

These themes are further borne out in the succeeding sections of the work, in terms of fulfilment in Solomon, so closely linked with this failure and loss through the period of the monarchy, restoration and renewal in the post-exilic community, and above all in Ezra. Thus I Chron. 10-29 (or better I Chron. 10-29+II Chron. 1-9) form the centre of the work.

THE DOWNFALL OF SAUL

10.1-14

The narrative proper begins without preface, other than the placing of the Saul genealogy at the end of the preceding chapter. The reader is brought suddenly out of the lists of names into a familiar story, for here as elsewhere the Chronicler assumes that his readers know the material to which he is referring. Sometimes, as here, he includes a complete narrative; elsewhere he makes only brief allusion to one which is to be found in the earlier books of Samuel and Kings. But in either case, as also when he introduces material which has no parallel in the earlier texts, he is inviting the reader to consider the meaning of the history, and for this purpose he arranges, selects and comments.

1-12. Here the narrative runs closely with that of I Sam. 31; the differences are for the most part small, though not necessarily unimportant. We cannot always be sure how far they are the result of deliberate alteration of the earlier form, or how far they represent the use by the Chronicler of a textform deviant from that known to us in the books of Samuel and Kings. The Qumran texts have shown the existence of various text-forms, and this inevitably makes for less certainty in deciding just what the Chronicler read. It is important that our reading of the Chronicler's work should not be simply a comparing of texts and supposing that we can discover an 'original'. We need to consider the Chronicler's work for itself, and to see the way in which he handles material which is to some extent known to us.

This narrative provides a good example. The small differences between the text here and in I Sam. 31 are important for the study of textual history, and at some points we may detect the Chronicler's own rewriting of the narrative. But the primary points lie in his actual use of this story and not of any other Saul material, and in his placing of the story

in a new light by the addition of a theological comment in
vv.13-14 which has no parallel in the Samuel text.

The reader, it is assumed, knows the story of Saul's kingship, of his prowess as a warrior and his failure as a king;
he knows how the figure of Saul is overshadowed in the narratives of I Sam. by that of David, the chosen king who is
being gradually recognized by all. His attention is drawn to
the final act, the doom of Saul and the disaster of Israel. So
a moral is drawn from disaster; such is the consequence of
disobedience. But at the same time the Chronicler makes the
point that the very establishment of David issues from a
moment of disaster. Where he might have omitted the whole
story of Saul and gone straight into the David narrative, the
Chronicler has in fact implied the significance of divine grace
in the setting of David the chosen one on the throne, the first
true king of Israel, set against the disaster to the rejected
Saul.

We may note that in v.6 the Chronicler speaks of the total
destruction of the house of Saul, and in this his account
differs from I Sam. The genealogy just given in fact con-
tradicts this, and 12.2 points in a different direction. But the
point being made is that there is no claimant to the throne
from Saul's house; the whole episode of Ishbosheth (Eshbaal)
is passed over in silence. Verse 10 contains a reference to the
putting of Saul's HEAD IN THE TEMPLE OF DAGON; this phrase
is perhaps accidentally lacking in I Sam. In this verse too we
have THEIR GODS in place of the proper name 'Ashtaroth' in
I Sam.; perhaps the naming of a goddess was felt to be too
shocking, though curiously the name of the god Dagon is
preserved.

13-14. This theological comment makes explicit the condemnation of Saul which, in the older account, is implied
in the positioning of the story. In I Sam. 31, the story is told
without comment, but we are led to understand the divine
rejection of Saul both because of earlier material and also
because of the overall pattern of the narratives. Here the
point is brought out by a precise indication of Saul's UN-

FAITHFULNESS (v.13 – the same word as is used for the apostasy of Judah in 9.1 and of the Manassites in 5.25). This unfaithfulness consists in disobedience to the divine COMMAND – an allusion in all probability to the Amalekite war story of I Sam. 15 – and in his consultation of A MEDIUM, the witch of Endor of I Sam. 28. To endeavour to find the divine will by means other than direct approach to God is equivalent to apostasy. (We may observe that the poetic fragment cited in I Sam. 15.22f., which is certainly later than the period of Samuel and shows the influence of prophetic thought, marks the same equivalence between such improper religious practices and apostasy.) The direct result of Saul's unfaithfulness is his death as a divine judgment and that THE KINGDOM is TURNED OVER TO DAVID (the same expression is used for the loss of the northern kingdom to Rehoboam in II Chron. 10.15). The story of judgment and failure ushers in the kingship of David.

THE SUPREMACY OF DAVID

11.1-12.40

11.1-3. These verses (corresponding to II Sam. 5.1-3) show David immediately after the death of Saul. He is AT HEBRON – though no explanation is given of this, since the story of his becoming king of Judah alone has been omitted. ALL ISRAEL anoints him as king, not as in II Sam. the representatives of the northern tribes, forced to accept him after the death of Ishbosheth. For the line of Saul has gone, warfare between David and that line is therefore unmentioned, and the two stages of David's kingship are merged. (In 3.4f. the lists in fact preserve a note of these two stages.) The Chronicler in taking over the II Sam. text of v.2 assumes that his readers know the stories of David's heroic exploits under Saul. David's kingship is ACCORDING TO THE WORD OF THE LORD BY SAMUEL (v.3); this provides a general allusion to the Samuel narratives, and in particular to the anointing story in I Sam. 16. At the same time, it is probably intended to point to the divine

declaration in v.2 which is to be understood as the word of
the prophet to David, though this is closely modelled on the
word of Nathan, cited in 17.7.

4-9. This section (corresponding to II Sam. 5.6-10) leads us
immediately to David's conquest of JERUSALEM (JEBUS), depicted as an act of ALL ISRAEL (and not just of David's army).
The Chronicler's text does not contain the very obscure
references to 'the lame and the blind', perhaps because the
text was not understood, but more probably because this
seemed to cast doubt on David's prowess. Nor is there any
reference to the 'watershaft' of II Sam. (NEB renders 'grap-
pling iron', though the precise significance is uncertain). There
is instead a tradition regarding the appointment of JOAB as
CHIEF (v.6). It is impossible to know whether the Chronicler
is here using a different text, or whether he is using this device
to explain the prominence of Joab who does not appear
(except indirectly, 11.39) in the following lists of David's
heroes. There is obscurity also in v.8: IN COMPLETE CIRCUIT
possibly depends upon an erroneously repeated word (II Sam.
has 'inward'). MILLO is of uncertain meaning: perhaps it
denotes a fortress, or perhaps some earthwork, a 'filling up'
(for the Hebrew word suggests this) either between the old
Jebusite city on Mount Ophel and its extension northwards
or in the terracing of the buildings on the steep slopes of
Mount Ophel. The last clause of v.8 could, with a small
(and attested) variant, be rendered: 'Joab spared the rest of
the population', which would suggest a tradition that Joab,
having killed the first Jebusite and thereby miraculously
reduced the defenders to impotence (cf. Jonathan's exploit in
I Sam. 14), showed himself a magnanimous conqueror.

11.10-12.40. The remainder of these two chapters is made
up of pieces of tradition and lists of names, all directed to
the same point. The Chronicler has just indicated his belief
that it was all Israel which appointed David as king and
which with him took Jerusalem. Now this support by all
Israel is made explicit by a listing of heroes and warriors
from the tribes who are described as joining with David. The

section is opened in 11.10 by a verse which stresses this point in relation to the MIGHTY MEN, the heroes of David's time, and the point is subsequently repeated at the beginning of the summarizing list at 12.23.

The opening verse is the Chronicler's own, and by it he has offered a new interpretation of the lists, and fragments of narrative, which follow in 11.11-47. Most of this (vv.11-41 – up to URIAH THE HITTITE) is to be found in II Sam. 23.8-39; the last verses present an additional list of names. In II Sam. these lists form part of a complex series of appendices to the book (II Sam. 21-24); here they are integrated into the presentation (as the Chronicler has also done for II Sam. 24, cf. I Chron. 21). There is clearly much ancient traditional information here, concerning THE THREE and THE THIRTY (or 'the Captains'), some of whose exploits have been preserved. In v.15 it is noted that they were with David AT THE CAVE OF ADULLAM, during the period of his outlawry and opposition to Saul, with which many of the narratives in I Sam. deal.

The two forms of the material show that there has been much textual dislocation. Thus, there is an obvious omission in vv.12-14: the verses found as II Sam. 23.9*b*-11*a* have been accidentally omitted, with the result that the story of ELEAZAR has now been partly conflated with the story of Shammah.

HE TOOK HIS STAND (v.14) represents a correction to correspond with the form in II Sam., but in the Chronicler the plural would be correct once the omission has taken place. The plural 'they took their stand' (RSVmg) represents an attempt to make the narrative cohere; it is intended to refer to Eleazar and David. We should, however, fill up the gap in the text and read both stories in full.

15-19. The narrative here is deeply expressive of the piety of David; the water won by heroism is as the life blood of the heroes, and to touch blood was forbidden in ancient Israel.

22. ariels The word probably means 'heroes' or 'champions' (so NEB), literally 'lions of God' or 'mighty lions'.

26-47. This list contains considerably more than thirty names; in II Sam. it is concluded with a note of the total as thirty-seven. The additional section may preserve the original ending of the list, but its differences of style suggest rather that the Chronicler has added here some material from another source, perhaps primarily to emphasize names of men from Transjordan, while the main list has names of men mostly from Judah and the hill country to the west of Jerusalem.

12. 1-22. These verses consist of various elements linked together as noting those who joined David at particular moments of his earlier career, and interrupting the catalogue of military support found in ch.11 and in 12.23-40.

1-7. *The introduction provided here – those who joined DAVID AT ZIKLAG – concentrates on THE BENJAMINITES, SAUL'S KINSMEN (v.2). This develops the theme found prominently in I Sam. that already under Saul the coming kingship of David was recognized by all – even by Saul and his family and his officers. WHO HELPED HIM IN WAR (v.1) is probably simply another expression meaning 'warriors'.

8-15. A list of warriors from Gad, beyond Jordan. Not only are they described as superlative warriors (v.14 should probably be understood as 'the least equal to a hundred, the greatest equal to a thousand'), but they also brave the flood waters of THE JORDAN IN THE FIRST MONTH: March-April in the year beginning in the spring. The latter part of v.15 probably continues this thought: WHEN IT WAS OVERFLOWING ALL ITS BANKS 'and making all the valley impassable ...'.

16-18. A very interesting piece of tradition is preserved here, recalling a number of the stories in I Sam. of the risk to David of betrayal. Verse 17 uses the theme, also found there, of David inviting God's judgment on betrayers (cf. the story of Nabal and Abigail in I Sam. 25). The assurance of loyalty is expressed in a poetic oracle (v.18), uttered in the power of the divine SPIRIT (RSV's use of a capital letter for 'Spirit',

---

* Heb. divides v.4 into two, as vv.4 and 5. The Heb. verse numbering is one higher from there to the end of the chapter.

here and elsewhere, is not very appropriate); as in the case of
Gideon (Judg. 6.34), the spirit is said to 'clothe itself in
Amasai' (CAME UPON is much too weak). Cf. also II Chron.
24.20. The poetic fragment, like a number found in I and II
Sam., is vivid and likely to be ancient: it is the counterpart
of the one cited in II Chron. 10.16. Blessing is upon all those
who associate with David because of the close bond between
David and God.

19-22. Manasseh Loyalists of this tribe, described as joining David at the time of Saul's last battle, are listed here.
Verse 19*b* is a parenthetic note to remind the reader of the
account in I Sam. 29. David's service with the Philistines was
a somewhat embarrassing aspect of the tradition concerning
him, and the fact that he did not actually fight against his
own people needed to be brought out to avoid misunderstanding. Verse 22 provides a summary, stressing the growth of
David's power and by implication the decrease of Saul's.
He came to have A GREAT ARMY, an army so great that it
could be described as AN ARMY OF GOD, probably here to be
seen as a phase expressing its superlative, almost supernatural,
quality.

23. This introduces a military census of tribal support for
David, and again draws out the point that this happened at
HEBRON, as part of the divine action to bring over to David
the kingdom of Saul (cf. 10.14; 11.10).

24-37. The contributions of the various tribes are listed here,
and it is noticeable that the more distant tribes have larger
numbers attributed to them. By these numbers the Chronicler
is evidently making the point – reiterated later – that while
fidelity in the south is self-evident, it should not be forgotten
that loyal men came to David (and hence to the true kingdom) from all the tribes. There are in fact thirteen tribes,
owing to the inclusion of Levi as a tribal group (v.26). Odd
pieces of tradition are noted, so that the list sounds somewhat like the blessings on the tribes found in Gen. 49 and
Deut. 33. For Benjamin, the stress is on the transfer of

ALLEGIANCE (v.29). For Manasseh, those who came are said to have been EXPRESSLY NAMED for the king-making (v.31). The men of Issachar have attributed to them a particular quality of wisdom, perhaps astrological (v.32).

38-40. The whole section is rounded off with renewed stress on the oneness of Israel at the kingship of David and the greatness of the celebration held at Hebron. That this unity is due to the purpose of God underlies the whole; that it is also an occasion of joy in Israel brings to the fore another characteristic of the Chronicler's understanding of his people's true life. Within his sometimes dry-sounding descriptions of events, the Chronicler has a very deep sense of the joy which belongs to the true people of God.

THE ARK – I

13.1-14

The immediate sequel to David's kingship and his capture of Jerusalem (chs.11-12) is given as the endeavour to bring the ARK OF GOD, ancient symbol of God's place as the focus of the life of the Israelite tribes, into the capital which is to be the religious centre.

The Chronicler links David's consultation WITH THE COM-MANDERS (v.1) to their presence at Hebron at the end of the previous chapter. He postpones the overthrow of the Philistines to ch.14, for, as v.3 makes plain, neglect of the ark is the cause of disaster, as IN THE DAYS OF SAUL. The reader is expected to recall for himself how the ark came to be at Kiriath-jearim (I Sam. 4-6); for the Chronicler's purpose, it is the bringing of the ark to Jerusalem (II Sam. 6) which forms the centre.

The narrative of II Sam. 6 is divided into two parts, and the sequel is found in chs.15-16. Here we have a section based very closely on II Sam. 6.2-11; it is introduced with the Chronicler's own characteristic emphasis on ALL ISRAEL as involved in this central religious task (esp. v.5). The military assembly of ch.12, culminating in festivity, becomes a primarily religious ASSEMBLY here (*qāhāl* used in v.2 and the verb in v.5 have this particular overtone). Such an assembly can give its judgment of what is right and can receive THE WILL OF THE LORD.

2. The rendering of this verse is not easy: it could run, 'if the LORD our God opens a way, let us send', or, 'if it is of the LORD our God, let us break out (or let us resolve) and send ...'. The text contains the verb (*pāras*) which appears also in v.11 ('break forth', Perez-uzza), and it may be that there is a deliberate play upon words here. The gathering of the remainder of the people is perhaps suggestive of a later date when scattered communities of Jews were to be found throughout the area, professing allegiance to Jerusalem though living under separate political organizations. It is stressed too that the bringing in of the ark can only be undertaken with THE PRIESTS AND LEVITES, a point which anticipates ch.15.

5. So ALL ISRAEL is ASSEMBLED, from its furthest borders, from THE SHIHOR – east of Egypt according to Josh. 13.3 – to THE ENTRANCE OF HAMATH (or Lebo-hamath) in the north (Josh. 13.5).

6-14. This narrative is essentially that of II Sam., though there are a few textual differences (in a number of instances the II Sam. text is clearly corrupt and needs to be corrected from this text). BAALAH, KIRIATH-JEARIM (cf. Josh. 15.9) was a Gibeonite city (Josh. 9.17). The use of A NEW CART is designed to be appropriate to the holiness of the deity (cf. also I Sam. 6.7). The apparently pious action of Uzza brings immediate divine wrath; the point is not explained, but the sequel in ch.15 makes it plain that none but a Levite should be concerned with the movement of the ark.

9. Put out his hand to hold the ark translates a different construction from that in II Sam.; it could suggest that he did not actually touch it: even the intention was enough!

The resulting anger and fear on the part of David delay the bringing of the ark to Jerusalem.

13-14. Obed-edom The tradition of its stay here is preserved by the Chronicler as allowing a pause in the narrative – which he uses for the material of ch.14 – and also as enabling him to stress that right care for the ark is to belong only to the Levites (ch.15). The identity of Obed-edom is unknown, nor is there any indication of the place in which he lived. In 15-18 there is named an Obed-edom who was a gatekeeper and another in 15.21 who was a levitical musician; nothing strictly identifies any or all of these, but it would seem to have been inferred by the Chronicler that the ark was being properly housed at this time. If this is so, then the RSV rendering of v.14 is quite acceptable; it would also be possible to render: 'the ark of God remained at (beside) the house of Obed-edom in its own house', i.e. that a shrine was provided for it, a temporary holy place on its journey to Jerusalem its final home. The blessing on the household of Obed-edom is mentioned here, but it is significant that this is not subsequently used as a motif connected with the further journey of the ark. That move is to be undertaken when it has been clearly recognized that only the proper personnel can handle the ark.

DAVID'S RENOWN
14.1-17

The Chronicler skilfully fills the three-month gap mentioned in 13.14 by using four pieces of tradition already built together in II Sam. 5.11-25 and providing them with a resumptive comment in 14.17. Chronology is not his consideration, and indeed the order of events as it is presented in II Sam. presents considerable difficulties. The themes of the four sections of the chapter are linked together to point to the FAME OF DAVID (v.17).

1-2. See II Sam. 5.11-12. The verses describe an embassy from HIRAM KING OF TYRE. The subsequent relationship between Hiram and Solomon at the building of palace and temple indicate that there was a trade pact. But it is so presented in this context that it would appear as if Hiram, recognizing the position of David, is sending a gift, almost paying tribute, to one whom he, as a representative of the outside world, owes allegiance. For David, as v.2 makes plain, is ESTABLISHED KING by God; tribute to David is the acknowledgement of God himself. The point is made explicit by v.17.

3-7. See II Sam. 5.13-16. These are notes of the WIVES and SONS of David IN JERUSALEM; the material has already been listed in 3.5-8. It is to be seen here as the expression of divine blessing in the sure establishment of a dynasty, the theme which will be taken up more fully in ch.17. We may note the inclusion of the name of SOLOMON, the only son of David with whom the Chronicler is to show concern. The names include BEELIADA, a compound with the divine title *ba'al*, for which the II Sam. text has the substituted form Eliada (cf. the note on the family of Saul in 8.33f.).

8-12. See II Sam. 5.17-21. This is the first of two traditions concerning the defeat of THE PHILISTINES. The Chronicler introduces his stress on David as KING OVER ALL ISRAEL (v.8). The theme is one of divine victory, utilizing, as does the narrative in ch. 13, the word *pāraṣ* ('break out, break through') as a motif. This is inevitably obscured in translation, though the RSVmg has some indication of it. We might render v.11*b*: 'God has *broken through* my enemies ... like a *breaking through* of waters. Hence the place is called "Baal (=the lord) of *breaking through*".' The placing of this 'breaking through' theme close to that of Uzza and the ark resembles the double use of the theme of Ebenezer ('stone of help') in I Sam. 4.1 and 7.12, the first negative, the second positive. The Chronicler makes a typical change in v.12; the gods of the enemy are BURNED, not taken as booty as is stated in II Sam.

13-16. See II Sam. 5.22-25. The second Philistine war story again has a divine action bringing victory. These two battle stories are like many to be found in the older traditions in that they play down the human element and stress divine action. The tendency to move still further in this direction is evident in the opening chapters of Joshua and in the battle narrative of I Sam. 7; the latter points forward to the Chronicler's own battle narratives which are theological occasions, demonstrations of the divine power and of the consequences of trust and mistrust.

17. The Chronicler's comment indicates that the embassy of Hiram and the defeat of the Philistines are to be seen as typical; the enduring Davidic dynasty is to be a symbol of the divine rule to which ALL NATIONS must submit in awe. A comparison has very appropriately been made with the themes of Ps. 2, where the nations are brought into submission to God in the person of his adopted son, the Davidic king.

THE ARK – II
15.1-16.43

The story of the bringing in of the ark, begun in ch.13, is now brought to its conclusion in the description of the great celebration, with the appointment of ritual and officiants associated with its presence in Jerusalem. The narrative itself is somewhat overlaid with lists and details, some part of which is likely to be due to later amplifications of the text. As a result, the relatively straight story found in II Sam. 6.12-23 is obscured; in certain important respects it has been modified. Verses 1-3 provide both an introduction and an explanation.

15.1. David's building of HOUSES FOR HIMSELF links the section with the opening of ch.14; the preparation of A PLACE FOR THE ARK and A TENT FOR IT tacitly suggests that the three-month interval (13.14) has been profitably employed. The implication is that the ark could not really have been brought into Jerusalem unless there had been proper preparation there. And this suggests that the use of the term PLACE is to be understood as suggesting a 'holy place', a 'shrine', a sense not infrequently to be found in the Hebrew word *māqōm*; the parallel TENT is also frequently used with a similar religious overtone.

2. A declaration, almost a decree, is made by David that only the Levites may carry the ark; this is a reiteration of the injunction found in Deut. 10.8, so that it may be clear that action is to be in accordance with the law.

3. Characteristically, too, it is ALL ISRAEL which DAVID ASSEMBLED – the religious assembly (cf. on 13.2) – to join in the action.

4-10. The setting is thus provided for a list of priests and Levites which really overlaps the content of what follows.

11-15. Here the real action is taken of commissioning the two leading priests and the heads of the levitical houses who are to be responsible for the carrying of the ark. Verse 13 makes it plain that it was disobedience to the law which brought disaster, and thus an explanation is given of the death of Uzza in ch.13. The opening of v.13 is not clear; it may mean 'since you were not there on the first occasion'. Priests and Levites prepared themselves by sanctification, by the appropriate cleansing rituals, to carry the ark (on poles on their shoulders, cf. Exod. 25.12-15), and so all is well.

16-24. Again the narrative is broken by a long list of officers. This links with two other points. First, we have the appointment of singers and instrumentalists; some of these names have already appeared in ch.6, though the details differ. We may note especially the appearance of ASAPH and HEMAN. The former reappears at 16.7 in a prominent position, and is also found in some psalm titles (e.g. Ps. 50); the latter name appears in the title of Ps. 88. It would appear that in these various sources of information we have some clues, though very obscure ones, to the development of the organization of psalmody and temple music. Second, we may note the emphasis placed on the GATEKEEPERS FOR THE ARK (vv.18, 23, 24); the various pieces of information here also point to develop-

ments. The importance of it rests in the stress on guardianship
and hence on purity (cf. on ch.9). This passage also includes
the obscure ALAMOTH (v.20) and SHEMINITH (v.21); the former
could be translated 'young women', but its occurrence in the
title of Ps. 46 suggests that it is in reality an unexplained
musical term. Much the same may be said of the latter, which
is found in the titles of Pss. 6 and 12; it might denote an
eight-stringed instrument.

21. to lead Another obscure word. A form from the same
root which RSV renders 'choirmaster' occurs in a number of
psalm titles, but it is very uncertain whether this is correct.
Since the root means 'to shine' – and hence is understood to
suggest pre-eminence, leadership – it could be that the word
really refers to some cultic action designed to make the deity
react favourably, to 'make his face shine' (cf. Num. 6.25,
which uses, however, a quite different word).

22. The terms translated LEADER, DIRECT are again quite
different. The whole question is so obscure that little is to be
gained from its discussion, the commentary on the Psalms
in this series contains some brief explanatory notes. The word
rendered MUSIC (cf. also v.27, where the text is confused) may
also be understood to mean 'oracle', for it indicates something
lifted or carried, and hence the lifting of the voice; it is used
as a technical prophetic term in a number of passages (e.g.
Isa. 13.1). Since elsewhere the Levites are associated with the
giving of prophetic oracles (e.g. II Chron. 20.14-17), such a
function would not be out of place. We might also wonder
whether it could not refer to the carrying of the ark, with
CHENANIAH denoted as the controller of the actual carrying.

25-29. We now arrive at a point at which the Chronicler
uses fairly closely the material of II Sam. 6. He introduces a
new stress on divine help (v.26); he develops the levitical functions and clarifies the references to garments, clothing the
Levites in the priestly linen. He may have wished to avoid the
suggestion that David was himself functioning as a priest (the

EPHOD came to be a priestly garment). Again it is ALL ISRAEL which welcomes the ark with a cultic shout (v.28). The Chronicler uses only the first part of the story of MICHAL THE DAUGHTER OF SAUL, and clearly this has been preserved to stress the point that the members of the house of Saul show themselves unable to recognize the true meaning of events; they are typical of unfaith.

16.1-3. These verses continue the older form of the story with only slight modification; it is clear that the feast of the ark is to be regarded as a great religious celebration, and the detail strongly suggests that it should not be regarded as a unique event in history but rather as a repeated enactment of the entry of God, symbolized in his ark. Psalms 24 and 132 also point in this direction, particularly the former with its words of welcome to the coming of the ark and its deity. From this angle we may perhaps best view both the older and newer forms of the narrative as presentations in narrative form of a cultic event.

3. portion of meat We may interpret 'date-cake'.

4-6. The impression of vv.1-3 is confirmed by a list of those who are to perform the rituals associated with the ark; three important cultic terms are used – TO INVOKE, TO THANK, AND TO PRAISE. The sense of the first is that of reminding God of his nature and of his actions in the past as an expression of confidence in his willingness to act now, a theme of many of the psalms of lament; the second suggests a link with the sacrifice known as the 'thank-offering' (cf. the title of Ps. 100); the third naturally points to the psalms which in Hebrew are called 'praises'. Thus we are again provided with some clues to the place of psalmody within the cult, and this is now further developed.

7. Asaph (cf on 15.16-24) appears here as leader of the group responsible for THANKSGIVING, and the text then offers an example of the kind of psalm appropriate to such an occasion. What in effect the Chronicler is telling his readers is that the contemporary practice of psalm-singing owes its origin and its authority to David, who first decreed what was to be done.

8-36. The psalm which follows might well have appeared in the Psalter. That it corresponds to certain passages found in other psalms is no objection to this, for we may observe that, for example, Ps. 108 is made up of two pieces found also in Ps. 57.7-11 and 60.5-12.

8-22. These verses correspond to Ps. 105.1-15. RSV has in fact quite improperly 'corrected' the text in v.13 by reading ABRAHAM where the Hebrew has 'Israel' ('Abraham' appears in Ps. 105). The reference to STRENGTH in v.11 is probably to be seen as a synonym for the ark (cf. most clearly Ps. 78.61, where RSV has 'power'; this subject is discussed by G. Henton Davies, 'The Ark in the Psalms', in *Promise and Fulfilment*, ed. F. F. Bruce, T. and T. Clark, Edinburgh 1963, pp. 51-61).

23-33. These verses correspond to Ps. 96.1-13a. Here we may note that vv.28-29 correspond also to Ps. 29.1-2, except that this psalm invokes 'heavenly beings' rather than FAMILIES OF THE PEOPLES. The latter may well represent a theological modification, a move away from the mythological term used at an earlier stage.

34-36. The closing verses of the psalm present different questions. Verse 34, it is true, may be paralleled in Ps. 106.1, and vv.35-36 in Ps. 106.47-48; but the former is a very common liturgical refrain (cf. e.g. Ps. 136.1). The other two verses are preceded by an introductory SAY ALSO, and may be regarded as an application of the psalm to a new situation – that of a scattered community after the exile – and a closing doxology, which appears at the end of Ps. 106 as the conclusion to one of the five books of the Psalter (cf. the comparable endings to Pss. 41, 72 and more briefly 89).

It is a misunderstanding to say that the Chronicler here quotes a group of psalm passages to illustrate liturgical practice. It is more accurate to say that he here includes a psalm, no doubt well-known to himself and his readers, which may be paralleled in the Psalter, as other psalm-passages may be paralleled. It provides us with an additional psalm comparable to others found outside the Psalter (e.g. Exod. 15.1-18; Judg. 5; I Sam. 2.1-10), though its material is familiar to us from other occurrences of essentially the same verses. There are in fact some textual differences which are of interest as showing the way in which the same text may be transmitted in more than one form.

37-38. The story of the ark is rounded off with an emphasis on the continuity of religious practice. Since the Chronicler is very evidently concerned with showing that the religious community of his own day, gathered around the post-exilic temple, is the heir to the true religious traditions of the past, it is clear that he is claiming that the descendants of these levitical groups can be regarded as the maintainers of the tradition. The ark had gone, perhaps already long before the destruction of the temple in 587, for it is not mentioned in the accounts of that; but what the ark stood for had not gone, and the fact that the psalms more often allude to the ark than refer to it by name may indicate that in the post-exilic period a celebration of the God of the ark and his entry in triumph continued, even though the actual physical symbol was not present. It is the essence of the celebration which counts.

39-42. Another aspect of the continuity of religious practice appears here. THE HIGH PLACE THAT WAS AT GIBEON was to give way to the Jerusalem shrine; yet it was to be given its proper value as a stage on the way, and the theme of Gibeon was to be picked up again in the narrative of Solomon. The tabernacle would be moved up to Jerusalem and associated with the ark in the third part of the story as it is told in II Chron. 5. The link is also expressed by the stress yet again on music and on guardians, and in the citing of the same religious refrain in v.41 as has appeared in v.34.

43. With the last verse the older narrative is picked up again. King and people alike return HOME, and the blessing which belongs to the celebration extends to the whole life of each HOUSEHOLD. An appropriate link is provided too for the narrative which follows in ch.17.

The place of music and psalmody in the worship of Israel which forms so central an element in these chapters is a matter of importance for our appreciation of the way in which so much of the religious tradition was kept alive for the ordinary worshipper. Just as in the liturgical practice of a number of the Protestant churches the confession of faith is properly expressed in the singing of hymns, so Israel acknowledged and entered into her tradition of faith by the use of psalms to which, as we may see here, the people respond with a word of affirmation (16.36). The Chronicler did not invent the idea that it was David who was responsible for such psalmody and music, but he gave a great impetus to the growth of a conviction that was ultimately to become hardened into the view that David wrote the psalms. For him the question was not the narrow one of authorship, which has bedevilled so much discussion of biblical questions; it was the concern about authority and continuity, expressed in relation to the life of a small religious community which needed to be recalled to the realities of its great tradition and enabled to appropriate that tradition fully.

THE HOUSE OF GOD AND THE HOUSE OF DAVID

17.1-27

This chapter corresponds very closely with its counterpart in II Sam. 7, and in the same way forms the sequel to the entry of the ark into Jerusalem. At this point we may see that the Chronicler is taking up material which has already undergone a complex process of development, for II Sam. 7 is to be seen as one of the key sections in the older interpretation of the history, that of the Deuteronomic writers. As a successor in part to that older interpretation, the Chronicler is here able to use the material with very little change.

There are two parts to the chapter. Verses 1-15 provide the setting and the divine word to David through the prophet Nathan. Here the theme is 'You shall not build a house for me, but I shall build a house for you', combined with the related

theme of David's son as temple-builder. Verses 16-27 are a
prayer on the theme of the house of David. In a number of
small touches, the Chronicler underlines his own understanding of this particular moment.

1. There is no mention of David being given 'rest from all
his enemies round about', an important element in II Sam.,
since it provides a link back to Deut. 12.10, where the ultimate building of the temple is associated with such 'rest'. The
Chronicler does not omit this because the main record of
David's wars follows only in chs.18-20, but because such a
statement would imply that there was a considerable interval
between the bringing in of the ark and the temple-building
project. The sequence for the Chronicler is clear. David is
king, he conquers Jerusalem, he brings in the ark (with only
a brief pause for preparation), he proposes a temple.

4. You shall not build me a house The direct prohibition
replaces a question. Here we may see the Chronicler by a small
change introducing a greater degree of unity into the passage.
The II Sam. text is not all of one piece, and it raises difficult
problems of interpretation because of this; it is not clear what
is the relationship between David's intention to build a temple
and the divine unwillingness to have one and the subsequent
promise that Solomon will build. Here the theme is clearer,
though something of the different levels nevertheless survives
in the following verses. David is not to build; Solomon will do
so. Subsequently (22.7ff.), we shall be told why David is forbidden to build.

12-13. When the promise that Solomon will build is made
clear, the theme of disobedience and chastisement is missing
(cf. II Sam. 7.14). This is not because the Chronicler was
unaware of the failure of the Davidic kings, but because for
him Solomon, the temple-builder, belonged to the age of
faithfulness. (The warnings in II Chron. 7.17ff. are directed
to the dynastic line and the people.)

14. In addition a change of pronoun here makes the house
(temple) MY HOUSE, and the kingdom MY KINGDOM; it is God's

rule which is being established, not that of a line of kings. Solomon will sit 'on the throne of the LORD' (29.23).

17. The text here is probably corrupted, as is the corresponding v.19 in II Sam. 7; RSV's conjecture FUTURE GENERATIONS provides a neat parallel to the preceding phrase, but remains uncertain.

19. A very slight emendation may be made to read: FOR THY SERVANT'S SAKE, O LORD, 'even thy dog's sake' THOU HAST WROUGHT ALL THIS GREATNESS. The worshipper may see himself in such a humble guise before the deity.

Already in the older form of the narrative, the promise to the house of David is more than a forecast of the four-hundred-year rule of that family in Judah; it points beyond to a hope of restoration of the Davidic line, adumbrated in the last verses of II Kings (25.27-30). For the Chronicler, to whom the restoration of the Davidic monarchy is not a real hope, the promise is to be interpreted rather in terms of the embodiment of God's rule through David in a community loyal to what David established.

DAVID'S WARS

18.1-20.8

The Chronicler continues his narrative with the material of II Sam. 8, but he has in fact made use of only a part of what follows from there to the end of II Sam. Although for the moment the temple-building theme appears to be almost lost to sight, it is in reality a main determinative factor in the selection of what to include and what to omit. David was not to build the temple; so the previous chapter has made clear. The task will fall to Solomon his son, his successor to the throne.

So a prior question must inevitably be: why was David not permitted to build? Chapter 17 indicates that the reason is the divine decree, but subsequently this is clarified by our being told that the prohibition was expressed in terms of a divine word revealing that David's involvement in war prevents him from building (22.8; 28.3). Here again we may see a reason for the omission in 17.1 of any reference to David being now at peace; it is Solomon who is to be given peace, and Solomon 'a man of peace' who will be the temple-builder. The selection therefore in chs.18-20 of the narratives found in II Sam. in which David is engaged in wars against his people's enemies – the nations around Israel – provides a clear basis on which this divine decree is to be presented.

Furthermore, the true succession found in Solomon is not to be doubted or put in jeopardy by any untoward events. That whole wealth of material which tells of David's other sons and their rebellious activities, as well as narratives which deal with other rebellions and with the fortunes of the house of Saul, are not relevant to the primary concern. So no part of II Sam. 9 or 13-20 or of Adonijah's rebellion in I Kings 1-2 finds a place in the Chronicler's work. Nor is the story of David and Bathsheba related, perhaps not simply because it is a story which casts a very unfavourable light on David; the Chronicler made good use of another unfavourable story in ch.21. It is not now needed because the choice of Solomon is the only possibility; the other potential successors are all left unmentioned apart from the appearance of names in the lists. (We may observe that the list in I Chron. 14 contains only Solomon of those who play any part in the older narratives; it is only in the opening of I Chron. 3, probably not an original part of the Chronicler's work, that we find the names of the other sons – Amnon, Absalom, Adonijah – around whom rebellion was to turn.)

It is interesting to observe how the presentation of the same point is so different theologically in the older and later writings. The compiler of the books of Samuel and Kings skilfully interweaves a great wealth of story to show how one and another of the sons of David were eliminated, and to make clear that the great failure of David in the affair of Bathsheba was to be the source of the divine promise of the acceptable successor Solomon (II Sam. 12). The Chronicler starts from the same premise that Solomon is divinely designated as temple-builder and therefore as successor. Largely by selection, but also by a different interweaving – particularly the use of ch.21 and the speeches and preparations of David for the temple – he leads up to the same culminating point.

Chapter 18 is almost identical with II Sam. 8. It traces some of David's campaigns against the surrounding peoples by which his establishment as a great ruler was achieved. The basis of these victories is made plain by the statement which appears as a sort of refrain in vv.6 and 13: THE LORD GAVE VICTORY TO DAVID WHEREVER HE WENT.

18.1. There is a link here to the Philistine theme of ch.14, and this theme is picked up again at 20.4-8. GATH AND ITS VILLAGES replaces an obscure expression in II Sam. where the text may be corrupt. It may be noted that the defeat of the Philistines did not lead to the actual occupation of their territory by Israel, unlike the areas of certain other peoples.

2. Moab The barbarous treatment described in II Sam. is omitted; presumably we should see in this an expression of the desire to present the character of David more favourably.

3-8. The defeat of the SYRIANS (or Aramaeans) under HADA-DEZER is connected with the question of the control of the trade routes to the Euphrates. The MONUMENT (v.3) or better 'victory stela' presumably indicates the Aramaean claim to control that area. The concept of the Davidic kingdom reaching to the Euphrates is to be found in ideal descriptions of its extent (e.g. Ps. 72.8). The word for GARRISONS is missing in the text of v.6, but is to be supplied from the parallel in II Sam. and in v.13; the word could in fact be rendered as 'officers' or alternatively as 'victory stelae'. Verse 8 has as an addition the statement that Solomon used THE BRONZE for important items of the temple furniture; by this the Chronicler links up the negative war theme – David prevented from building – with a positive one; David's wars are themselves linked to the temple. In this the Chronicler is in fact developing a theme already found in the older narrative and repeated here in v.11, which refers to the dedication of booty to God.

9-13. The defeat of the Aramaeans leads to the KING OF

HAMATH becoming tributary to David. The theme of battle is summarized in v.11 and again after a mention of the defeat of Edom (vv.12f.) in v.13. Ps. 60 (title) ascribes the victory at THE VALLEY OF SALT to Joab, not to ABISHAI.

14-17. II Sam. 8 included a section on David's royal organization, preserved also in II Sam. 20.23-26; it corresponds very closely to the similar statement for Solomon in I Kings 4.2-4. It is preserved here naturally enough, since it emphasizes the JUSTICE AND EQUITY of David's administration. We may note in the list of officials that ZADOK the priest appears to be associated with the family of Eli, though this is not found in the fuller details of ch.24. AHIMELECH THE SON OF ABIATHAR appears to be the wrong way round (cf. II Sam. 20.25), for it was Abiathar who was most closely associated with David. DAVID'S SONS (v.17) are described simply as chief officials, not priests as in II Sam., though the term so translated is not necessarily so restricted in meaning.

19.1-19. The narrative of ch.19 corresponds closely with that of II Sam. 10, with some small differences of wording and slight dislocations of text, as for example in v.3 (cf. II Sam. 10.3). The Ammonite theme runs through this chapter and the next, but it is closely interwoven with a further series of campaigns against SYRIANS (Aramaeans). This group of stories again serves to emphasize the extension of David's rule and the disarray of his enemies.

10-15. We may again see in a battle narrative that the giver of victory is God himself. Joab exhorts his men to courage, but the issue rests with God to DO WHAT SEEMS GOOD TO HIM. So it is that the SYRIANS and AMMONITES immediately take to flight, before there is any real engagement.

20.1-3. This continues the Ammonite theme and is remarkable for its containing only the beginning and end of the narrative found in II Sam. 11-12, omitting entirely the David-Bathsheba theme. The text is close to I Sam. 11.1 together with 12.26, 30-31. As it stands, there is some inconsequence.

20.1. David remained at Jerusalem This follows quite naturally from the opening, but serves in II Sam. to introduce the Bathsheba story. Here it is isolated.

2. No explanation is given of how David came to be at Rabbah. It may be that there has been an accidental omission from the text corresponding to II Sam. 12.27-29. If the text is rendered in v.2 THE CROWN OF THEIR KING, it is being claimed that David became as it were successor to the Ammonite royal line, a not inappropriate sequel to the shameful treatment meted out to David's ambassadors in 19.1-5; if the marginal rendering MILCOM (which has the same consonants) is preferred, then the crown belonged to the Ammonite deity and we can sense a ridiculing of the impotence of an alien god.

3. The precise sense here is not clear, but it seems unlikely that David subjected the Ammonites to the barbarous treatment suggested by the marginal rendering 'he sawed' them; more likely is the sense found in II Sam., which indicates forced labour by captives.

4-8. These verses correspond to II Sam. 21.18-22, and again deal with the conflict with the Philistines. An association is made in this particular passage between the PHILISTINES and THE GIANTS, the Rephaim – a term sometimes used to denote the earlier inhabitants of the land and particularly those inhabitants thought of as superior in strength and stature (cf. Gen. 15.20; Deut. 3.11); the term is also used to denote the spirits or shades of the dead, suggesting supernatural beings. Among them is included LAHMI THE BROTHER OF GOLIATH the GITTITE (v.5) killed by ELHANAN; in the II Sam. text, the death of Goliath himself is claimed for Elhanan, and it would appear that the Chronicler, knowing that his readers would be familiar with the story of David's defeat of Goliath, has introduced an explanatory phrase to resolve the problem created by the double tradition. The name LAHMI may in fact be a corruption of 'Bethlehemite', designating Elhanan as coming from there (cf. II Sam. 23.24). Where II Sam. has this material among the traditions of David's mighty men, utilized by the Chronicler

in ch.11, here it is used to round off the war theme. The Philistines, already in the earlier traditions the centre of hostility
as representing the alien world of those who do not accept
allegiance to Israel's God, the world of the uncircumcised,
are here too presented as the symbol of the forces overthrown
by David.

THE CHOICE OF THE TEMPLE SITE

21.1-22.1

The narrative of the census and plague and of David's
acquisition of Ornan's threshing floor as the site for the
temple is very closely based on II Sam. 24; but the differences
in overall presentation and in detail are of great importance.
(A more general discussion of the relationship between the
two narratives may be found in *The Cambridge History of the
Bible*, Vol.1, ed. P. R. Ackroyd and C. F. Evans, Cambridge
University Press 1971, pp.86-90.) Most obvious is the fact
that whereas II Sam. 24 forms part of the complex appendices to that book, here the narrative is closely integrated into
the overall structure. And whereas in the II Sam. form no
explicit link is made between the story of the threshing floor
and the site of the temple, here the climax is reached when
David recognizes the divine choice of place in which the
temple is to be built. (That the story is preserved in II Sam.
because it was believed to relate to the temple-site is probably
true; but the entire lack of mention of the relationship points
to the story being originally an independent sanctuary legend,
which has now been combined with the census and plague
themes.)

The story as now presented is central to the whole David
narrative. It continues the temple-theme and provides the basis
for the subsequent commissioning of Solomon and the actual
building described in II Chron. It also paves the way for the
Chronicler's fuller affirmation that, though David was not permitted to build the temple – and the reason for this is to be
disclosed in 22.8 – he could nevertheless be regarded as its

founder, both as the one who made all the necessary preparations and also as the organizer of the worship and personnel
of the shrine. The Chronicler ventures as near as he may to
affirming that it was really David who was responsible rather
than Solomon; the latter is depicted basically as the one who
carried out what had already been ordained.

21.1. The first major change appears here. The older narrative
speaks simply of God's anger being again kindled against
Israel, and it is apparent that this makes a reference back to
the similar narrative in II Sam. 21.1-14, which is likely to
have stood originally next to II Sam. 24. (The intervening
material constitutes two stages of expansion – David's heroes,
21.15-22+23.8-39, and two psalms, 22+23.1-7.) For this the
Chronicler has SATAN STOOD UP AGAINST ISRAEL. Here we have
a figure known to us from scenes in the heavenly court (Zech.
3; Job 1-2), one of the attendant beings – described in Job as
among the 'sons of God' – who comes in course of time to be
more sharply differentiated and changes from being a sort of
official accuser to be an instigator of evil. Yet, though he
INCITED DAVID TO NUMBER ISRAEL, and hence divine anger
was incurred against David and his people (v.7), Satan is not
here to be seen as independent of God or simply as opposed
to him. As in the passages mentioned in Zechariah and Job,
Satan or the Satan (the presence or absence of the definite
article may or may not show a greater or less sense of in-
dividuality) is operating within the divine purpose, and what
he does is still within divine control. He may be seen as testing
David's loyalty to God. Furthermore, there is no possibility
of man shifting the blame for his action to an alien force;
David and his people must bear absolute responsibility.

2. The sin to which David is led is that of conducting a
census; no precise reason is given for this, but v.5 makes
it evident that it is connected with military purposes. Nor are
we told why such a counting of the people is sinful. In Exod.
30.11-13, a census is indicated as a moment when special
precautions are necessary, the paying of a ransom by each
man 'that there be no plague among them when you number

them'. It is likely that behind this there lies an ancient belief
that such a numbering infringes on the area of divine rights.
We could readily understand the census being subsequently
interpreted, in view of its military connections, as indicative
of a lack of trust in the God whose prerogative it is to give
victory, whether by few or many. The Chronicler's battles
frequently exemplify this point. Such a view is, however,
somewhat at variance with the listing and numbering of families and tribes found in the opening chapters (cf. further the
comment in 27.23f.).

3. Joab's questioning of David's action may be seen as an
expression of a conservative piety, perhaps originally in reaction against the development of what may be seen as
undesirable governmental practices.

6. Joab excludes LEVI from the count, in accordance with a
principle laid down in Num. 1.47ff. So too BENJAMIN, though
no reason is given for this. Since v.5 indicates a number for
ALL ISRAEL, and then has a separate number for JUDAH, we
may wonder whether originally the Chronicler's account excluded Levi, Benjamin and Judah – the religious orders and
the true people of the faithful kingdom – and that subsequently
a figure for Judah was added by a scribe who thought that
Israel here meant the northern tribes, as it often does in the
older writings. It is possible that Benjamin is excluded because
Jerusalem and Gibeon, the holy places, lay within that area;
but this is only a guess. All the detail of the census is omitted
from v.4.

7. Divine judgment of an unspecified kind leads to David's
repentance.

9-12. The choice of three alternative punishments is offered
by GAD, the SEER.

15-16. The figure of the destroying angel known, for example,
in the story of judgment on the Assyrians in II Kings 19.35,
is considerably developed in the Chronicler's account; in v.16

he is depicted as being BETWEEN EARTH AND HEAVEN, which is the Hebrew way of saying 'in the air', WITH A DRAWN SWORD; this has been thought to be a vivid way of describing the appearance of a comet in the sky, for such natural phenomena were readily understood as indicative of divine action. In fact this fuller text is to be found in a manuscript of Samuel from Qumran, and the Chronicler may therefore have found this element already in his source. With a slight emendation, v.15 could be read: 'And the angel stretched out his hand' TO JERUSALEM TO DESTROY IT; this would make a better sequence of thought.

17. David's acceptance of sole responsibility may also be slightly emended to read: IT IS I WHO HAVE SINNED, 'I the shepherd'. BUT THESE SHEEP, WHAT HAVE THEY DONE? – a reading also to be preferred to the text as it stands.

18-25. This is a slightly deviant version of the negotiations with ORNAN – so the name appears here instead of Araunah. In v.20, he and HIS FOUR SONS see the angel; it is not clear what function the sons have in the narrative, and some commentators have suggested emending the text to make it refer to the sons of David, noting that if the four listed first in 14.4 were present they would include Solomon. The detail of the conversation has been influenced by the comparable one between Abraham and the Hittites at Hebron for the purchase of the cave of Machpelah (Gen. 23); the emphasis on the FULL PRICE (vv.22, 24) probably comes from that narrative (Gen. 23.9). More details are added to conform to proper sacrificial practice. The price paid (v.25) is very large (SIX HUNDRED SHEKELS OF GOLD, as against fifty shekels of silver in II Sam. 24.24), as befits a site which is to be so sacred.

Ornan the Jebusite The part played by him in this narrative is not explained; it has been thought that he was the previous ruler or priest of the city. The appearance of his sons in this passage might suggest that they too were to play a part in the cult on this site. He is depicted as engaged in an ordinary secular occupation, but v.22 makes David ask for

THE SITE OF THE THRESHING FLOOR, and again in v.25 there is reference to THE SITE; the word used (*māqōm*) is, as we have seen (p. 60), one that often carries a religious meaning. Is there here a relic of a tradition that it was already a holy place which was taken over and became the site of a shrine for Israel?

26-27. fire from heaven The acceptance of the new holy place by God is demonstrated in this way (cf. I Kings 18.38) and the judgment is brought to an end; here the words of v.15 are picked up again.

28. sacrifices The affirmation that this is now to be the place where sacrifices are to be offered brings the narrative to its real point.

29-30. the high place at Gibeon An explanatory passage shows why David was prevented from going here; clearly the choice of the new site lay within the purpose of God.

22.1. In the final verse there is an echo of the Bethel story in Gen. 28 (cf. v.17 there); such an echo may incorporate a polemical note. This site, Jerusalem, is the only holy place; no other, whatever its antiquity or sanction, can be allowed a claim. Here is a note which could be directed against dissident groups such as the Samaritans, who could claim greater antiquity for places such as Shechem and Bethel over against the temple at Jerusalem, which belonged only to the time of David and Solomon. Polemic or not, the claim for Jerusalem is being made with the authority of a divine revelation and the word of David.

The provision of the true site marks the beginning of the actual building of the temple, and the remainder of the David narrative centres on preparations both of material and of personnel.

PREPARATIONS FOR THE TEMPLE

22.2-23.1

The following chapters are largely, though not entirely, a composition independent of the earlier narrative in the books of Samuel and Kings. Here and there an allusion shows the Chronicler engaged in writing a kind of expansive commentary on the earlier material. His theme of the building of the temple is now being combined with its counterpart, the succession of Solomon, and the fact that in the older material II Sam. 24 is followed by I Kings 1-2, in which the succession of Solomon is described, provides a motive for the introduction of his succession at this point. But it is subordinated to the primary concern with the temple.

22.2-4. The survey of building preparations, both in respect of materials to be used and in the appointment of foreign craftsmen, is a point to be taken up again in II Chron. 2.17f. The Chronicler avoids the suggestion that forced labour duties were imposed on native Israelites; their co-operation is to be enjoined in I Chron. 29.

5. This introduces the commissioning of Solomon and is therefore better opened without RSV's FOR. That Solomon is YOUNG AND INEXPERIENCED has been picked up from the prayer of Solomon at Gibeon (I Kings 3.7: 'I am but a little child [better 'a young or inexperienced person']; I do not know how to go out or come in'. The Chronicler's version of that story II Chron. 1.10 omits this theme of inexperience). Solomon's inexperience stands out in sharp contrast to the magnitude of the task; for the temple is to be OF FAME AND GLORY THROUGHOUT ALL LANDS. Such an idea of the centrality of the Jerusalem shrine may be found in prophetic oracles (Isa. 2.2ff. = Micah 4.1ff.; Zech. 14.16ff.) and in psalmody (e.g. Ps. 48).

7-13 (14-16). The commission itself is loosely based on

elements in the injunctions to be found in I Kings 2.1-9, but only the themes of vv.2-3 are used: BE STRONG and OBSERVE THE STATUTES ... (of) MOSES (v.13). The primary charge is TO BUILD A HOUSE FOR THE LORD (v.6, picked up again in the following verses). The explanation of David's inability to build because of the guilt of bloodshed (v.8) is based on the earlier statement of I Kings 5.3-4 (Heb. 17-18) that his wars left David no opportunity to build the temple; but the change is a significant one. Bloodshed in war, involving ritual guilt, and the building of a shrine are here said to be irreconcilable. By contrast with this, Solomon will be able to build, as A MAN OF 'rest' (better than RSV's PEACE in v.9). This verse in facts builds upon two word-plays; the more obvious one is the quite correct linking of the name of SOLOMON (Heb. SHELŌMŌ) with the Hebrew word rendered PEACE (SHĀLŌM – often better rendered 'prosperity, well-being, wholeness'), but there is also a play on the word for 'rest', and here the Chronicler makes use of an element which is omitted in 17.1 (cf. the note there). Solomon is A MAN OF 'rest'. I WILL GIVE HIM 'rest' FROM ALL HIS ENEMIES (the RSV translation entirely misses this second element, as do NEB and the Jerusalem Bible; it is correctly given in RV). The declaration of divine promise in v.10 is closely based on the oracle delivered by Nathan in 17.12ff., though the clauses are differently arranged.

The commission proper is followed by an exhortation of a sermonic kind, a feature of the Chronicler's method which recurs frequently. The divine presence is the assurance of success in the task of temple-building; the granting of wisdom to Solomon described in II Chron. 1 is anticipated in v.12, and this wisdom is directed primarily to obedience to the law of Moses. A final exhortation to courage and strength is again one which finds frequent echoes in such passages throughout the work.

14-16. These verses stress the preparations already made, with some link to vv.2-4, but with amounts of silver and gold which are clearly beyond the bounds of possibility; yet by

these immense figures, the Chronicler is stressing the central
place which the temple is to occupy, and thus there is a
link to the assurance of v.5 that the temple is to be of
significance for all lands. The opening phrase WITH GREAT
PAINS could be rendered in various ways: it could be 'in my
poverty', an exaggerated statement to contrast with the
immensity of the wealth mentioned; or it could be 'in my
humility', which would suit the acknowledgement by David
that he is only the preparer of the temple building; or yet
again 'in my trouble', i.e. in spite of the pressure of warfare
during my reign. Of these, 'in my humility' is perhaps the
most attractive, though no certainty can be reached. Verses
15-16, joined together in RSV, as in other modern versions,
may also be treated as separate statements, as in RV; we
would then read: '... craftsmen skilled in all kinds of work.
(v.16) Of gold, silver ... there is no reckoning.'

17-19. This is an anticipation of the full exhortation to the
community in I Chron. 29; the insertion of this duplicating
statement here could be due to the breaking of the main
material by the inclusion of 23.2-27.34 (see below); the mention of Solomon's accession in 23.1 would seem to need such
a word to the people as a whole before it took place. The
exhortation stresses the coming of peace: the second sentence
in v.18 may better be rendered as future, 'And he will give
you peace', the statements that follow being then affirmations
of what God has already decreed.

23.1. In its mention of David's old age this verse provides
a reminiscence of the court intrigue described in I Kings 1,
but all the details of that intrigue are passed over; Solomon
is the sole claimant to the throne, the divine choice as successor. Both this statement and the narrative in I Kings may
well imply a period of co-regency, desirable when a ruler by
reason of old age or illness (cf. Uzziah in II Chron. 26.21)
is unable to carry the full responsibility. This verse may be
regarded as a kind of heading to the narrative of I Chron.
28-29, which provides its true sequel.

THE OFFICIALS OF TEMPLE AND KINGDOM

23.2-27.34

At this point, with the preparations for the temple described as under way and with Solomon appointed as successor to David, we should expect the completion of the narrative as this is to be found in I Chron. 28-29, where the exhortations to Solomon and the people are set out in a fuller form than those which we have just seen in ch.22. Instead, virtually four chapters are devoted to lists of names and details of temple and other organization, of a kind which we have already seen within the narratives, particularly in chs.15-16. The overlapping in detail of the material of these chapters within themselves, as well as their evident relationship to lists which appear elsewhere within the Chronicler's work, shows that we have another example of the process by which either the Chronicler himself or his successors, or more probably both, made use of this method both to underline the Davidic authority for the institutions known to them in their own time and also to make certain claims and assertions about that organization. The differences, for example, in the gatekeeper lists of ch.26 from those found elsewhere in chs.9 and 16, suggest that we should see in all this material reflections of changing situations, modifications in the organization, the rise and fall of particular families, some indications of manoeuverings for position, if not actual struggles for power. When we consider the evidence available for later years – for example in the second century BC – of the conflicts between families and parties within the community, we should not be surprised to find that such struggles existed also at an earlier date. A detailed examination of the various lists shows the extreme complexity of the matter, and there is no agreement as to how far the compiler was making use of earlier material – even perhaps material going back to the Davidic age – or how far he was using contemporary information for his own particular purposes. Nor is there agreement as to how far the material of these chapters was included as a deliberate insertion by the original author or how far their present complex state is due to several stages of accretion. The diversity of the material and its variations in comparison with other lists in the work point rather in the latter direction, but complete consistency is not necessarily a mark of an author whose primary concern is interpretation. What remains as the most significant point to the reader of the whole work is the claim which is being made in these lists that the institutions, both religious and secular, of the later period have the authority of David. For the community to which the work was addressed there is the implicit appeal that if they are to be the true people of God they must see themselves as the successors to what was decreed by David and must express in their own life and organization the values which are set out in the Davidic material.

23.2. This may perhaps be regarded as still part of the preceding narrative; it could be a broken fragment of the summons to the whole leadership which appears at 28.1.

3-23. This is a list of the levitical families under the three sons of Levi: GERSHOM, KOHATH and MERARI; their functions are set out (vv.4-5) as having CHARGE OF THE WORK IN THE HOUSE OF THE LORD – that is, of the conduct of worship in general and perhaps also of repair work, as OFFICERS AND JUDGES, as GATEKEEPERS, and as musicians.

3. Thirty years old and upward The enumeration here follows the prescriptions of Num. 4.3, 23, 30; Num. 8.24 has twenty-five years old, whereas in vv.24, 27 here and in II Chron. 31.17; Ezra 3.8, we find twenty years old. The different regulations may reflect different situations, perhaps periods when a shortage of Levites of the proper age led to a lowering of the point of entry to office. The counting of the Levites here contrasts sharply with its absence in 21.6.

4. officers The term is used in a number of instances – though the English term does not always correspond to the same Hebrew word – and probably denotes scribes or clerks.

13-14. Aaron and Moses Particular comment is made on the status of these among the descendants of Levi. The position of Aaron and his descendants is made the special concern in ch.24; Moses is given less prominence, but he is regarded as THE MAN OF GOD, a term often used to denote a prophet but clearly having a potentially much wider connotation.

22. daughters of Eleazar This curious note seems to be connected with a claim to full position through the female line.

24-32. There follows a definition of the duties of the Levites, with vv.25f. indicating a certain change envisaged as a result of the establishment of the temple in the place of the earlier tabernacle. Like the comparable material in ch.9, the concern appears to be with the establishing of the continuity of status for those who engage in the temple service, and much of the detail of the following verses repeats what is found in ch.9. A reference to THE TENT OF MEETING in v.32 points to the awareness that at the period to which this is supposed to refer, the tent was still at Gibeon. Verse 27 is probably out of place; it is an explanatory note to the change to twenty years old in v.24. Verse 25 emphasizes again the granting of peace and the permanence of the divine dwelling at Jerusalem, an idea which had to be qualified, for example by Ezekiel at the time of the temple's destruction, but one which is to be retained because of the assurance it gives of the continuity of worship even across such a disastrous break.

24.1-19. These verses are devoted to the priestly orders, noting that they are descended from two sons of Aaron, ELEAZAR, to whom sixteen duty rotas are assigned, and ITHAMAR, who appears as less prominent with only eight. An allusion is made in v.2 to the account in Lev. 10.1f. of the calamitous death of the other two sons, NADAB AND ABIHU, a story which the reader is assumed to know. The arrangement of the priestly orders according to twenty-four rotas of duty is of considerable interest. Its continuance in the New Testament period is known from the reference to Zechariah, the father of John the Baptist, as belonging to the order of ABIJAH (Luke 1.5, cf.

v.10 here). The naming of JEHOIARIB (v.7) as FIRST suggests the possibility that the present form of the list may be linked with the events of the Maccabaean period, since Mattathias and his sons, the so-called Maccabaean family, belonged to that order (I Macc. 2.1). The concern with such regularity of ordering is also to be seen prominently expressed in the rules of the Qumran community.

20-31. A further levitical list appears as a kind of supplement to the material of ch.23.

25.1-31. This chapter covers the organization of music, and has close links with chs.15-16.

1-3. We may note the prominence here of the function of prophecy as associated with the Levites (cf. on 15.22); the precise sense, however, is not clear. Is the term perhaps being used in a rather looser sense for 'divine inspiration', since the reference is to prophesying with musical instruments of various kinds? The association of music with prophecy (cf. most clearly the Elisha story in II Kings 3.15) may point to some procedure by which the playing of music in worship was seen to be related to the revealing of the divine word.

4-5. Greatest prominence is given in the lists to HEMAN and his family, and he is described as THE KING'S SEER (v.5). The variations in position of the different groups may again point to changes of status at different times. There is, however, a curious feature about the names in the second half of v.4 (from HANANIAH onwards); one or two of these names are very odd both in form and meaning (GIDDALTI – 'I have made great'; ROMAMTI-EZER – 'I have exalted help'), and it has been suggested that we have here a fragment of a psalm which has at some point been read as if it were a list of names. The words could be rendered:

> Show favour to me, O Yah, show favour to me;
> You are my God:
> I magnify and exalt (you), my help;

> As I dwell in hardship, I speak (or I faint):
> Grant visions.

(It is probable that the text is corrupt at a number of points.) A rather remote analogy to such a transfer of the words of a psalm to names has been found in Sumerian texts, but it would seem more likely that a misplaced psalm fragment – perhaps originally part of a larger poetic insertion comparable to that found in ch.16 – has been understood to be part of a list. Perhaps it was originally intended to provide an example of the inspired utterances which belonged to these levitical functionaries. The association of some psalms with the leading names here points to such a possibility.

8. teacher and pupil This indicates the existence of an instructional system for the music, though it is possible the two terms simply form an expression suggesting completeness.

9-31. The remainder of the chapter lists the musicians arranged in twenty-four orders like the priests.

26.1-19. gatekeepers The list here, similar to that of the Levites, may be compared with the material to be found in chs.9 and 16 and in Ezra 2=Neh. 7. The names of the family groups are listed (vv.1-11) and the allocation of them to their particular duties. Special attention is devoted to the divinely blessed family of Obed-edom (cf. 13.14).

18. parbar This word, indicated in RSV as of unknown meaning, appears to be of Persian origin and most probably denotes a 'colonnade'. A number of topographical details concerning Jerusalem are found here; cf. the further indications in Neh. 3.

20-28. This is a list of another group of Levites responsible for the TREASURIES of the temple and THE TREASURIES OF THE DEDICATED GIFTS (v.20). (Ahijah in this verse is probably an error; we should read 'fellow-Levites'.) Ancient temples were naturally enough treasure-houses of accumulated wealth and rich gifts dedicated to the deity for particular reasons, per-

sonal and public. The temple as a source of wealth appears
in a number of Old Testament narratives (e.g. the buying-off
of Sennacherib by Hezekiah in II Kings 18.13-16). The references to spoil from David's campaigns (v.27) provide a link
back to chs.18-20; the inclusion of a reference to Samuel
and Saul, Abner and Joab is not necessarily an indication
of an ancient document or of authentic information, for it
may simply enshrine popular belief. In the time of Hezekiah's
reform, there is reference to the presence in the temple of a
bronze snake associated with Moses (II Kings 18.4), but it
is unlikely that this object really had so ancient an origin.
More probable is the view that the temple through its history acquired a great many objects of which the real origin
was forgotten, and these came to be popularly associated
with great figures of the past. According to I Sam. 17.54,
David had taken the head of Goliath to Jerusalem, and the
latter part of that verse may mean that the armour was
placed in the tent-shrine. Since Jerusalem was not yet in
Israelite hands, this is clearly an anachronism, but it would
occasion no surprise if there were a belief that these and
other objects from the time of David and earlier actually
survived in the shrine. The mention of Saul in a more favourable manner in a work which is so hostile to him may
suggest the use of some popular tradition of this kind, preserved in spite of its difference of outlook.

29-32. Perhaps these verses belong really with ch.27, for
although the list of Levites appears here to be continued,
the real subject concerns more general administrative activity;
OFFICERS (clerks) AND JUDGES are indicated as appointed for
the tribes WESTWARD OF THE JORDAN (v.30) and for those on
the east (v.32). An odd piece of tradition is preserved in the
precise reference to the carrying out of a search for suitable
officers in THE FORTIETH YEAR OF DAVID'S REIGN (v.31). The
last phrase of v.32 indicates oversight in matters religious and
secular, and we might perhaps see in this – and in the fuller
picture of organization in ch.27 – a reflection of the need in
the period of Ezra and later (cf. Ezra 7) to extend the control

outside the territory of Judah to include members of the community living further afield. That such an extension should claim Davidic authority would again be fully intelligible. It was during the Persian period and later still under Greek rule that political power came to be increasingly in priestly hands, the high priest becoming the embodiment of both secular and religious authority.

27.1-22. Some parts at least of ch. 27 may well go back to old information, reflecting early administrative organization such as we find attested for the reign of Solomon; but it is also probable that the Chronicler, making use of older material, is projecting this into the Davidic age as showing a pattern which is still to be regarded as relevant. This concern for the ordering of the community, both political and religious, has a certain analogy in the idealized portrayal of the new land in the last chapters of the book of Ezekiel (47-48). The central temple with its proper personnel and worship is there seen as surrounded by a newly organized land, its tribes appropriately situated geographically in relation to the centre. What the book of Ezekiel projects into a visionary future, the Chronicler or his successors project into the Davidic age. So here the tribes (though Gad and Asher are not mentioned) are organized and numbered, and material is used for this which is in part related to the lists of mighty men in ch.11.

23-24. The apparent conflict between this material and the census narrative of ch.21 may have led to the comments here. The exclusion of those under twenty, presumably regarded as the age of maturity as it is the age of full membership at Qumran, opens the way to suggesting that the full number would not be known, since it depended on divine promise (cf. Gen. 15.5; 22.17). It is then suggested that Joab did not finish the census, though this is somewhat differently explained in 21.6.

25-31. These verses, which may well be based upon older material, are concerned with the royal estates and their

administration. Such royal property is frequently alluded to
in the Old Testament; it might be acquired by purchase (e.g.
I Kings 16.24), or by expropriation of a criminal's property
(e.g. I Kings 21). Its administration would be an important
concern. Again there is a parallel to the Ezekiel material,
where the prince has lands adjacent to the area of temple
and city (Ezek. 48.21f.).

32-34. The section concludes with a further list of royal
officials; these appear to be the personal staff of the royal
household rather than the public officers listed in 18.15-17.
For THE KING'S FRIEND cf. II Sam. 15.37; 16.16ff.; the position was evidently one of considerable importance. There is
allusion to the narratives of Absalom's rebellion in the mention of AHITHOPHEL and HUSHAI, and of the successors to
Ahithophel, whose death by suicide is not mentioned, but
is evidently assumed to be known to the reader (cf. II Sam.
16-17).

The effect of all this material, even though it interrupts
the course of the narrative, is to emphasize the provision of
complete order for the people's life by David. Its implication to the later readership must be clear. A recovery or preservation of their true life as the people of God is linked
with their recognition that such a proper organization had
once existed and could be regarded as providing the guarantee
for stability and order in their own time.

THE COMMISSIONING OF SOLOMON
28.1-21

1-2. The theme begun in 23.1 (2) is resumed, with the summoning of an assembly which by its long list of terms suggests
the inclusion of all those who have been mentioned in the
previous chapter. The text has probably been amplified to
correspond to the insertions made in the preceding chapters.
The assembly is addressed by KING DAVID. We may sense
here that the Chronicler is countering the story of I Kings 1

by stressing that he ROSE TO HIS FEET. This is not the senile
David of I Kings, unable to keep warm in old age and subject to the influence of intrigue on behalf of the son of
Bathsheba. It is a David who in a ripe old age is still in
full possession of his faculties, ready to hand over the task
to his son and go to his death as a great king should (cf.
29.28). A similar transformation of Moses at his death may
be seen by comparing Deut. 31.2, where he is much weakened,
with Deut 34.7, which emphasizes his continuing vigour.

2-8. The first part of his address is to the whole assembly.
and it repeats in considerable measure the material of the
address to Solomon in 22.7-13. The temple was David's intention; it was to be A HOUSE OF REST – the word picks up the
theme of 22.9 (see p.79) and further that of II Sam. 7.1 and
Deut. 12.10 echoed in other Deuteronomic passages, and in
Ps. 95.11. So it is not just that the temple is to be a permanent, immovable dwelling for God; rather, it is connected
with the establishment of God's people in the land which is
the objective of divine promise (see below v.8). The ARK
here appears to be paralleled by THE FOOTSTOOL OF OUR GOD.

3. The reason for David's inability to build is repeated.

4-5. The choice of Solomon from among the sons of David
is here substantially amplified; it is comparable to the divine
choice of David himself. This choice is expressed in a form
which may be paralleled elsewhere: he is TO BE KING OVER
ISRAEL FOR EVER; within Israel, it was the tribe of JUDAH
that was chosen (cf. Ps. 78.68); within Judah, it was the family
of Jesse; within that family, it was this son David (cf. I
Sam. 16.1-13). For the narrowing of the divine choice, compare the choice of Gideon, with the sequence 'Israel, Manasseh,
the clan within the tribe, Gideon within the clan' (Judg.
6.15), and also the choice of Saul by lot as king (I Sam.
10.20f.). It is in fact a theme which is more broadly expressed
in the opening chapters of names in I Chron., as also in
the conception of a narrowing of the divine covenant in
Genesis. The parenthetic reference to David's MANY SONS (v.5)

points the reader to the rich narrative of II Sam. 10-19; I Kings 1-2.

An important new element appears here, for now it is made clear that the throne upon which he is to sit, the throne of David, is in fact THE THRONE OF THE KINGDOM OF THE LORD OVER ISRAEL (cf. 29.23; cf. also note on 17.14). The status of the king in ancient Israel has been a much debated subject. It is clear that the king is never depicted as divine, as a god-figure; it is also clear that, however much he is described in terms which do full justice to his humanity and in particular to the failure of kings to conform to a right standard, he is nevertheless no ordinary man. For he can be described as the adopted son of God (Ps. 2.7); his relationship to God is such that he appears both as representative of the people to God and as mediator of the divine blessing to the people (so often in the Psalms). Ps. 45.6 has a phrase the exact rendering of which has been much debated. Literally it runs: 'Your throne, O God, is for ever and ever', but it is addressed to the king, and the words have been used as an argument in favour of understanding the Israelite king as having divine status. More recently (cf. NEB) a rendering has been proposed: 'Your throne is like God's throne', but even if this is correct it still makes plain the close association between the divine rule and the rule of the king as the chosen representative of God. The fact that we find in the Chronicler such clear evidence of an understanding of the royal throne being in effect the divine throne suggests both a certain idealizing of kingship in a period when kingship no longer existed, but also a clear recognition that the rule of the king is the rule of God. For the Chronicler, with his attempt at clarifying the position of the people of God, such an affirmation is important as suggesting that the embodiment of the ideals of Davidic kingship in an age when kingship cannot be a political reality is to be seen in the acceptance of the reality of divine rule, in a theocratic ideal.

6. This verse uses the theme of 22.10.

7. Here the themes of 22.13 are taken up.

8. A new theme is now added, one which is the *Leitmotiv* of the book of Deuteronomy; obedience is enjoined on the people, for obedience is associated with the perpetual possession of THIS GOOD LAND. Where Deuteronomy (as do the books which follow it) appeals to a community which has lost the land of promise to understand the conditions of its recovery, the Chronicler, from a later date, sees the continuing promise of God and his people's position as still dependent on that promise and on obedience. It may be that, considering the weak and constricted position of the little provincial area of Judah, he is also pointing to the conditions upon which alone a full possession of the land can be envisaged (cf. p. 304 on Neh. 9.36f.).

9-10. Solomon is addressed here; the verses are a sermonic exhortation, expressing a deep sense of the relationship between man and God. What is said to Solomon may be seen to be said to the whole community; the God known to David – THE GOD OF YOUR FATHER – is the one who SEARCHES ALL HEARTS AND UNDERSTANDS EVERY PLAN AND THOUGHT. He is willing to BE FOUND (cf. Isa. 55.6); but IF YOU FORSAKE HIM, HE WILL CAST YOU OFF FOR EVER (v.9).

11. The verbal commission is followed by the handing over of THE PLAN of the whole series of temple buildings, a plan divinely given.

12. This could be rendered better: 'the plan of everything which was with him by the (divine) spirit, in respect of the courts . . .'

13-19. The plan, as here developed, includes not simply the design of the buildings, but the ordering of priestly duties and the temple VESSELS, here given a particular weight as objects of gold and silver. This theme of the temple vessels is to recur, not only in the actual description of the building in II Chron. 4, but also in connection with the destruction of Jerusalem and its temple (II Chron. 36.18ff.) and with its restoration (Ezra 1 and again in chs.7-8). Such an emphasis is not to be seen simply in terms of the Chronicler's obvious love of worship and of everything connected with it; it is to be seen as a theme which points to the continuity of worship from the moment of the planning of the temple right through to its contemporary use. What the worshippers of the Chronicler's own time do is one with the worship of the temple's founders.

That the temple is built by a divinely granted plan (vv.11, 19) makes a link with the making of the tabernacle in Exodus (cf. Exod. 25.9, 40), where such a plan (the same word is used) is shown to Moses by God.

19. The precise text and wording are not clear. The Hebrew has a sudden change to a first person form: 'All this is in the writing (document) from the hand of the LORD: by me he has brought to fruition all the works indicated in the plan.' The change indicated in RSV is a small one and it removes the awkward change of person, but such shifts are not uncommon in Hebrew, and by making David speak at this point, the author lays particular emphasis on his words.

20-21. The exhortation to Solomon is resumed with a reiteration of the themes of vv.9-10 and of the preceding verses; here there is added too the emphasis on the priests and Levites and their duties, and on the willingness of the people to respond, a theme which is taken up in ch.29.

THE COMMISSIONING OF THE PEOPLE AND THE SUCCESSION OF SOLOMON

29.1-30

1-5. The immediate sequel to the exhortation to Solomon is a similar one to the people. He is YOUNG AND INEXPERIENCED (v.1), a phrase which picks up the wording of 22.5; the greatness of the task of building the temple is emphasized here, as also in that verse, but a different word is used, rendered PALACE, a word which occurs only in the later writings of the Old Testament in this sense or as meaning castle or fortress (e.g. Neh. 1.1 cf. p. 265). The theme of accumulation of materials for the temple is elaborated in a different manner, with emphasis on their precious nature and rarity, and to this general statement of preparations is added the indication that David set an example to his people by dedicating to the temple his own private TREASURE (vv.3ff.). So in 5*b* the appeal is made that the people should OFFER WILLINGLY, a theme which echoes that of Moses' appeal to the people for the building of the tabernacle (Exod. 25.1-7). The phrase CONSECRATING HIMSELF is literally 'filling his hand', a technical expression used for the ordination or consecration of priests, as in Exod. 28.41, where the phrase is translated 'ordain them', and stands alongside terms for 'anoint' and 'consecrate' or 'sanctify'. If this is what the phrase means here (so RSV), then there is an extension of its meaning to suggest that the willingness of the people's offering constitutes an act of consecration of themselves to God. It is not just the gift that is dedicated, but the giver. But it may be that the phrase is here used in a non-technical manner, simply in the sense of 'being willing to fill one's hand', i.e. to give with total generosity.

6-7. The appeal is followed by the response, as may be seen in a number of the Chronicler's narratives, and as we may see also in Hag. 1.12-14. The list in v.7 includes DARICS, a word which occurs elsewhere in the Old Testament only in Ezra 8.27; it is an anachronism here, for it belongs to the Persian period and it denotes coined money as distinct from weighed gold. Coinage is attested only from the eighth century BC onwards, at first in Asia Minor.

8. treasury Its existence in the temple is assumed, again anachronistically. The Chronicler is clearly thinking in terms of the practices and institutions of his own day.

9. A familiar stress is that on rejoicing; such generosity carries with it a true rejoicing. The Chronicler often brings out this aspect of religious experience. A similar theme is to be seen in Exod. 38.24f.

10-19. This is one of the best examples of prayer-forms used

by the Chronicler. We may see in such prayers the expression
of the liturgical practice of his own time, drawing upon the
rich Israelite tradition found at its fullest in the psalms.

10-12. The first part is an act of praise, recalling the ancestral
faith (THE GOD OF ISRAEL OUR FATHER), THE POWER of God,
and his control of the whole world. His is THE KINGDOM, a
theme appropriate to the context of Solomon's accession
(cf. v.23). Everything rests in the hand of God. Verse 11
here is comparable to the doxology to the prayer of Jesus
in some MSS of Matt. 6.13.

13. And now The second part of the prayer would seem to
begin here; the RSV paragraphing is less satisfactory. The
words form the introduction to the main section of the prayer.
This is on the analogy of the letter style in which the initial
greeting – here represented by the praise of vv.10-12 – is
followed by the real substance of the letter introduced
commonly by these words (cf. the letter in Ezra 4, esp. v.12).
So the sense is: 'Here we are thanking thee and praising thy
name (the Hebrew has participial forms in these phrases suggesting the continuity of the action), *but* – and the word is
strongly emphasized – what is our status before God?' The
comment on this is in a series of statements.

14. All that men give to God is in fact from God.

15. Emphasis is on the theme of impermanence found, for
example, in Ps. 39.12f. and in Job 14.2. The word rendered
ABIDING may also be rendered 'hope', as the RSVmg indicates;
the Hebrew word may in fact bear either sense. Alternatively
it has been suggested that it means 'security'.

16. The theme of giving is again brought out.

17-18. We now move to a different theme, that of the accept-
ability of a people known to God, now revealed in their true
nature as willing and joyous givers. So the appeal is that
the ancestral God (v.18) will keep always alive this attitude
of loyalty and generosity.

19. An addendum makes a final prayer for Solomon, bringing back the general theme of the prayer to the immediate situation. Here we may see how the Chronicler, utilizing already familiar prayer-forms, adapts them to the particular setting in which they stand.

20-22a. These verses describe the people's response in an act of worship, and the carrying through of a great festival on the following day. Perhaps there is here in the Chronicler's mind a reminiscence of the story of Adonijah in I Kings 1.9f., for he held a great feast in honour of his acclamation as king, though he was not in fact to be the successor of David.

22b-25. The accession of Solomon is now described. The words THE SECOND TIME (missing in LXX MS Vaticanus) in v.22 are to be regarded as a later insertion made because of the reference to his accession in 23.1; this statement, which may be seen as a heading to what follows, has been misunderstood as suggesting that there were two stages in the accession. Perhaps at the back of the annotator's mind is the recollection of the double kingship of David – first Judah and then Israel – or the apparent double appointment of Saul in the complex of narratives in I Sam. 9-11. The plurals THEY MADE, THEY ANOINTED are equivalent to the passive 'he was made, anointed'; it leaves open the question of who performed the actions. He is KING and PRINCE, a term which means 'the one in front, i.e. leader', used of Solomon in I Kings 1.35, and also of Saul and David. It is a term very frequently used by the Chronicler, possibly because in the later period the fact that kingship had ceased made the use of 'king' seem at times rather out of place, though evidently the term 'leader, prince' was an early one in Israel's thought about leadership. The anointing of ZADOK at this moment blends together the information of I Kings 1.39 and 2.35; the precise point at which Zadok came into prominence is by no means clear in the earlier narratives (cf. note on 6.48-53). The anointing of the high priest was a post-exilic custom. Verse 23 both reiterates that the throne of the Davidic king is the divine throne (cf. 28.5; 17.14) and offers a summary of the coming reign of Solomon, again emphasizing that he is king of ALL ISRAEL. So allegiance to Solomon is pledged by ALL THE LEADERS AND THE MIGHTY MEN (v.24), including the other SONS OF KING DAVID – a sidelong glance at the position of Adonijah in I Kings 1-2. The position of Solomon is compared favourably to his predecessors, a statement which is not to be taken literally but to be seen as a conventional polite formula of courtly language (cf. e.g. II Kings 18.5).

26-30. The final summary of David's reign is given in a form which will be found again for other rulers; it is the Chronicler's version of the formulae found in the earlier writings. Again there is the echoing phrase ALL ISRAEL (v.26), and a recall of the two periods of his reign, even though the division between them has been slurred over in the account (v.27). Verse 28 brings him to a proper death, unlike that of I Kings 1-2; there is no loss of power or personality here. The full account of his reign is described as to be found in the CHRONICLES OF SAMUEL THE SEER, ... NATHAN THE PROPHET, ... GAD THE SEER (three different words are used, though the distinction which once existed between these terms has long since been lost). We may see the Chronicler here essentially making a reference back to those parts of the earlier work in which these three prophetic figures appear. The CHRONICLES or 'acts' or 'words' of the particular prophet may be regarded as those narratives in which they can be seen as directing events under God. This is extended to make the point that the history of David, and the whole history of God's people, is carried through under the divine will, mediated through the agency of his prophets. The point will be brought out again at different stages of the narrative; it is a reminder that we are dealing with theological interpretation rather than with historical account.

These last two chapters of I Chronicles are of particular interest because they give us so much insight into the Chronicler's own thinking. They are typical of the kind of comments which are made, not directly, but by means of sermon and prayer and narrative, drawing the reader's attention to the underlying principles which are to be appreciated. Some part of the Chronicler's outlook as expressed here may be seen in his transfer to David of some of the themes set out in II Chron. 6 (I Kings 8) in the prayer which is there ascribed to Solomon, though it quite evidently shows a reflection on the whole existence and significance of the temple. We may see the influence also of the tabernacle narratives of Exodus and of the ideals expressed in Ezekiel 40-48. The picture of David which emerges here, as from the preceding chapters – even though it is modified and extended by the additions made to the original work – is that of the one to whom the temple and its worship are to be attributed, as the one who carried through what the law of Moses laid down; the authority for what men do now in worship, in the Chronicler's own day, lies in the attestation of David's action under God. The Chronicler's David is an ideal figure, though there is no reluctance to use an unfavourable narrative (ch.21) when this points to the divine grace which overrules even the failure of David. But the Chronicler's intention is not just to paint an ideal figure of the past; it is to show how in that figure there has been expressed the basis upon which worship and life are to be maintained. It is an ideal in the past which is a projection of the Chronicler's convictions about the present.

SOLOMON

II Chronicles 1-9

It would be equally proper to treat this section of the
Chronicler's work as simply part of the David/temple narrative. The division between the two books of Chronicles is
not original, so that the opening chapters of what is now
termed II Chronicles are to be read straight on from what
precedes. This section portrays the actual carrying through
of what David had planned; it is a putting into effect of
plans already made.

Yet Solomon as the actual temple builder has a position
which deserves special treatment. In addition, the Chronicler
has made use of the wisdom of Solomon as a theme, closely
linked to that of the temple, which is seen to be the supreme
expression of the granting of wisdom to the king. He has
presented this picture of Solomon by making use of a considerable amount of the material to be found in I Kings 3-11.
No use is made of the accession narratives of I Kings 1-2,
though we have seen some possible allusions to them in the
preceding chapters. There are also substantial omissions from
the Solomon narratives. The discreditable material is not
included, in particular the final condemnatory passage in I
Kings 11; nor is the organizational information of I Kings
4 to be found here, perhaps because the Chronicler saw David
as the administrator of the kingdom too (cf. I Chron. 27,
though this may be a later addition). There are also substantial changes within the sections which have been taken
over. The selection made enables the Chronicler to carry
somewhat further an emphasis found already in the earlier
presentation; the Solomon narratives are set in a framework
of emphasis on his wisdom. The granting of this is the main
theme of II Chron. 1, and the story is rounded off in ch.9

largely with its expression in the visit of the queen of Sheba. If the supreme example of Solomon's wisdom is seen in the building of the temple, which forms the theme of the whole of the intervening chapters, his wisdom also expresses itself in his reputation as a ruler and in the wealth and prosperity of his reign. So his trading ventures are closely bound in with the wisdom theme, and at the same time they serve to undergird his building activity which depended so largely upon that prosperity.

THE WISDOM AND PROSPERITY OF SOLOMON – I

1.1-17

1. The account of Solomon opens with a resumptive statement of the establishment of his rule and of the presence and support of God for him. It picks up the comment in I Chron. 29.23-25, and forms a counterpart to the statement of I Kings 2.46*b* which there indicates the overcoming of the opposition which confronted the king at the outset of his reign. Similar phrases are used of other kings in 12.13; 13.21; 17.1; 21.4, though they are not as much elaborated as the one for Solomon.

2-13. These verses correspond substantially with the narrative in I Kings 3.5-15, but there are some very important differences. These are partly due to additions and omissions, some reasons for which may be suggested. But partly they show a considerable freedom in relating the story, with departures from the words and phrases of the original in such a way as almost to suggest that the Chronicler was here telling a familiar story largely in his own words. Should we perhaps see here an example of a homiletic technique, very familiar from the preaching of many ages and contexts, in which a biblical narrative – which has perhaps been read as part of the liturgy or which can be assumed to be known to the hearers – is paraphrased, the additions and omissions, the changes in wording, all being due to a desire on the part of

the preacher to bring home the real significance of what is
already familiar?

2-6. What the older story shows as a private visit to THE
HIGH PLACE AT GIBEON is here a public pilgrimage, undertaken by the whole ASSEMBLY, the religious convocation of
ALL ISRAEL. This is no visit to another sanctuary, one of the
high places whose use by Solomon is regarded in I Kings
as a point at which praise of him must be qualified (I Kings
3.3). It is a necessary procedure because, as vv.3b-5 here
explain, until the temple was built certain of the great religious
objects of the past were preserved there: THE TENT OF MEET-
ING OF GOD constructed by MOSES (v.3), and the BRONZE ALTAR
made by the craftsman BEZALEL (v.5, cf. Exod. 27.1f.; 38.1f.,
where it is made clear that the altar was in fact of wood overlaid with bronze). Verse 4 reminds the reader that THE ARK,
the other great religious symbol, has already been brought
into A TENT PITCHED FOR IT IN JERUSALEM (cf. I Chron. 13;
15-16). These notes explain that it was proper for Solomon
to be at Gibeon, but we may wonder whether behind this
form of the narrative there is not something more. It is conceivable that the Chronicler is, as it were, tidying up the
religious traditions. To someone who might ask what became
of the tabernacle and all its furniture, he provides the
answer that it was preserved and used until it ceased to be
needed with the building of the temple. But we may suspect
a further motive. His concern with the Jerusalem shrine is
such as to suggest a polemical note (cf. on I Chron. 22.1); it
is to be this place and no other. The significance of Gibeon
is only hinted at in the Old Testament (cf. note on I Chron.
9.35-38, and cf. Josh. 9.23); that it had a special place in
some forms of ancient tradition which are now overlaid and
obscured appears very likely. In the post-exilic period we can
detect various 'reform' movements – we have fairly full information about the later stages of the Samaritan and Qumran
communities, though the origins of both remain difficult to
describe with any precision. There may well have been other
'reforming' groups which have left little trace, and it would

occasion no surprise if we were to discover that there were some who believed that Jerusalem, having been destroyed and thus divinely judged, was to be regarded as contaminated; true continuity with the ancestral faith was perhaps to be sought in a return to some other more ancient centre – might it be Shechem? or Bethel? or Gibeon? The Chronicler could be countering such pressures by saying at one and the same time: Jerusalem is the one and only true shrine, the true successor of ancient practice, and: those things which belong to other shrines or those things which have been said about them, really belong to Jerusalem or have been properly transferred there (cf. further on 3.1). This has been implied for Bethel in I Chron. 22.1. Confronted with a well-known and surely popular story of Solomon at Gibeon, the Chronicler turns it away from any suggestion that Solomon was engaged in some improper practice to the affirmation that Solomon was here recognizing the presence there of holy objects which must in due course be taken up into the Jerusalem temple, but which should not be neglected in their temporary resting place at Gibeon. So Solomon's sacrifices at Gibeon (v.6) are an act of proper piety. But Gibeon has now been superseded (cf. also J. Blenkinsopp, *Gibeon and Israel*, esp. ch.8).

7-13. On the occasion of this act of worship – a single act here and not a habitual procedure as in I Kings 3.4*b* — a divine revelation is granted to the king. The term 'dream' is not used, perhaps because in course of time revelation by dreams had come to be regarded as open to abuse (cf. the strictures in Jer. 23.25ff.). The offering of a request to the newly anointed king is reflected in the words of Ps. 2.8; it may be seen as normal royal formula. The response of Solomon to this is in a text considerably shortened in vv.8-9, with the removing of any possible suggestion that David could have been disloyal. The prayer form (cf. on I Chron. 29.10ff.), has the opening statement of the divine nature (v.8), followed in v.9 – which should begin with the word 'now' – by the request, in terms of the fulfilment of the promise to David. Quite different expressions are used in the request for WISDOM AND KNOWLEDGE in v.10, though the text echoes the wording of I Kings 3; the deprecatory statement about Solomon's inexperience is omitted, perhaps because it has already been used in the words of David in I Chron. 22.5; 29.1. The Chronicler passes over I Kings 3.10, which speaks of God's pleasure at Solomon's request, and moves on to a similar but not identical statement of the granting of both this and of RICHES, POSSESSIONS AND HONOUR, magnified with the same kind of courtly language as we have seen in I Chron. 29.25. Solomon's return TO JERUSALEM (v.13) makes no reference to sacrifices before the ark; only when the temple is built will this become possible and proper. The Chronicler makes no use of the illustration of Solomon's wisdom in the story of the two harlots (I Kings 3.16-28), perhaps because he thought it improper, but more probably because he could assume that his readers would know it well.

14-17. This is an almost word for word transcription of the text of I Kings 10.26-29; only the addition of GOLD in v.15 – a simple piece of magnification – shows any real difference. Since this material appears again in 9.25-28, we may wonder whether it has been added here by a later scribe, perhaps one who felt that it would be proper at this point to give an illustration of the way in which the prosperity promised was shown; its position in ch.9 corresponds to its position in I Kings, so that is where we should expect to find it. The closeness of the textual correspondence – where 9.25-28 shows a freer handling of the material – may point to its having been copied in from the text of I Kings by a later hand.

16. Kue Cilicia in southern Asia Minor.

Egypt This appears to be either an erroneous insertion under the influence of v.17, or a corruption of a less well-known name Musri (Egypt=*miṣraim*), also an area in Asia Minor; this is possible also in v.17, though it seems less likely since the real point seems to be to indicate trade in both directions. Nevertheless, the main concern, as v.15 shows, is to underline the fabulous wealth of the kingdom under Solomon.

PREPARATION FOR THE BUILDING

2.1-18

Much the same freedom in the use of the source material is to be found in this chapter as in ch.1, though for the most part the Chronicler's text is due to a skilful interweaving of elements to be found in other contexts in Kings and to a heightening of the glory of the temple and of Solomon.

1. * **to build a temple ... and a royal palace for himself** (better 'his royal palace'). The narrative begins with Solomon's purpose, though the word rendered PURPOSED is hardly so strong; literally it means 'said' or 'thought'. We may note that this expression of Solomon's turning to the building of temple and palace has been extracted from the middle of the Kings account of the negotiations with Hiram, where it appears as I Kings 5.5. The Chronicler clearly felt it undesirable that the carrying through of what had been laid upon Solomon should first be expressed in words directed to the king of Tyre.

2. This is a duplicate of v.18, and since the material belongs in the latter position, it is likely that it has been added here. Possibly a later scribe thought that some explanation of the SKILLED WORKERS of v.7 was needed, and erroneously identified these with the labourers of the corvée (see below).

3-16. These verses are roughly paralleled by I Kings 5.2-11, but we note that it is Solomon who initiates the negotiations, whereas in Kings Hiram sends messengers to Solomon on his accession, evidently with a view to continuing a relationship already established with David. Throughout the initiative

* This verse is 1.18 in the Hebrew, so that the Hebrew verse numbers are one less than the English in ch.2. A shift is also observable in the parallel passage in I Kings 5, where the Hebrew ch.5 begins at the English 4.21, with the effect that the Hebrew verse numbers in ch.5 are 14 higher than the English.

is with Solomon. There is first a recall of the previous relationship, described in I Chron. 14.1, where (see note) Hiram
(written here as HURAM) appears virtually to pay tribute to
David (and cf. on v.14 here). The thought has influenced the
presentation of the negotiations here.

4-6. These verses considerably modify the Kings form of the
narrative, bringing out in much greater detail the nature of
the worship which will be offered in the temple. The reason
for this is seen in v.5, which picks up the theme of I Chron.
22.5 and amplifies it into a statement of the supremacy of
the God of Israel; v.6 picks up words which are to be found
in the prayer of Solomon at the dedication (6.18), but modifies
them so as to remove still further the idea that God can
dwell in an earthly building. Where the older text recognizes
the problem of the relationship between the eternal God and
an earthly dwelling, the Chronicler goes a stage further:
WHO AM I TO BUILD A HOUSE FOR HIM – an expression of
humility in the presence of God – EXCEPT AS A PLACE TO BURN
INCENSE BEFORE HIM? (or better 'to offer sacrifice, worship',
for the term has a broader range of meaning). The temple
is not a dwelling for God; it is the place in which men may
worship him.

7. 'And' **now** This introduces the main content of the message – the letter form is being used, though its opening
greeting has been substantially expanded and modified. It
is a request for A MAN SKILLED TO WORK; the Chronicler has
brought the theme forward as the first request, whereas in
I Kings it appears only later as a minor element (I Kings
7.13). The parallel of Bezalel, the skilled craftsman of the
tabernacle in Exodus, is in mind, and the breadth of the
skill required is much greater than is found in Kings. He
is to work with THE SKILLED WORKERS, the native craftsmen,
of JUDAH AND JERUSALEM, and here the Chronicler slips
naturally into thinking of the community of that restricted
southern area which he knows in his own time. The craftsmen
have been PROVIDED by DAVID (cf. I Chron. 22.15f.), so that
what is being asked is not Tyrian skill as such, but co-opera-

tion. The Chronicler is playing down the alien element in the tradition of temple-building.

8-9. The requests for material represent a rearrangement and amplification of I Kings 5.6. ALGUM TIMBER (or better 'almug', cf. I Kings 10.11f. and so too in the Ras Shamra texts) is not certainly identifiable. It is evidently a wood used for furniture and decorative work (cf. 9.11). In exchange for the materials Huram is asked to supply, Solomon lays down what he will pay, not leaving Huram free to name his price (I Kings 5.11). The word rendered CRUSHED (somewhat freely) is an error for a very similar word meaning 'provision, board' which appears in the Kings text: I WILL GIVE ... WHEAT 'as provision' FOR YOUR SERVANTS ...

11-16. Huram's response takes the form of a letter. The double beginning is not very elegant, and we should probably take the cue from the Kings text and reverse the order of these two verses. Then we have, first, Huram's word of praise to the supreme creator of Israel, a due acknowledgement by a non-Israelite of the true God, and following on this the text of a letter which begins with an acknowledgment that the choice of Solomon is because God LOVES HIS PEOPLE (v.11), and leads on (NOW, v.13) to the substance of the letter. It is a straight response to the requests of Solomon. The craftsman appears here as HURAMABI, but perhaps since the name appears elsewhere (4.11), simply as Huram, we should read this as 'Huram my master (craftsman)'; the name may have been influenced by the name Oholiab, Bezalel's assistant (Exod. 31.6). He is in fact almost an Israelite, for his mother was of the tribe of Dan, and it is this that counts. We may note that the stress in Ezra 9-10 and Neh. 13 in the matter of foreign marriages is on foreign wives. In I Kings 7.14, Hiram's mother is from Naphtali; perhaps we may see here too the influence of Exod. 31.6. Huram's position *vis-à-vis* Israel is shown by his use of the title MY LORD for David (v.14). The commercial negotiations are accepted in vv.15-16; the Chronicler adds, from his contemporary knowledge, that the timber will be brought TO JOPPA (cf. Ezra 3.7; Jonah 1.3).

This was the site of the port in later years; it has been shown
that at an earlier date it was further north of the mouth
of the river Yarkon (Tell Qasileh, north of Tel Aviv).

17-18. The theme of I Chron. 22.2-4 is taken up here; the
corvée is imposed on non-Israelites only, and not, as the Kings
text indicates, on all Israel (cf. I Kings 5.13ff., but note that
this is qualified in 9.20-22, utilized by the Chronicler in
8.7-9).

THE BUILDING OF THE TEMPLE

3.1-5.1

Chapter 2 envisages the building of a temple and a royal
palace; the latter is subsequently mentioned in 7.11; 8.1;
9.11, where it is relevant to the context. But whereas I Kings
devotes a section to details of the complex of buildings which
form the palace (I Kings 7.1-12) – though it is subordinated
to the temple – the Chronicler gives no account at all of the
palace building. His concentration is on the temple. But
even here there are considerable differences, and for the most
part his account is a substantial abbreviation of the Kings
material (cf. note on 4.10-22). He seems to be selecting simply
those elements which he regards as most significant; there
is some magnifying of numbers and measurements and decora-
tion, but there is also some simplification, which suggests
that the Chronicler was being influenced at one and the same
time by a concern with the glory of a temple for the worship of the supreme God and by the actual second temple, the
one which he himself knew. It is likely that from some of
the details, we may deduce information about that temple
which is otherwise not described. The reduction of space given
to the description of the temple is perhaps a further illustration of the point made by the Chronicler in the previous
chapter; the temple is in no sense a dwelling for God, but a
place of worship (cf. note on 2.6).

3.1. This verse makes an important further identification of the temple site. The THRESHING FLOOR OF ORNAN (cf. I Chron. 21.1-22.1) is said to be MOUNT MORIAH, known to tradition as the place where Abraham had been commanded to sacrifice Isaac (Gen. 22). The Chronicler is unlikely to have invented this identification; it is already implicit in Gen. 22.2, which says that God will show which mountain in the land of Moriah is his choice, a clear pointer to the choice of Jerusalem, the holy mountain of God. Furthermore, the subtle word-play of Gen. 22 is picked up by the Chronicler here: God 'will provide' (Gen. 22.8) is literally 'God will see for himself'; the place of revelation is termed 'Yahweh will see' or 'provide', and subsequently 'today it is called the mountain of Yahweh who shows himself' (Gen. 22.14; there are problems of text and interpretation here which go beyond our present concern). So the phrase THE LORD HAD APPEARED TO DAVID HIS FATHER suggests a parallel between the divine revelation to Abraham and that to David. The ancient religious tradition of Abraham is taken up into the choice of the temple site which had apparently been independently revealed to David; the same holy place must be designated in each story. The theme of continuity of religious faith and practice is given a further extension. There may again be a polemical note, for there is evidence to show that the Samaritan community identified the mountain of the Abraham story with Gerizim (cf. J. Macdonald, *The Theology of the Samaritans*, SCM Press, London 1964, pp.329, 394).

3.2-4.22. This section covers some of the details of the building and contents taken from parts of I Kings 6 and 7. The date is given (v.2) with less detail than in I Kings 6.1.

3-9. The Chronicler deals first with the temple itself, its MEASUREMENTS (the text in v.3 is not entirely clear but the sense is evident), and some of the details of its construction and ornamentation.

4. height That given is nonsensical, and is due to an error by which A HUNDRED AND TWENTY has been read in place of 'twenty cubits' (*me'āh we'eṣrīm* for *'ammōth 'eṣrīm*). Possibly there has been some influence from the description of the temple of Herod. The old standard for the cubit probably designates the larger or royal cubit of about twenty inches (cf. R. B. Y. Scott in *New Peake's Commentary*, Nelson, London 1962, p.37).

6. Parvaim Not known; its gold was evidently of particular purity and excellence.

8. The most holy place Literally: 'holy of holies', the term for the inner shrine used in later writings to stress its sanctity; the older word is *debīr* – the 'rearmost' place.

9. upper chambers These seem to be indicated for the inner shrine in the last clause, but are otherwise not attested. Since the Chronicler does not deal with all the elaborate details of the rooms adjoining the temple (cf. I Kings 6.5-6, 8-10), it may be that this note has been added to complete the picture.

10-17. These verses deal with two major elements in the temple, THE CHERUBIM in the inner shrine and the two mysteriously named PILLARS which stand before the temple as in other ancient shrines. Whether there were such objects in the post-exilic temple is not known.

10. The wording is not entirely clear; perhaps instead of the phrase OF WOOD we should have 'in image form'.

14. veil This is not mentioned in the description in I Kings, but because of a textual error in I Kings 6.21.

16. necklaces The conjectural rendering is based on a rendering of the letters of the word for the inner shrine (*rābīd* for *debīr*).

4.1. altar This appears by error to have fallen out of the I Kings description.

2-6. the sea Its real significance remains uncertain, but it is here defined as FOR THE PRIESTS TO WASH IN. The description also covers THE LAVERS.

7-9. This is a description of the LAMPSTANDS, TABLES and BASINS, the COURTS and their DOORS.

10-22. This passage is almost word for word the same as the text of I Kings 7.39*b*-50. It is strange that after such free handling of the previous material, the Chronicler should suddenly produce so slavish a copy (cf. on 1.14-17), and we may suspect the addition of this passage by a later scribe who felt that the details should be given more fully; at some points there is here a difference over against the previous passage.

17. the clay ground We should render 'place of casting', or 'foundry'.

5.1. The whole description is drawn together with a note that what David had prepared was also brought into the temple. And with this brief account, the way is open for the more important acts of dedication and prayer.

THE ARK AND THE TENT

5.2-14

The text of this section follows closely the passage in I Kings 8.1-11, but there are certain important differences, and in all probability the deviation would be greater were it not for modifications which have taken place in the Kings text. The occasion is a great celebration held to inaugurate the newly-built temple, and first to bring into it the ark (cf. I Chron. 13; 15-16).

3. the seventh month The feast is the feast of tabernacles.

4. the Levites Their place as the carriers of the ark is made plain; only when the ark is taken into THE INNER SANCTUARY (v.7), where none but priests may go, is it handed over to them.

5. tent of meeting, holy vessels These are also brought up; but the text at this point is not entirely clear. The corresponding verse in I Kings 8 is probably a later addition, perhaps

already made before the time of the Chronicler, perhaps
influenced by Chron., for Kings has no concern with the tent
of meeting. For the Chronicler, however, the incorporation
of the tent with its association through Gibeon back to the
wilderness period (cf. on ch.1) is a subject of significance.
Probably the reference to Levites is intrusive and we should
read: (v.4) the Levites took up the ark (v.5) and they brought
up the ark. But at the tent of meeting and all the holy vessels
that were in the tent, the priests brought them up.' Then it
would be clear that the priests who were at Gibeon, not here
mentioned, had their particular share in the action.

9. to this day This may be seen as a survival from an older
source when the ark still existed, or better may be regarded as
equivalent to 'in perpetuity'.

11-14. There has been a substantial elaboration of the text
here. RSV marks most of this by brackets, but probably the
parenthesis should be extended to the end of the hymnic
refrain in v.13, for in I Kings the opening clause of v.11 is
immediately followed by the description of the cloud filling
the shrine. In the addition, we may see the concern of the
Chronicler with music – this makes a close link back to the
procession of the ark described in I Chron. 15-16 to which
this chapter may be seen as a sequel. The reference to the
priestly DIVISIONS (v.11) is perhaps of later origin, since it
depends on the supplementary material of I Chron. 24. The
last clause of v.13 needs a small emendation to read: 'the
house was filled with the cloud of the glory of the LORD'.
Verses 13b-14 in fact anticipate 7.1-2, and it may be that the
Chronicler intended to delay the appearance of the divine
glory until after the prayer of Solomon, where it comes aptly
as a response to the final words of the prayer (cf. on 6.40-42);
a later scribe may have supplemented the text from I Kings.
   The chapter provides an example of the difficulties of
analysing the text of Chronicles. Where two closely parallel
texts exist side by side, either may influence the other, as
may be seen also in the case of the synoptic gospels.

THE PRAYER OF SOLOMON

6.1-42

Apart from a number of small deviations and a major change at the end (vv.40-42), the Chronicler has followed the earlier text of this section (I Kings 8.12-50a). It is not surprising that this should be so. The prayer attributed to Solomon contains a variety of elements, some of them of such a general quality that no precise dating is possible. But the clear references to exile and the basis for return expressed in the latter part of the prayer point very plainly to an eventual exilic compilation, and so too does the emphasis on the temple as a place of prayer rather than as a place of sacrifice. Some parts of the prayer can then be seen to take on a new meaning for the members of the post-exilic community, and as the Chronicler uses it we may see it through the eyes of that community as speaking to continuing and changing needs.

1-11. The first part is couched in the form of an address to the people, though it also has much of the character of both prayer and sermon. It opens with an ancient poetic fragment, which points to the idea of the divine theophany being from THICK DARKNESS, as at the Sinai revelation (Exod. 20.21), and in relation to the Jerusalem sanctuary as indicated in some of the psalms (Ps. 18.9, 11; 97.2). The poem draws together the ancient appearing of God and the question of his relationship to the newly-built temple. The remainder of this passage rehearses material concerning David and his intention to build, which has already been used in David's closing words in I Chron. 28.2ff. (cf. also I Chron. 22.6ff.). In vv.5b-6a there is a passage not found in I Kings, but it is probable that it was accidentally omitted there because of the repetitive wording (cf. I Kings 8.16).

11. covenant This is simply with ISRAEL, not tied to the Exodus events as in I Kings.

12-13. The second part of the section opens with a descriptive statement, and here again the text preserves material missing from I Kings. It seems likely that because of the similarity of the ending of the two verses 12 and 13, the material of the latter was accidentally omitted from I Kings (after 8.14). That this is so is indicated by the statement in I Kings 8.54 which refers to Solomon rising from a kneeling position. That is only mentioned in this missing verse. There exist ancient portrayals of kings or priests on raised platforms for the offering of prayer, so that this was evidently an established custom (cf. W. F. Albright, *Archaeology and the Religion of Israel*, Johns Hopkins Press, Baltimore [3]1953, p.153. For a picture possibly portraying this cf. ANEP. no.490, and C. M. Jones, *Old Testament Illustrations*, Cambridge University Press 1971, fig.173). Elsewhere too we have indications of the king having a special 'standing place' in the temple (cf. 34.31).

14. The prayer proper opens with the appropriate act of praise and descriptions of the supreme God.

16. 'And' **now** The main part of the prayer begins. Its first element concerns the perpetuity of the Davidic line. Note that WALK IN MY LAW takes the place of I Kings 'walk before me'; the change is suggestive of the emphasis on the law as a way of life in the post-exilic period. The stress on a Davidic ruler probably indicates that such a hope continued in the time of the Chronicler, though there is little indication of active political concern with Davidic rule in his work.

18-21. This is a general introduction to a series of 'prayer situations', raising the question of the relationship between the God who is too great for HEAVEN AND THE HIGHEST HEAVEN and the place of men's worship, and asking that when men pray TOWARDS THIS PLACE God will HEAR FROM HEAVEN. (The Chronicler uses 'from heaven' in each case where Kings has 'in heaven'.)

22-23. These verses envisage a situation where a legal dispute necessitates an OATH BEFORE THY ALTAR, a procedure by which a decision can be made between guilt and innocence. The text speaks of REQUITING THE GUILTY where Kings has 'condemning the guilty' (i.e. declaring which is the guilty party).

24-35. The following section covers a variety of situations of need of a more public kind, and the position of the FOREIGNER who comes to offer his prayers because he has heard of THY GREAT NAME, AND THY MIGHTY HAND, AND THY OUTSTRETCHED ARM (v.32), a theme particularly appropriate to the later situation, since it was with the exile that the community realized the relevance of God's dealings with it to the nations which would thus acknowledge him.

36-39. These verses envisage the situation of exile, and would be particularly relevant to a time when members of the religious community were scattered over many lands. But whereas the Kings text links this with the Exodus theme, seeing in the deliverance from Egypt the basis of hope for restoration from exile (a view to be found reflected in the prophets, notably in the Second Isaiah), the Chronicler links it back to the Davidic theme in vv.40ff.

40. This is partly dependent upon I Kings 8.52.

41-42. In contrast, these verses are part of a psalm. This is related to but not identical with part of Ps. 132. Verse 41 corresponds to Ps. 132.8-9 (cf. also v.16a) but the wording is not quite the same; v.42a corresponds to Ps. 132.10b; v.42b has a theme found in Ps. 132.1a and in Isa. 55.3, but it is differently presented. Since we have numerous examples of psalms which appear in different forms, it is better to suppose that the Chronicler here makes use of a text which has not otherwise survived than to suppose that he has gathered odd fragments together (cf. on I Chron. 16.8-36). The psalm brings in again the theme of THE ARK which has already had such prominence. PRIESTS and SAINTS (better 'loyal ones') REJOICE, for to be CLOTHED WITH SALVATION is comparable to the wearing of festal raiment. The ANOINTED ONE is the term for the king, at a later date to become the technical term Messiah; but in the post-exilic period it could also be properly used for the high priest (cf. e.g. Dan. 9.26). The STEADFAST LOVE for David is better seen as a plural expression speaking of the 'loyal acts', and these may be understood either in the sense of those loyal acts which David performed, and in particular his preparations for the temple, or in the sense of that loyalty which God has shown to David, his faithful acts of love to the founder of the dynasty. These last verses, seen in the light of the Chronicler's central interest in David, point to his resting of confidence in his own time on what was established under David and on what the Davidic promises could mean for the community.

THE DEDICATION AND ACCEPTANCE OF THE TEMPLE

7.1–22

The Chronicler omits here a section in I Kings 8 in which Solomon blesses the people, not because he thought such a blessing improper for someone other than a priest (cf. 6.4), but because the prayer, reaching its climax in the appeal to God of 6.40–42, should be answered at once by a divine response. In ch.7 the two themes of acceptance and dedication are interwoven; it is God who accepts and consecrates (vv.1, 12, 16), it is Solomon and the people who dedicate (vv.5, 9). The two actions are counterparts the one of the other. But primacy rests with the divine action.

1. fire ... from heaven ... the glory of the Lord ... filled the temple In this first expression there is an echo of I Chron. 21.26, the acceptance of the threshing-floor as a holy place, and of 5.13f., which appears to anticipate what follows more logically here.

2-3. The effect of the divine glory is paralleled in 5.14. Further, it is emphasized that both FIRE and GLORY were visible to the whole people, who prostrated themselves and offered the word of praise summarized by its title or refrain (cf. I Chron. 16.34, 41). The description is clearly related to the tabernacle consecration in Exod. 40.34-38.

4. Here the Chronicler picks up the text of I Kings 8.62-66 and follows it fairly closely.

6. This is an addition stressing the part played by THE LEVITES as musicians, and again recalling the instituting of their duties by David. By the quotation: FOR HIS STEADFAST LOVE ENDURES FOREVER (cf. v.3 and I Chron. 16.34, 41), a link is made both with what precedes in this account and also with the precursor of the temple dedication in I Chron. 15-16.

7. altar This is specifically ascribed to Solomon (cf. 4.1).

8-10. These verses elaborate the information about THE FEAST; here it appears as THE DEDICATION OF THE ALTAR SEVEN DAYS and THE FEAST (i.e. tabernacles) SEVEN DAYS. This represents an extension of the Kings version, in which the dedication and tabernacles coincide, lasting seven days, and the people are dismissed on the eighth day; the Hebrew text in Kings has, however, been glossed by a reference to another seven days, and a total of fourteen days is mentioned. This would appear to be a gloss based on the Chronicler's elaboration. The dating of the celebration is not, however, entirely clear in our text. The holding of what RSV renders as A SOLEMN ASSEMBLY ON THE EIGHTH DAY is not clear: does it come after the first group of seven or after the second? Nor is it clear what it is, for the term suggests 'stopping' or 'closing', perhaps a restriction on work (cf. the same pattern in Neh. 8.18). It would appear than an attempt has been made to clarify the celebration in relation to the practice laid down in the law (cf. Lev. 23.34). We know that there were various stages in the development of tabernacles, and not all the evidence fits together precisely.

9. the dedication Note that it is that OF THE ALTAR, a reminder of the meaning of the temple as a place of worship (cf. v.12 and note on 2.6).

10. The celebration ends appropriately in rejoicing.

11-22. These verses correspond to I Kings 9.1-9, but again with some modification and expansions. The Chronicler introduces into v.11 an emphasis on Solomon having SUCCESSFULLY ACCOMPLISHED all that he PLANNED TO DO; it is a reminder that what has been done has been under the hand of God (cf. I Chron. 28.20).

12. The reference to Gibeon is omitted; Gibeon now belongs to the past, a stage of religion which has been overtaken. The second half of the verse expands by stressing that the temple is A HOUSE OF SACRIFICE (cf. above on v.9).

13-15. These verses interrupt the sequence by drawing out the willingness of God to HEAR and FORGIVE; God himself promises a full response to what Solomon has asked in his prayer. The words of v.15 echo those of the appeal in 6.40.

16. The I Kings text is again followed here, stressing the divine act in consecration and in the choice of the temple.

17-22. The sequel draws out the contrasting results of obedience and disobedience. There are one or two points of detail to be noted. We observe that, as in so many Deuteronomic sermons, the positive element is much shorter than the negative (cf. e.g. Deut. 28; Jer. 42.9-22); yet the promise is there to be picked up again after disaster.

18. The text is modified here. The relationship with David is described in covenant terms rather than as promise, though the difference is perhaps not great; and the Kings reference to 'the throne of Israel' is modified to a promise of A MAN TO RULE ISRAEL. This phrase may be an echo of the Davidic promise in Micah 5.2 which perhaps has 'messianic' overtones; it is also possible that it represents a qualifying of the promise so as to suggest that there will always be a ruler, divinely appointed, but not necessarily a king. With monarchy a dream of the past, the Jews under Persian and Greek rule may have needed to see such a re-interpretation of ancient promise.

19. Here we move into the negative part of the sermon, and it addresses the people as a whole and not just Solomon. The

second-person address is followed in the Hebrew text – which
here corresponds to I Kings, where we have a reference to the
cutting off of Israel – by third-person forms. RSV alters this
to make the sequence easier, but it is proper to see here how
the preacher unconsciously moves out of the context in which
he is putting the words, into a more reflective statement about
the history of his people. He knew that the disaster here
spoken of as a threat had become a reality of history, for
both the Deuteronomic historian and the Chronicler looked
back on the fall of Jerusalem in 587 BC. The disaster, both in
terms of the exiling of the people (I WILL PLUCK 'them' [YOU]
UP FROM 'my' LAND [RSV has THE LAND in error]) and of the
rejection of the people (I WILL CAST [the temple] OUT OF MY
SIGHT) is to be a matter of comment by the nations. This is
the counterpart of the coming of foreigners to worship in
6.32f.; here the nations are astonished that this should happen
to the people brought out of Egypt.

21. which is exalted must strictly be translated 'which was
exalted'; the Kings text has a different verbal form, which
may represent future or present. The evidence of some of the
ancient translations suggests the possibility that both texts are
defective, due to the loss of a similar phrase, and that we
should render: 'this house which was exalted but which becomes a ruin'. (The words for 'exalted' (*'elyōn*) and for '(in)
ruin' (*le'īyīn*) are very similar, and this could have led to the
error.)

22. evil a more accurate rendering is 'calamity' (cf. also
Isa. 45.7, where RSV has 'woe', and so also Amos 3.6).

THE ACHIEVEMENT OF SOLOMON

8.1-16

The main part of ch.8 forms a sort of appendix to the
completion of the temple, as does the parallel text in I Kings
9.10-25, which is followed fairly closely at some points but
substantially modified at others. The reasons for most of the

changes can be clearly seen, but there is also some disorder which perhaps derives from textual corruption.

1. This is simply a summary, mentioning again the palace, which in the Chronicler's work recedes into the background.

2. This provides a remarkable example of the way in which an unfavourable piece of material has been turned to quite different use. In the parallel in I Kings 9.11-13 (14), the cities are described as given to Hiram by Solomon; Hiram inspected them and gave them a derogatory name. It may be that the earlier narrator included this little piece of information because he thought it amusing that Solomon had pulled a fast one on Hiram. For the Chronicler, the whole transaction was impossible; it could only be that HURAM (as he appears here) HAD GIVEN the cities to Solomon, no doubt as part of the tribute which was fitting for an alien ruler (cf. on I Chron. 14.1). So it is related that Solomon REBUILT THE CITIES and brought in Israelite inhabitants. It is quite clear that this transformation has been brought about; the passages stand in exactly comparable positions in the texts and there is no room for the various theories which have attempted to reconcile these quite contradictory statements. We must see the hand of the Chronicler at work, commenting piously on a familiar story.

3-6. There are a number of differences and rearrangements in this passage, which deals with various building matters.

4. Tadmor This important city in Syria (Palmyra) is substituted for Tamar, a relatively unimportant place in the south. (The Kings text has been corrected by a marginal note so as to introduce this change.) Tadmor was particularly prominent in the later period, a site of great Hellenistic building. So, having made this change, the Chronicler expands the text to include a conquest and rebuilding of the area of HAMATH, perhaps partly in dependence on the David traditions (II Sam. 8.3ff.; cf. I Chron. 18.3ff.).

5. There is also some extension here, but Gezer is not mentioned. The Kings text tells us that it was still in Canaanite hands, but was conquered by Pharaoh and given as dowry with his daughter on her marriage to Solomon – an understandably unacceptable idea for the Chronicler.

6. Curiously the names of Megiddo and Hazor have fallen out, perhaps by accident; the development of STORE-CITIES, and of chariotry and all that went with it, is an important aspect of the development of Israel's power under Solomon. Though the buildings thought to be stables, but more probably to be regarded as stores, excavated at Megiddo, are now known to be later than Solomon, there is still ample evidence from various sites to show the degree to which military policy was carried through at this time.

7-10. The text of I Kings 9.20-23 is followed fairly closely, with some small changes. We have seen that the theme of the corvée imposed only on alien inhabitants has already been used in 2.17 and that the Chronicler does not include any reference to forced labour imposed on Israel. Verse 8 emphasizes that this is to be a permanent arrangement.

11. Another careful change of wording. The Chronicler says nothing about Solomon's marriage with PHARAOH'S DAUGHTER, though it occupies a prominent place in I Kings 3.1. We have noted the absence of the Gezer reference found in I Kings 9.16f., but the theme of her house which occupies a place in the palace descriptions (I Kings 7.8) is here used with a religious explanation.

the places to which the ark of the LORD has come are holy Entry into a cult place is limited, and in later Jewish practice women were restricted to certain areas; how far back such practice goes we do not know. Solomon expresses such a pious attitude when he says 'a wife of mine' SHALL NOT LIVE IN THE HOUSE OF DAVID ... (so more accurately than RSV).

12-15. The corresponding verses in Kings are elaborated by a detailed account of the obedience of Solomon to all the cultic duties laid down in the Mosaic law. Some part of this – vv.14f.

– may well be later than the Chronicler, for it depends on the additional material in I Chron. 23-26.

16. The point is reinforced in the final summary; everything is depicted as performed to fulfil what David had laid down, and the last phrase sums this up by saying: SO THE HOUSE OF THE LORD WAS 'fully in order' (RSV COMPLETED is a less adequate rendering).

THE WISDOM AND PROSPERITY OF SOLOMON – II

8.17-9.28

The Chronicler has followed the structure of the Kings narratives of Solomon in presenting the central theme of the temple within a framework of material depicting his wisdom and prosperity. But whereas the negative material of I Kings 11 then overshadows the glory of Solomon and paves the way for the disruption of the kingdom, the absence of this enables the Chronicler to end the story of Solomon on a high note. The twofold theme of wisdom and wealth, set out in the Gibeon vision of ch.1, is picked up here in the trading ventures and the visit of the queen of Sheba, already interwoven in I Kings and used here with few alterations. The section also serves to underline the theme adumbrated in the prayer of ch.6 (vv.32f.), and before this in the emphasis on the supremacy of Yahweh in 2.5, namely that the nations will acknowledge Israel's God, and this may be seen expressed in the recognition of Solomon's divine appointment as king on the throne which belongs to God and his wisdom as the gift of God (cf. esp. 9.3, 5, 8, 23).

8.17-18. The themes of wealth and wisdom run together. These verses (cf. I Kings 9.26-28) describe the trading ventures, supported by HURAM, from the ports of the Red Sea. The wording in the two forms of the material differs slightly; Solomon, according to the Chronicler, himself WENT TO EZION-GEBER AND ELOTH. The part played by HURAM is thus by implication reduced. This is continued in 9.10f., 13f. and 21.

9.1-9, 12 the queen of Sheba This story has been woven into the account of Solomon's trading ventures; its background is the trade relationship between Palestine and Arabia. From a somewhat later date there is evidence of queens in the latter area, so that the story has some verisimilitude. It is, however, a stylized account, designed to bring out the acknowledgment of both wisdom and wealth by a representative of the outside world, as in the use of this theme in Matt. 12.42. The Sheba story was later to be developed in elaborate traditions, especially in Ethiopia (cf. E. Ullendorff, *Ethiopia and the Bible*, Schweich Lectures 1967, Oxford University Press, London 1968, ch.III).

1-2. The contest of wits is a familiar theme of ancient story; the bringing of gifts is emphasized, though underlying the text is a clear reference to its being an exchange of courtesies. The tribute offered is of the costliest (cf. v.9).

4. his burnt offerings This reference is found by emending the text to conform to I Kings, where, however, it is probably already in error. The Chronicler actually has a reference to 'his upper chamber'; a small emendation would give 'his stairs by which he went up to the temple'. The last is the most probable in a context which deals with description; a reference to sacrifices is much less in place. That there WAS NO MORE SPIRIT IN HER means that she was awed at Solomon's grandeur.

6. the greatness of your wisdom The text is more explicit here.

7. Happy are your wives As also in I Kings, this represents an emendation of the text attested by some of the early versions; it is surely correct in I Kings, but we might wonder whether the change was first deliberately made here by the Chronicler in view of his omission of the derogatory material of I Kings 11; Solomon's wives were anything but a credit to him!

8. throne This becomes God's throne (cf. on I Chron. 28.5).

10-11. The verses interrupt the story, but stress further sources

of Solomon's wealth. On ALGUM ('almug') wood cf. 2.8; it is
here described as used for musical instruments, and for STEPS,
though the Hebrew word suggests 'causeways'; I Kings suggests
'supports', though the precise meaning of the word is uncertain.

12. The story of the queen of Sheba ends here; the text of
this verse is confused, as is also that of I Kings 10.13. It is
possible that each verse is lacking a phrase, and here we might
fill out to WHATEVER SHE ASKED BESIDES 'what he gave her in
return for' WHAT SHE HAD BROUGHT TO THE KING. The omission could be accidental, or could have been due to a desire to
emphasize that she offers tribute, whereas Solomon gives of
his bounty.

13-28. These verses have some overlap with 1.14-17 and re-
count further aspects of Solomon's wealth. Here vv.13f. and
21 continue the details of trading ventures and tribute from
various lands, thus placing the Sheba story in context. Verses
15-20 concern the use to which some of this wealth is put,
with details of decorations in the palace and of the royal
THRONE.

18. Note that there is no reference to a 'calf' (I Kings 10.19),
perhaps because of its alien religious associations (cf. I Kings
12.28).

20. The last clause links to the comment of v.27 (cf. 1.15).

21. Tarshish The fact that this can be seen to be in the
western Mediterranean (cf. Jonah 1.3) seems to suggest trading
ventures with Huram other than in the Red Sea; SHIPS OF
TARSHISH may be understood as those engaged in long-distance
trade.

21. peacocks This word, though it has been connected with
an old Tamil word *takai* and hence has been seen as evidence
for trade with India, appears more probably to be another
word for a type of monkey.

22-28. This further summarizing statement again emphasizes

the WISDOM of Solomon which is sought out by ALL THE
KINGS OF THE EARTH (v.23), who bring their tribute.

24. myrrh The word most probably denotes a perfume of
some kind, though it could also be translated 'weapons'; but
this is out of context in the list.

25. On the chariotry, cf. on 1.14 and 8.6.

26. The Chronicler introduces a statement of the broad extent
of Solomon's rule which is not in I Kings at this point (but
cf. I Kings 4.21).

29-31. Appropriately, the picture of wealth and wisdom leads
directly into the summary of Solomon's reign. This corresponds to I Kings 11.41-43, but the sources of the information
are given, as in the case of David (I Chron. 29.29), as prophetic works. THE HISTORY (literally 'words') OF NATHAN points
to I Kings 1; THE PROPHECY OF AHIJAH recalls the narrative,
not here used, in I Kings 11.26-40; THE VISIONS OF IDDO have
no basis in the Kings material. Josephus was to identify Iddo
(Jadon) with the unnamed prophet who pronounced judgment
on Jeroboam in I Kings 13, but there is no reason to suppose
that the Chronicler made this identification. Perhaps we should
in reality see the Chronicler using the names simply to make
plain the comparison with David.

The high point in the story is past. The whole achievement
of David and of Solomon as his executor marks a standard
to which the later life of the kingdom may be compared, and
an ideal to which men may look.

THE TRUE KINGDOM AND ITS FAILURE

II Chronicles 10-36

The lists in I Chronicles 1-9 have already prepared the reader
for the concentration on the south – Judah and Benjamin –
as the true Israel. Thus the Chronicler in his account of the
history from the death of Solomon to the fall of Jerusalem
deals virtually only with the south, the true kingdom, the true
Israel. The north secedes as an apostate community, from
which from time to time faithful people return to their true
spiritual home in Jerusalem and the south. Appeals and warnings mark the relationship between south and north; the more
sensitive of the northern inhabitants are able to recognize
their error (cf. esp. ch.28).

The apostasy of the north is under the hand of God (cf.
10.15); the people of the south too, the true Israel, is found
wanting, and the account, as in the books of Kings, moves
relentlessly to the climax of doom on Judah and Jerusalem.
But the structure of the narratives which lead to this point is
different in the Chronicler's work. The Deuteronomic writers,
at any rate in the latter part of the narrative, tend to alternate
good and bad rulers – Ahaz, Hezekiah, Manasseh, Josiah –
over-blackening some and idealizing others. Something of this
tendency may also be seen in the Chronicler, but his bad
rulers are not infrequently shown to be repentant, and his
good rulers equally show how readily faith becomes unfaith,
success leads to pride. There is a pattern in both the accounts;
it enables the authors to offer a theological judgment on the
history of their own people. The Chronicler's judgment owes
much to his predecessors, but he is never slavishly tied to their
way of presenting the story, and in his pictures of sin and
repentance, faith and unfaith, he opens up a view of man as
able to respond to the divine will, a hope tempered with a

knowledge of the realities of human experience, a view which can encourage obedience and foster loyalty in the community of his own time.

A. THE TRUE KINGDOM

II Chronicles 10-13

THE SECESSION OF THE NORTH

10.1-11.4

The narrative follows very closely the text of I Kings 12.1-24. It takes over the theme (cf. v.15) that the events are a 'turn-about' effected by God himself, while at the same time the people of the north who secede are the disloyal, in rebellion AGAINST THE HOUSE OF DAVID 'in perpetuity' (v.19). The north becomes, indeed, the symbol of disloyalty.

The question of the relationship between the two texts is not, however, quite so simple as this. It is very evident in Kings that the order of events and the position of Jeroboam are far from clear, and the Septuagint offers an alternative in which the story of Rehoboam at Shechem is related without any reference to Jeroboam; his place is indicated only sub-sequently in a long passage which makes use of various parts of the material drawn together in a different manner. It is therefore possible that the original Kings narrative did not introduce Jeroboam until after the northern tribes had decided to secede. It may have been the Chronicler who made Jero-boam a prime mover in this action, introducing the references to him in vv.2f. and 12; subsequently, these references were also copied into the Kings text, resulting in the present some-what confused narrative. Here again we have an example of the problem of deciding the original forms of the texts and the degree to which they have influenced one another.

Some confusion arises from the fact that the Chronicler's source here used the phrase 'all Israel' to indicate the northern tribes – and so he has copied it in vv.1, 3 and 16. (In fact, in

the second occurrence in v.16, the word 'all' is not in the
Kings text as we have it; probably it was in the text used by
the Chronicler.) In 11.3, however, he uses ALL ISRAEL in its,
to him, proper sense of the true united community, though
now it is seen to be limited to Judah and Benjamin.

10.2. This refers to the story of Jeroboam's flight to Egypt,
narrated in the chapter of Kings (I Kings 11) which the
Chronicler has omitted. He could assume that his readers
knew the story; at the same time, by introducing Jeroboam
in this way, he seems to suggest that it must have been some
wrong on Jeroboam's side which had brought this about, for
his description of Solomon hardly admits the interpretation
offered in Kings. In the sequel, the HEAVY YOKE imposed by
Solomon is mentioned, and Rehoboam's refusal to heed the
request for alleviation is, by implication at least, shown to be
foolish. But, as we are now invited to read the story – and
this is to some extent already the case in Kings – what Rehoboam did was to be seen as bringing about the inevitable
apostasy of the north. Even this, in some strange way, was
to be understood as the result of the divine purpose.

6-11. A modification is introduced in v.7. The Chronicler
avoids the suggestion that the king should 'be a servant' to
the people; the more innocuous BE KIND and PLEASE THEM
were probably felt to be more fitting to the Davidic king. The
contrast between the two groups consulted is vividly drawn.
The OLD MEN, better 'the elders', for this gives a sense of their
official status, are to be seen as the men of experience, who
have a position in the community. Here they are figures of
national importance; in a village community (cf. Ruth 4.2),
they would be men of local standing. The YOUNG MEN are
unlikely to be an official group, though it has been argued
that they constituted an assembly of men of military age existing alongside the eldership. The derogatory tone of the narrative towards these young men hardly suggests that they had
such status. It is more probable that we should see here a
feature often to be found in wisdom writings; age with its
experience is to be preferred to callow youth.

15. it was a turn of affairs brought about by God This comment, and the statement that this was in fulfilment of the divine word spoken BY AHIJAH THE SHILONITE, mark the central point of the narrative. Here again is an allusion to the narrative of I Kings 11. We have seen that the Chronicler refers to 'the prophecy of Ahijah' as a source for the reign of Solomon (9.29); the retention of the reference here underlines his view that events are intelligible in the light of the divinely given word. It will be a theme developed more fully for the final disaster to Judah (cf. ch.36).

16. The text accidentally lacks the word for SAW, the result of a scribal slip. The poetic passage quoted in this verse, as also in I Kings 12, appears in addition in II Sam. 20.1, a rebellion narrative not used by the Chronicler. Instead, he cites the reverse of these words in I Chron. 12.18 as an expression of loyalty to the Davidic house. (There is in fact more poetry in this chapter, particularly in vv.10f., 14.)

17. This is an odd verse, and its structure is unusual. Literally it runs: 'and the Israelites who were living in the cities of Judah, and Rehoboam ruled as king over them'. The first clause may be treated as meaning 'as for the Israelites ...', loosely attached to the latter; but we may wonder whether the text is defective, and whether it may not originally have anticipated Rehoboam's return to Jerusalem and made a statement about his establishment as king there. At all events it lays the emphasis that the true Israel is now to be found in the south (cf. 11.3).

18. the people of Israel The Chronicler has substituted this for 'all Israel' in Kings; probably the immediately preceding reference to the true Israel pointed to the need for modifying the text to avoid the suggestion that 'all Israel' was involved.

11.1–4. The account of the establishment of Rehoboam in Jerusalem and of his being forbidden TO FIGHT AGAINST ISRAEL, TO RESTORE THE KINGDOM follows immediately. What has been decreed by God (v.4, cf. 10.15) must not be resisted by man.

The Chronicler has omitted I Kings 12.20, which tells of
Jeroboam's election as king of the north.

THE TRUE KINGDOM UNDER REHOBOAM

11.5-23

The reign of Rehoboam, as it is depicted by the Chronicler,
shows an alternating pattern of obedience and faithlessness
after the disaster of the secession of the north. In this, the
Chronicler makes use of some parts of the material in I Kings
12, but prefaces this with a quite different picture which has
as a counterpart in Kings only a few small points regarding
the apostasy of the north.

5-12a. A list of cities in Judah and Benjamin fortified by
Rehoboam paves the way for the loss of these cities to the
Egyptians in 12.4. There has been much discussion about the
origin of this list, some scholars believing that it derives from
early information, perhaps even belonging to the time of
Rehoboam, others arguing that it is later, reflecting the conditions of Josiah's reign. Our knowledge of the fluctuating
conditions of the kingdom of Judah is really insufficient for
a satisfactory conclusion to be drawn. But whatever the origin
of the material, it is used by the Chronicler to point to the
firm establishment of the true kingdom, with fortified cities
well provisioned and under proper leadership.

12b-17. It seems proper to begin the next paragraph with
v.12*b* rather than with v.13, for the whole of the passage to
v.17 is concerned with showing the consolidated true kingdom. We may render: 'Now Judah and Benjamin were his',
(v.13) AND THE PRIESTS AND THE LEVITES ... Not only did the
two faithful tribes belong to the true kingdom, but it also
contained all the true religious officials – ejected from
office by Jeroboam and his sons. This is not found in I Kings;
it is the Chronicler's inference from the account of Jeroboam's establishment of alien worship in the north; no true
religious official could remain under such conditions. With

them came also the faithful: THOSE WHO HAD SET THEIR
HEARTS TO SEEK THE LORD GOD OF ISRAEL (v.16). This is
an important theme. The true kingdom is a gathered community. Jeroboam's idolatrous policy (v.15) becomes the setting up of HIS OWN PRIESTS FOR THE HIGH PLACES – the
condemned local sanctuaries – FOR THE SATYRS, the goat gods,
perhaps thought of as demonic beings, and THE CALVES, the
representations associated with Jeroboam in I Kings, symbols
of fertility and power which were to become objects of worship rather than associated with the invisible deity. The reader
is here expected to know the narrative of I Kings 12.25ff. The
result of the coming of the faithful from the north is that
THEY STRENGTHENED THE KINGDOM OF JUDAH; it is more firmly
established in its faithfulness. This was to last FOR THREE
YEARS (v.17); the period is not arbitrary, for it links with the
story to follow of unfaithfulness. Rehoboam and his people
were to forsake 'the law of the LORD' (12.1), and this is by
inference in the fourth year, so that in 'the fifth year' judgment falls (12.2).

18-22. The unfaithfulness is prefaced by an account of Rehoboam's wives and family. Where the Chronicler omits all
suggestion of Solomon's harem, he introduces material regarding Rehoboam's. The information is not entirely easy to
follow, since it conflicts with certain other statements. ABIJAH
is here son of MAACAH THE DAUGHTER OF ABSALOM; but in 13.2
the mother's name is given as 'Micaiah the daughter of Uriel
of Gibeah'. In I Kings 15.2 the first statement appears almost
in identical form; but in v.10 the same woman appears as the
wife of Abijah (Abijam), not as his mother. The various pieces
of information cannot be simply reconciled. Should we perhaps see a deliberate use of information by the Chronicler
to make a particular point? Rehoboam's first wife (v.18) is a
granddaughter of David (as Rehoboam was grandson) and
also on her mother's side descended from David's brother
Eliab; she is a very genuine Davidide, and surely a true queen
for the Davidic king. His second wife Maacah, who is given
preference by Rehoboam and whose son Abijah was chosen

as successor, is described as DAUGHTER OF ABSALOM. The Chronicler has not related the story of Absalom's rebellion, but his readers would know it as well as he. There is no certainty in fact that the same Absalom is involved, but the Chronicler may well have believed them to be identical. Abijah was to prove a faithful king (ch.13), though he was descended from an unfaithful member of the Davidic house. Is this intended to pave the way for the unfaithfulness of Rehoboam in 12.1?

23. he dealt wisely This verse seems to point in another direction, namely to his wisdom in organizing the districts of the kingdom with their fortified cities. But the text is not perhaps quite so certain. The opening words could be a corruption of 'and he built'; the last clause is certainly corrupt, and while RSV follows a commonly accepted redivision of the words, another possible suggestion would be to emend to: 'he sought (i.e. worshipped) the gods of his wives'. The verse may contain both a duplicate of part of the statements in vv.5-12 and also a statement of apostasy. In that case, there would be an even clearer pointer to the judgment which inevitably falls in the next chapter. The Jerusalem Bible in fact makes this final phrase the introduction to ch.12.

REHOBOAM – FAITHLESSNESS AND REPENTANCE

12.1-16

1. he forsook the law of the LORD As has already been adumbrated in ch.11, the moment of the full establishment of Rehoboam's kingdom appears also as a moment of pride and apostasy. This concise indication of failure replaces the long catalogue of religious evils to be found in I Kings 14.22-24 which introduces the divine judgment in the form of Egyptian invasion. Here the Chronicler has first set out (vv.2-8) his interpretation of that invasion, and then, closely following the I Kings material, the consequences for Jerusalem in payment of tribute (vv.9-11). At the end (v.12), he resumes his interpretation with a brief note.

2. The significance of the passage for the Chronicler clearly lies in its exemplary character; this is the inevitable consequence not simply of royal disobedience, but of the people being UNFAITHFUL TO THE LORD.

3. The immensity of the Egyptian attack is stressed; the SUKKIIM were probably Egyptian mercenary troops. SHISHAK (Egyptian: Sheshonq, 945-924 BC) was a powerful ruler whose invasion of the Palestinian area is recorded in an inscription at Karnak. This lists more than 150 places claimed as captured; it is of note that among them only Aijalon (cf. 11.10) belonged strictly to Judah, though there are some places in the region south of the kingdom. Shishak's main objective, not mentioned in the biblical accounts, appears to have been the control of the centre and north, presumably as a preliminary to further advance, though he was not in the event able to undertake this. The biblical accounts concentrate on Judah, the implication being that Judah was able by using temple and royal treasures (vv.9-11) to buy off the Egyptian threat. But the Chronicler goes much further, for he depicts the capture of THE FORTIFIED CITIES OF JUDAH and an actual threat to Jerusalem. Of this there is no indication in the Egyptian records, and it seems probable that he is depicting this situation in terms of another, namely that of Sennacherib's invasion in 701 BC (cf. II Chron. 32.9-22; II Kings 18-19; Isa. 36-37). The promise of partial (or perhaps speedy) deliverance – so v.7, where SOME DELIVERANCE can mean either 'deliverance on a small scale' or 'deliverance in a short while' – and the withdrawal of total WRATH on Jerusalem parallel the themes of remnant and of the sparing of the city to be found in the accounts of the Sennacherib period. And we may see the compiler looking further forward too and seeing here a foreshadowing of the overthrow of Jerusalem in 587 BC, which in its turn was to be followed by response and restoration.

5-8. The judgment is expressed by the prophet SHEMAIAH (cf. 11.2), whose pronouncement, like other such prophetic words (e.g. Isa. 7.9), depends upon a neat word-play, here on the

word 'abandon'. Such prophetic interventions are to be found
frequently in the narratives that follow. The response of king
and leaders is an act of self-humbling and of acknowledgment
of the justice of the divine action; such an acceptance was to
be an important element in the interpretation of the exile.
Total judgment is therefore withdrawn, but, again with a
word-play, there is to be servitude; by being subject to Shishak,
the true people of God will learn what is MY SERVICE and what
THE SERVICE OF THE 'kings' (rather than kingdoms) OF THE
COUNTRIES, the outside, alien world (v.8). Such servitude was
to be the familiar political situation of the post-exilic community for which the Chronicler wrote (cf. Neh. 9.36). Is he
perhaps here exhorting them to use even this servitude to
learn more fully the nature of their position as servants of
God?

9-11. These verses follow the I Kings text closely, but they
are linked into the Chronicler's treatment by his resumptive
comment in v.12.

12. Here again the theme of there not being A COMPLETE
DESTRUCTION is underlined. The last clause is not clear. RSV,
like other translations and commentaries, understands it as
suggesting that things were not too bad for Judah. An alternative and better rendering would be: 'and on (in) Judah
too (i.e. in addition to Jerusalem alluded to in the previous
phrase) there were benevolent words', a promise of good.

13-16. This is the concluding summary of Rehoboam's reign,
closely linked with the comparable material in I Kings,
though adding a reminder of his failure in v.14, and introducing the source of the information as THE CHRONICLES OF
SHEMAIAH THE PROPHET AND OF IDDO THE SEER (cf. I Chron.
29.29 and II Chron. 9.29). To this the Hebrew adds 'to be
enrolled (by genealogy)', cf. RSVmg; it may be the remnant
of a longer phrase, perhaps 'including the official genealogy'
or 'and so too the enrolling of (?) the Levites'.

ABIJAH AND THE NORTH

13.1-14.1

13.1. Abijah Little information is given about Abijah
(Abijam) in I Kings 15, but the bare statements there are
expanded with a little homily on David, his faithfulness and
his one failure concerning Uriah. Unusually the Chronicler
includes a cross-reference to the chronology of the north,
but this is probably because in this section he is concerned
to express divine judgment upon the north in the person
of its apostate ruler.

2. war between Abijah and Jeroboam The theme is picked
up from the earlier statement.

3. The war theme is presented as an encounter between two
very unequal forces, those of the north being twice those
of the true kingdom; the importance of this is only brought
out in vv.13ff., but first the Davidic king makes his appeal
to the north and to Jeroboam its ruler to recognize the true
situation.

4-5. Mount Zemaraim Perhaps to be connected with the
town of that name near Bethel, mentioned in Josh. 18.22.
Stationed here, Abijah calls on the north to remember that
true kingship belongs to the Davidic house established by
eternal covenant (for COVENANT OF SALT as indicating an
inviolable covenant, cf. Lev. 2.13; Num. 18.19). The covenant
with David is comparable to the covenant with Israel.

6-7. We may note that the speech comments on Jeroboam's
part in the events, a feature which shows this to be a sermonic
elaboration (cf. the mention of Samuel in his own speech in
I Sam. 12.11). Stress rests here upon Jeroboam's rebellion and
on Rehoboam's youth and inexperience; Jeroboam REBELLED
AGAINST HIS LORD (the text has the plural 'lords', which we
could understand to mean God); he was joined by WORTH-
LESS SCOUNDRELS, literally 'sons of Belial', a word which later

becomes a name for an evil spirit, but originally meant either
'confusion' or 'the swallower', i.e. Sheol, the realm of the
dead. Such men, by their behaviour, reveal themselves as
belonging to the realm of evil.

**8-12. the kingdom of the LORD in the hand of the sons of
David** By contrast, the true people of God is too strong for
one who puts his trust in superior numbers and in GOLDEN
CALVES. For the north has excluded true priests and has
associated itself with alien religious practice; its priesthood
is worthless. A strong mocking note is evident here, and it is
possible that we should see a polemic against Samaritan
priests or other dissident groups in the time of the Chronicler.
The true people is known by its obedience; there is a further
word-play on the same word as in 12.5, though here in
vv.10 and 11 it is translated 'forsake'. The continuity of its
status is shown by its true priesthood, its proper sacrifice,
its temple vessels. Here again we may detect polemic against
other worship in the Chronicler's own day which claimed to
possess the true 'apostolic' succession. In a great climax in
v.12, the north is reminded of the presence of God as the
leader of his true people, and of the utter impossibility of
fighting against God (cf. Acts 5.33-39).

13-17. The confidence of Abijah is confirmed by the battle
description. Not only does Jeroboam have superior numbers;
he is also shown as a clever military strategist. Judah is caught
between two armies, a theme derived perhaps from the battle
of Joab with Ammonites and Aramaeans in II Sam. 10. The
people, however, CRIED TO THE LORD, AND THE PRIESTS BLEW
THE TRUMPETS (v.14) – a reminiscence of the siege of Jericho
(Josh. 6). THE BATTLE SHOUT, appropriate to the very presence
of God (cf. I Sam. 4.5ff.), marks the moment for God himself to act. The army of Judah is involved only in the pursuit
and the slaughter (vv. 16f., 19). Here, as in other battle
narratives in these chapters, the ancient theme of the 'holy
war', in which Israel is consecrated to battle and is regarded
as fighting in a war which is really Yahweh's war, has been
developed into a descriptive form (cf. also I Sam. 7).

18. The emphasis rests upon the reality of divine power and deliverance, and the Chronicler's own comment underlines the point.

19. The consequences are set out with a note of places acquired for Judah, perhaps a reference to the post-exilic community which may have laid claim to these areas.

20-22. Further, the contrast is drawn between Jeroboam's decline and, by implication, his sudden death, and Abijah's prosperity and power. The narrator sums up the story with another allusion to a prophetic source: THE STORY OF THE PROPHET IDDO. The actual word used – *midrash* – is known to us particularly from its later Jewish employment for writings of an explanatory or expository kind. It is found in the Old Testament only here and in 24.27, where the RSV has 'Commentary'. It may mean little more than 'book', or it may indicate already the beginnings of that more expansive material of which the Chronicler's own writings provide a good example.

14.1. The English Bible begins a new chapter with the statement of Abijah's death; in the Hebrew this verse forms the conclusion to ch.13.* The final clause of the verse in fact summarizes the first part of the reign of the next king, Asa, and the Jerusalem Bible is probably right in treating this as the beginning of the next narrative.

B. FAITH AND UNBELIEF IN JUDAH'S LIFE

II Chronicles **14-27**

ASA THE FAITHFUL

14.2-15.19

The alternating pattern of faith and unbelief which is to be so characteristic of the narratives concerning the kings of

* The Heb. verse numbers are therefore one less than the English in ch.14.

Judah is here further developed; a sharp contrast is drawn between Asa the faithful who enjoys peace and divine protection and Asa as he puts his trust in human resources (ch.16).

14.2-7. The opening passage, echoing the words of v.1*b*, lays its stress upon the granting of peace and well-being. So in v.5, THE KINGDOM HAD REST UNDER HIM and similarly in v.6, together with the further statement there that THE LORD GAVE HIM PEACE. The I Kings material (15.9-15) depicts Asa as a reforming ruler; here the point is made more explicit, and the relationship between the removal of alien religious objects, listed in vv.3-5, and the well-being of the land, is drawn out. It is essentially the same theme which is taken up in vv.6-7, where the accompaniment of obedience is expressed in terms of protecting the land with FORTIFIED CITIES, set out in greater detail in v.7. At first there seems an odd contrast between the emphasis on peace and this protective building; one might suppose that if God gives peace, there will be no need of military preparation. But we should perhaps see in this the same kind of theme as will appear in the Nehemiah (and Ezra) narratives; the community, if it is to remain the faithful and pure people of God, needs to be protected from the outside world.

7. the land is still ours The phrase may be seen as a reminder to the reader that a time was to come when the land would be lost and the people of God exiled from it; possession of the land goes with obedience, with true searching for God.

8. This verse may be linked with the protective theme, or may be seen as providing a link to the narrative of vv.9-15.

9-15. Judah's protective army, impressive as it may appear, is not much more than half the size of the immense force ascribed to ZERAH THE ETHIOPIAN. Strictly this unknown figure is a Cushite, and it may be argued that, since the engagement is placed south-west of Jerusalem at MARESHAH, one of the Judaean fortresses (cf. 11.8), and the pursuit goes only as far as GERAR, south of Gaza (vv.13f.), the origin of the story might be in some story of raids into Judaean territory by beduin from these outlying areas. But such searching for a historical base for the narrative is not really of much value; the Chronicler's intention is clearly to magnify the nature of the threat to Asa, and so to underline the faith expressed in his prayer in v.11. Only God can help; it is on him that the people rely; against him man cannot prevail. The theme of reliance suggests a possible link with such a passage as Isa. 10.20, where RSV renders the Hebrew word more literally as 'lean', and where the contrast is explicitly drawn between wrong reliance and true 'leaning upon God'. It is a theme picked up again in ch.16.

To such trust the response from God is seen in the total overthrow of the enemy, and again the 'holy war' idea is expressed, both in the total destruction, as if the enemy had been put to the ban (cf. Josh. 6.17), and also in THE FEAR OF THE LORD which is upon the whole area (v.14). This concept is to be found in the conquest traditions (e.g. Exod. 23.28, where the older translations have 'hornet', but the proper sense is 'panic'), and it may be seen also in such a narrative as that of Gideon's overthrow of the Midianites (Judg. 7). The emphasis rests again on God's power and action; the enemy WERE BROKEN BEFORE THE LORD AND HIS ARMY (v.13), literally 'his camp', which suggests the concept of Israel as the people of God organized in military formation as in the opening chapters of Numbers. Verse 15 adds a new element, perhaps with a clearer pointer to an engagement with beduin tribes.

15.1–7. It is in the light of this experience of faith and the power of God that Asa is met by AZARIAH THE SON OF ODED, whose words are subsequently described as PROPHECY (v.8). He preaches a short sermon to the king and people, an example of what has very appropriately been described as the Chronicler's use of contemporary 'levitical preaching' (see von Rad, 'The Levitical Sermon in I and II Chronicles', cf. p. 15). It is a sermon which combines two main elements:

appropriate allusions to prophetic teaching, and pointers to
the historic experience of the people. Verse 2 finds its counterpart in Jer. 29.13f.; vv.5f. in Zech. 8.10; v.7 in Jer. 31.16 and
Zeph. 3.16. It is clear that the Chronicler or the levitical
preachers of his day made use of phrases drawn in some
measure from the biblical material which has come down
to us. The allusions to history are not so easy to follow.
RSV quite properly translates some of the verbal forms as
past tenses, and thus we are led to look for such a period
as that of the end of the time of the Judges (esp. Judg. 17-21)
as a time of disorder. But much of the phraseology here has
no precise reference to the past, and the allusions to
Zechariah's prophecies, to the insecurity of the time of restoration after the exile, to the need then for COURAGE (v.7, cf.
Hag. 2.4), may perhaps indicate that the preacher is not
simply invoking the past but seeing it as paralleling the later
experience of the community and providing points of contact with the needs of his own time.

8-15. This may be seen also in the response of the king. The
words of prophecy lead into a full-scale religious reform,
comparable to those attributed to Hezekiah (chs. 29ff.) and
Josiah (chs.34f.). We observe that there is a repair of THE
ALTAR such as is described in Ezra 3 for the restoration
period; there is a gathering of faithful sojourners from
EPHRAIM, MANASSEH AND SIMEON, just as we find that the
renewed temple after the exile is dedicated with the presence
of those who separated themselves from defilement (Ezra 6).
It takes place in THE THIRD MONTH (v.10), probably to coincide
with the feast of weeks (Pentecost), the name of which is
possibly alluded to by a word play in vv.14f. (*shebū'ōth*,
the title of the feast, and the root *shāba'*, to swear, and its
derivatives). A COVENANT is made of total obedience, with
a severe injunction against those who refuse (vv.12f.). In
later centuries, the giving of the law on Sinai was to be
associated with Pentecost; it is possible that we have here
from the time of the Chronicler an early indication of this
association of the feast with historical tradition, just as at

an earlier date both Passover and Tabernacles had been given such links with the great saving events of the Exodus.

16-19. The picture is of a community rejoicing at new-found obedience, enjoying peace and well-being UNTIL THE THIRTY-FIFTH YEAR OF THE REIGN OF ASA (v.19). Some extra detail of reform is given in vv.16-18. MAACAH, the queen mother, a position of some considerable significance in the kingdom's life, was not spared from degradation, for she had made some unspeakable alien religious object – its precise nature being unstated. This is BURNED outside the city AT THE BROOK KIDRON (v.16, cf. 29.16); a much fuller statement of the kind of action involved is found in II Kings 23.4, 6, on which cf. Exod 32.20. Verse 17*a* appears to contradict 14.3f., and this, together with the rather overloaded reform material of these two chapters, may suggest that the narrative is not all of one piece. But the component parts all turn around the same primary theme. Faith and well-being belong together in the people's life.

ASA THE FAITHLESS

16.1-14

The long peaceful period of Asa's reign lasted, according to the Chronicler, until his THIRTY-FIFTH YEAR (15.19). At this point, the narrative in I Kings 15.16-22 is picked up. There it is set out as one example of the continual warfare between Israel and Judah; here it becomes an indication of how a good king could, in the last years of his reign, be led totally astray from faith.

1-6. Confronted with an Israelite threat, which cut the route from Jerusalem northwards at RAMAH – the text indicates that Baasha 'rebuilt' Ramah, i.e. he fortified it to protect his own kingdom and threaten Judah – Asa sent ambassadors to the king of Aram (SYRIA), invoking a long-standing treaty and asking for help in return for payment. As a result of Aramaean attack, Baasha withdrew and Asa was able in his turn to

fortify frontier posts and thus protect Jerusalem against
attack. We may observe that in his desire to show how long
years of peace follow upon faith and reform, whereas lack
of faith brings speedy disaster, the Chronicler has contra-
dicted the chronology which we find in I Kings; for according
to that record, Baasha had ceased to reign years earlier.
Nothing is gained by trying to harmonize the figures.

7-9. The significance of this narrative for the Chronicler is
brought out in a prophetic word of judgment, spoken by
HANANI THE SEER, evidently thought of as the father of another
prophet named Jehu, who appears in I Kings 16.1 pronouncing
judgment on Baasha, and also in II Chron. 19.2. The judgment here is in the form of a sermon, like that of Azariah in
15.1-7. It is linked to prophetic words; the theme of reliance,
as in 14.11 (cf. Isa. 10.20), is one that is expressed in a
number of passages in Isaiah which warn against reliance
upon Egypt (e.g. Isa. 31). The words: THE EYES OF THE LORD
RUN TO AND FRO THOUGHOUT THE WHOLE EARTH (v.9) are taken
from Zech. 4.10, where they are used in a quite different
context; their theme is the protection afforded by such all-
seeing power. That Asa has DONE FOOLISHLY recalls the words
of Samuel to Saul (I Sam. 13.13), found also in David's
acknowledgment of unwisdom (I Chron. 21.8 = II Sam. 24.10).
The example of the battle against the Ethiopians in ch.14 is
used to point the obvious moral (v.8). But this placing virtually
side by side of a narrative in which immense dangers are met
with faith and one in which there is reliance merely on
human and indeed foreign aid, brings out forcibly the contrast between faith and unbelief. Even so good a king as Asa
can fail, a point which is to be made also for other and
greater kings. It is a telling warning against religious complacency.

7. the army of the king of Syria The reference to its escape
seems strange. There is some evidence for substituting 'Israel'
for SYRIA (this is followed in NEB), and the error in the
text would be very easily intelligible in the context. It is
possible that the meaning is that had Asa had faith he would

have vanquished not only the immediate enemy, Israel, but even the other alien power, Aram.

10. Asa's response to the prophetic word is shown to be even more indicative of his lack of faith. The prophet, like Jeremiah, is put in THE STOCKS (cf. Jer. 20), and SOME OF THE PEOPLE, presumably sympathizers, were cruelly treated. But judgment would follow.

11. This is a brief note of the source book of his narratives – hardly to be identified with I and II Kings if we may judge from the Asa narratives as they appear here.

12. The Chronicler uses the theme of his illness (I Kings 15.23) to stress an even further lack of faith. For IN HIS DISEASE HE DID NOT SEEK THE LORD a sharp contrast with Hezekiah in a similar situation (32.24-26; cf. II Kings 20.1-11; Isa. 38). His resorting to PHYSICIANS may be interpreted in the light of Ecclus. 38.1-15, which relates prayer and healing, or it may be understood as a reference to undesirable practices, since the word, literally 'healers', may also be understood as having connections with the spirits of the dead. Necromantic or magical practices may be in the Chronicler's mind. The failure of Asa to appeal to God for help might have been suggested to the Chronicler in part by the interpretation of his name; a fuller form of his name might be 'Asa-el', which could be understood as 'God heals'.

13-14. The concluding comment appears in some measure to rehabilitate Asa, for he is given an honourable burial. Is this to suggest that he finally saw the error of his ways, or is it to remind the reader that he had been a good king who fell from grace? The word for VARIOUS KINDS (of spices) in v.14 appears to be of Persian origin, reflecting the period of the Chronicler's activity.

JEHOSHAPHAT THE JUST

17.1-19

The Chronicler devotes four chapters to Jehoshaphat, incorporating most of the very meagre information in I Kings (15.24; 22.41-49) and using also the long narrative of I Kings 22.1-35, which is there presented rather as part of the Ahab tradition. The whole structure of the section is very different from that in I Kings; the whole of the Elijah and Elisha narratives have been passed over (with only a brief reference to Elijah in 21.12ff.), and, naturally enough, only that one part of the narratives of Ahab which can be used to provide teaching about true faith (cf. 18 and 19.1-3) reappears here. The sources of the Chronicler's new material have been much discussed. It may be that actual documentary material was available, though, if it was, it by no means follows that it originally had anything to do with Jehoshaphat. More likely is the supposition that the name of the king has provided the basis for homilectic development, as we have seen to be possible in the case of Asa. Jehoshaphat, 'Yahweh judges', suggests a twofold line of thought; to judge is to deliver, a theme adumbrated in ch.17 but more fully developed in ch.20. It also suggests the teaching mission and the judicial reform which appear in chs.17 and 19. In these two ways, the nature of God himself is traced within the narrative material.

The theme of ch.17 is in reality the protection of Judah, the true people. This is the significance of the statements about fortifications in v.2 and about the armed forces in vv.12-19; it is a reiteration of the point already made in chs.11 and 14.

1. strengthened himself against Israel This may be intended to emphasize the countering of any danger from the apostate north; but it is possible that we should understand the Hebrew to mean 'he showed himself strong over Israel', i.e. as ruler over the true people.

3-6. riches and honour The result of religious reform, as Jehoshaphat followed the wise policy of his father's earlier years. (The addition of 'David' in v.3, see RSVmg, is probably simply due to a copyist writing a common formula 'his father David', not observing that the context demanded a reference to Asa.)

7-9. Jehoshaphat's reform, like those of Hezekiah and Josiah, is now taken a stage further in the instructing of the people of Judah in THE LAW. A body of officials, lay PRINCES, LEVITES and PRIESTS, go on circuit to ensure total obedience to the law. We may probably see in this a projection back of the work of Ezra, whose commission (Ezra 7) demanded the acceptance of the law as the mark of the true member of the community. The name TOBADONIJAH in v.8 is probably due to an accidental recopying of the two previous names.

10-11. the fear of the LORD The attitude of the surrounding lands is the counterpart to the state of obedience and right conduct by the king. Judah is protected from war, and PHILISTINES and ARABS pay tribute. The reference may reflect a stage in the life of the post-exilic community when some of the areas bordering the province of Judah came within its aegis. An obscure passage in Zech. 9.5-8 may reflect a similar situation.

12-19. Judah is strengthened and protected.

JEHOSHAPHAT AND THE NORTH

18.1-19.3

The Chronicler has taken over almost unchanged the story found in I Kings 22.1-35. In its Kings context, the story serves to point sharply to the distinction between true and false prophecy, typified in the single figure of Micaiah set against the four hundred. It belongs within the series of Arab narratives, and as such underscores the judgment on Ahab's house by Elijah, though it does preserve in the king's heroic death a hint of a different estimate of this northern ruler.

For the Chronicler, the prophetic element in the story is clearly important. But his greater concern is with the position of Jehoshaphat, quite unnecessarily involved in dangerous contact with the apostate north and escaping only by an act of divine intervention from a disaster which he has courted.

18.1. At the start, we are reminded of Jehoshaphat's GREAT RICHES AND HONOUR; but, despite this, he was so foolish as to enter into A MARRIAGE ALLIANCE WITH AHAB of the north; the detail of the alliance is passed over here (cf. II Kings 8.18).

2. A courtesy visit to Ahab, the occasion of a great feast, provides the moment for Jehoshaphat to be 'enticed' into war with the north against Aram at RAMOTH-GILEAD, an important place in Transjordan, the scene of more than one contest between Israel and Aram. The RSV INDUCED is not strong enough to express a word which is used (e.g. in Deut. 13.6) for seduction into apostasy.

3. The words of Jehoshaphat identifying his own people's interests and concerns with those of Ahab are taken direct from the account in I Kings, but here, with the Chronicler's so great emphasis on the apostasy of the north, they come to have a stronger meaning. To identify the true people with the apostates is an act of appalling folly.

4-27. As in the I Kings narrative, it is Jehoshaphat who appears as the pious king; he asks that the divine oracle be sought, and when the four hundred prophets offer victory, he is sufficiently sensitive to ask if there is not ANOTHER PROPHET OF THE LORD (v.6), with the implication that the true word has not yet been heard. The kings ON THEIR THRONES, in festive robes (v.9) in the 'open space' before THE GATE OF SAMARIA (although the word means threshing-floor, it is quite evidently not used in that sense here), the leader of the prophets expressing in symbolic action WITH HORNS OF IRON his conviction of divine victory, make a dramatic setting for the entry of the true prophet, who will speak only WHAT MY GOD SAYS (v.13). His pretended conformity to the four hundred is recognizable as spurious even by the evil Ahab (v.15). He pronounces judgment, and grounds his prophetic utterance in the description of a vision of the heavenly court, closely parallel to that of Isa. 6. The true prophet, as Jeremiah was to affirm (Jer. 23.22), is one who has stood in the council of God, to overhear or even to participate. At the end of this part of the narrative, a scribe who has identified Micaiah with his namesake Micah of more than a century later has added the opening words of Micah's prophetic collection (Micah 1.2); it is an interesting example of midrashic comment.

28–34. In the battle scene which follows, the point of the earlier narrative remains. Ahab may change clothes with Jehoshaphat, but it does not help him. Jehoshaphat's cry (v.31) does not lead, as in the earlier form, to his being recognized, but to divine intervention in which the enemy are drawn away. Without direct statement it is implied that the bowman whose shot killed Ahab was in fact directed by God. He did it, as the Hebrew says, 'in all innocence' (this appears to be the correct sense rather than the alternative which has been proposed of interpreting the word as meaning 'in full strength'); but his action was being overruled. So Ahab died, with the Chronicler preserving, curiously, the note of his heroism in remaining PROPPED UP IN HIS CHARIOT FACING THE SYRIANS UNTIL EVENING.

19.1–3. For Jehoshaphat, the sequel awaits his return to Jerusalem IN SAFETY. For then he finds himself confronted by the prophet JEHU THE SON OF HANANI (cf. on 16.7), judged by the divine WRATH for his supporting of THE WICKED, the opponents of God. Yet the consequences of judgment are averted by his right actions. The warning serves to introduce a fuller account of Jehoshaphat's good deeds and of his faith.

JEHOSHAPHAT, REFORMER OF JUSTICE

19.4-11

4-10. There is no evidence in the Kings material to support
what is here said about Jehoshaphat. Much of what is said
about the reform of justice is of a general, somewhat homiletic kind. The people are BROUGHT BACK TO THE LORD (v.4).
Justice is in the presence of God; it must therefore be without any PERVERSION (vv.6f.). The judges are to act IN THE FEAR
OF THE LORD (v.9). They will decide issues of murder and
manslaughter, and problems of the interpretation of law
(v.10). Proper justice enables the community to avoid both
divine WRATH and human GUILT (cf. a similar point exemplified
in Deut. 21.1ff.).

The language in which the charges are given for the administration of justice is strongly reminiscent of Deuteronomy,
particularly of Deut. 16.18-20 and 17.8-13. This suggests that
this passage represents at least very largely a projection back
into an earlier period of the practice or the desired practice of
a later age. It is perhaps best seen as an attempt at applying
in a new situation the kind of requirements represented most
clearly by Deuteronomy. In the light of the general impression which the Chronicler's work creates, this would most
naturally be a reflection of the needs of his own time, an
expression of his own hopes and ideals as well as of the
realities of the contemporary situation.

This does not mean that there may not have been earlier
moves for the better organization of justice. The failures of
justice which are indicated in the prophetic literature would
point to such a need at an earlier period. But we have no
real basis for ascribing historicity to the present account.

11. Perhaps the clearest indication lies in the injunction
that there shall be THE CHIEF PRIEST as supreme IN ALL
MATTERS OF THE LORD – the administration of all concerns
in which religious issues arise, which could well include questions of membership of the religious community; and also a

personage described as GOVERNOR OF THE HOUSE OF JUDAH –
the term is a very general one, meaning simply 'leader', 'leading person' – IN ALL THE KING'S MATTERS. The precise interpretation of this is very uncertain.

chief priest The expression (literally 'head priest') is one
which appears in the Deuteronomic literature and in the
Chronicler (including one occurrence in Ezra 7.5); there is
another expression, literally 'the great priest', which occurs
in a similarly wide range of writings, including Haggai and
Zechariah, and also Neh. 3.1, 20. The form here could therefore perfectly well refer to the post-exilic high priest as having something already of that authority which may be seen
in the Greek and Roman periods.

governor The term is not that normally used in the post-
exilic writings, but the division of authority looks so much
like what we find in Haggai and Zechariah that it would
appear very probable that it too reflects the later situation.

the king's matters What is meant could be quite generally
questions of military duties, forced labour, taxation and the
like, but it could, in the period of Persian rule, denote those
matters which are governed by the demands of the *Persian*
king. In that case, the Chronicler could here be seen enjoining on his contemporaries the need to pay due regard to the
demands of the foreign authority, to recognize the division
between the requirements of that authority which must be
accepted and the proper carrying out of the laws which
govern the life of the religious community. We may possibly
see here evidence of the Chronicler as one concerned to discover a right basis of order which will enable the Jewish
community to be itself under the constraints of foreign rule.

JEHOSHAPHAT – FAITH AND DELIVERANCE

20.1-37

Only the concluding verses of this section (vv.31-37) have

any parallel in the Kings text. The remainder is a battle
narrative which reveals very clearly the characteristics of the
Chronicler's understanding of the divine ordering of men's
affairs. It has sometimes been thought that the story could
represent an elaborated version of the battle with Moab in
II Kings 3, but the differences are too great. The precise
topography of the story has suggested to some commentators
that there must be a historical basis for it, though such
precision is as much the mark of legend as of history, and it
may be noted that the really precise details appear in a
strongly sermonic passage in vv.15-17. If there is history
underlying the narrative, it is more probable that an incident
– a raid into Judaean territory, perhaps connected with Nabataean movements in the post-exilic period – belonging to a
time nearer to that of the Chronicler has been utilized by
him. The explanation of the place name BERACAH (v.26) which,
because of its meaning 'blessing', might be expected to have
a story attached to it, could possibly be the nucleus of what
is now both a liturgical account and an important reinterpretation of themes belonging to the 'holy war' ideology.
Attempting to discover historicity here is really of very
little value in the assessment of the significance of the passage.

1. after this A loose chronological connection is made with
the preceding narrative by the opening. An alliance of groups
to the east and south-east of Judah is described.

the Meunites These (cf. I Chron. 4.41; II Chron. 26.7) were
perhaps connected with the region of Petra, the Nabataean
capital to the south-east of the Dead Sea. The Hebrew text
has an erroneous double reference to the Ammonites.

2. The attack is reported to Jehoshaphat. The names of the
enemy, and the reference in v.10 to MOUNT SEIR, a synonym
for Edom, confirm that the correct reading here is EDOM,
not Aram. The confusion, due to the closely similar letters,
occurs more than once in the Old Testament.

Hazazon-tamar Unknown, but its locality is indicated by the well-known EN-GEDI, on the western shore of the Dead Sea just north of Masada.

the sea Here it can only mean the Dead Sea, though this is normally given a fuller title, e.g. Salt Sea.

3. The report of the attack produces FEAR, but also a proper response; the king SET HIMSELF TO SEEK THE LORD and A FAST WAS PROCLAIMED in ALL JUDAH.

5-9. This first stage of the liturgy – for such it really is: response in inquiry to God and fasting – is followed by a con- fession of faith by Jehoshaphat, leading into prayer. Here there is an appropriate acknowledgment of the supremacy of Yahweh and of his uniqueness, themes common in hymnic psalms. There is a recall of the conquest events, which pro- vide the basis of present hope. The allusion to ABRAHAM as FRIEND of God is paralleled in Isa. 41.8, and the immediate link to the building of the temple recalls the implicit reference to Abraham in the siting of the temple on Mount Moriah in II Chron. 3.1. The confidence that God will HEAR AND SAVE in any emergency (v.9) is strongly reminiscent of Solomon's prayer in ch.6, with the effect that the present narrative is set out as an example of the reality of the divine promise.

9. judgment A better suggestion is 'floods'.

10-11. Precise reference to the immediate need includes an allusion to the events of the wilderness period (cf. Deut. 2); that Israel was forbidden to encroach on territory allocated to Edom, AMMON and MOAB here becomes the basis for emphasizing the maintaining of the inheritance of Israel. Encroachment on Judaean territory in the exilic age by these peoples may be a further element of background experience to this particular statement.

12. The final appeal of the prayer expresses both absolute confidence in the reality of divine power and awareness of human weakness; in such a situation OUR EYES ARE UPON THEE (cf. Ps. 123.2).

14-17. The answer to such prayer for the community comes in the liturgy in the oracle of salvation, here pronounced by A LEVITE, a member of the Asaphite guild of singers, who is empowered by the SPIRIT OF THE LORD to prophesy. In the books of Chronicles, the place of earlier prophets is not infrequently taken by such Levites, whose preaching and teaching function is also emphasized. It is perhaps also to express this that the name of this particular Levite is given as JAHAZIEL, 'God gives vision' (v.14). The oracle begins and ends, like the comparable oracle of salvation in Isa. 41.10-13, with an injunction: FEAR NOT.

The battle is not yours but God's   This recalls I Sam. 17.47.

16. go down   The command reminds us of Judg. 7.9.

17. take your position, stand still, and see the victory of the LORD   The words are closely reminiscent of Exod. 14.13, as Israel stands at the edge of the sea with the Egyptians in hot pursuit.

18-19. The assurance is greeted by king and people in an act of worship, of prostration before God; and by the levitical singers engaging in an act of praise.

20. early in the morning   At what is often the moment of divine victory (cf. e.g. Josh. 10.9f.; also Ps. 30.5), the army advances, to be exhorted afresh by the king in a brief sermon. It is based partly on Isa. 7.9, but the words from there of belief and assurance are paralleled by the words: BELIEVE HIS PROPHETS, AND YOU WILL SUCCEED. Here we may see how the words of the prophets, spoken to one situation, are being regarded as living oracles, renewed and reapplied to other situations. There is a move towards the emergence of a canon of holy writings; here, as often in the Chronicler's sermonic passages, the problem of the relationship between the word of God attested in the past and the needs of the contemporary moment is tackled by a placing together of a prophetic word and an injunction to see in that word a message of life.

21. In further preparation, the king designates those who

are to sing praises, following in this the example of his fore-
father David, and the appropriate act of praise is sung before
the advancing troops.

praise him in holy array, found also in Ps. 96.9 and used in
I Chron. 16.29, may denote the holy garments of the singers,
or they may be a brief quotation indicative of the glory of
the deity who reveals himself in holy splendour. The refrain
quoted (cf. Ps. 136.1) has also been used in I Chron. 16.34.

22-23. The moment of praise is the moment of God's victory. No rationalizing explanation of the battle is appropriate;
the supposition that the various enemy groups failed to recognize each other misses the point that it is God himself – by
what means is not stated – who is seen as throwing the enemy
into confusion and destroying them utterly; they are treated
as under the ban in the holy war.

24-30. The result is like that in one of the narratives of the
overthrow of the Assyrians in II Kings 18-19; Isa. 36-37; for
there too (II Kings 19.35) the whole enemy army is found by
Judah to be dead; nothing remains but the despoiling of the
corpses. The climax is an assembly in the place of 'blessing',
the VALLEY OF BERACAH (v.26, cf. p. 148), and in a great festive
entry to JERUSALEM and its temple. The FEAR OF GOD is upon
all lands, and Judah enjoys peace.

The whole account is both liturgical and theological. In
danger the community must turn to God, in whom alone help
is to be found. Praise, confession of faith and prayer constitute the right approach; to those who turn to him, God
answers with the assurance of his saving power. This salvation is not brought about by human means; it is God himself
who acts. What rests on his people is the response of praise,
the commitment to him in total trust, the act of thanksgiving.
In such experience those who are outside the community will
see and acknowledge the nature of their God. It is a strongly
quietistic doctrine, with its extreme emphasis on divine action;
but it is expressive of a very confident faith. Without knowing
precisely the kind of situation to which the Chronicler spoke,

we may nevertheless suppose that there were in his generation, as for example in the times of the prophets, those who
imagined that hope lay in skilful political manoeuvre, in
alliances, in military power. A later generation than that of the
Chronicler, confronted by a threat to the faith and life of
the community in persecution and oppression, was to hear the
same essential emphasis in the manifestos of the book of
Daniel; and later generations still were to discover to their
cost the disastrous consequences of warfare and intrigue. The
Chronicler's emphasis is not the whole truth, but it contains
essential understanding of the nature of religious faith.

31-33. The conclusion to Jehoshaphat's reign comes as an
anticlimax. Here is the statistical and other information with
the reminder that the king acted rightly, but that there was
still disobedience in the people's life.

34. Reference is made to the sources, with another prophetic
compilation, that of JEHU THE SON OF HANANI (cf. 19.2),
indicated. Verses 31-34 are based on I Kings 22.41-47, but
show some modifications.

35-37. The final verses modify their counterpart in I Kings
22.48-50, and no doubt they appear here because in that context they stand at the end of what limited material there is
about Jehoshaphat. In the light of the preceding chapters, they
serve to point yet again to the theme of unbelief. Alliance for
war in ch.18 is balanced here by alliance for trade; the ven-
ture is disastrous, as prophesied by yet another prophet,
ELIEZER, only mentioned here. The point is clearer if we
adopt an alternative rendering for the end of v.35 and the
beginning of v.36: 'He (Jehoshaphat) did wrong in that he
allied himself with him (Ahaziah) in building ships....' It was
not necessary to say that a king of the north did wrong; in the
Chronicler's view that was self-evident. But here was a king
who should have learnt from experience, as the Chronicler
has described his reign. The death of Jehoshaphat in 21.1 concludes the narrative, but serves also to open the next.

JEHORAM–THE CONSEQUENCES OF WICKEDNESS

21.1-20

The very brief account of Jehoram, son of Jehoshaphat, in II Kings 8.17-22 notes only his evil ways, the sparing of Judah for David's sake and the rebellion of Edom. This material, utilized by the Chronicler, is elaborated with fuller explanation of the nature of the evil and its consequences.

2-4. The other SONS OF JEHOSHAPHAT – according to v.13, BETTER THAN Jehoram – who had been given positions of honour by their father are murdered by Jehoram, together with some of the leading men of the kingdom. The implication seems to be that they disapproved of Jehoram's evil ways. It is worth noting that the Hebrew text refers to Jehoshaphat in v.2 as KING OF 'Israel', and to the leading men in v.4 as PRINCES OF 'Israel'; there is some support for altering the text to read JUDAH as RSV has done, but it is more probable that the word Israel is used as elsewhere to denote the true kingdom.

6. The evil ways of Jehoram are explained from the wife (Athaliah) who influenced him and was herself to play a prominent part in subsequent events (chs.22-23). But total judgment does not fall because of God's COVENANT ... WITH DAVID, the promise that there would be a perpetual LAMP, a continuing life, for the royal house.

7. The substitution of HOUSE OF DAVID (the royal dynasty) for 'Judah' in the Kings text shows the Chronicler's concern for the Davidic line.

8-10. Judgment falls first in the revolt of EDOM and a similar revolt of LIBNAH, south-west of Jerusalem on the Philistine border; the latter might be linked with the Philistine troubles mentioned in v.16. The course of the narrative is not entirely clear, and some commentators emend the text to make it say that Jehoram was defeated by Edom. It would appear that

what is meant is that he was in effect defeated, being himself
SURROUNDED WITH HIS COMMANDERS, but just succeeded in
escaping the Edomite encirclement.

10-11. These rebellions are explained as due to the apostasy
of Jehoram and his making of HIGH PLACES.

12-15. At this point the Chronicler has introduced a new
method of passing prophetic judgment on the Judaean king's
failure. Instead of a prophetic speech, delivered in person, he
speaks of A LETTER – or perhaps more generally 'a writing' –
FROM ELIJAH THE PROPHET. The information of II Kings 2
shows that Elijah can hardly have been alive at this moment,
though the chronology is by no means absolutely certain. The
Chronicler may simply have taken no note of this, and assumed
that Elijah the prophet who spoke judgment upon the house
of Ahab in the north could still actively give a comparable
judgment upon a king who was imitating the ways of THE
HOUSE OF AHAB (v.13). Or he may have had in mind the situation in which he himself lived, when written records of the
prophets' messages were available for reapplication; so he
emphasizes that the words of the prophets last, even if they
themselves must die (cf. Zech. 1.5f.: '... the prophets, do they
live for ever? But my words and my statutes, which I commanded my servants the prophets...'). Prophetic words are
gaining canonical status. The absence of Elijah and Elisha
from the main narratives of the Chronicler is not altogether
strange, since their concern was entirely with the north. But
here he picks up the significance of Elijah's prophetic activity.
What was said of the north is equally applicable to Judah. To
turn from the right way – here linked with Jehoshaphat and
Asa – to follow the ways of the north and particularly of
Ahab, and to murder BROTHERS ... WHO WERE BETTER THAN
YOURSELF, leads inevitably to terrible judgment.

16-17. The sequel in judgment is twofold. It is first in terms
of an attack on the kingdom by PHILISTINES and ARABS, leading to the massacre of the sons of Jehoram except for his
youngest JEHOAHAZ.

18-19. Then it is in INCURABLE DISEASE, and a death IN GREAT AGONY. He died dishonoured.

20. and he departed with no one's regret Literally: 'without any desire'. The RSV paraphrase is very likely, but the phrase could mean 'without any interest (in him)', and we may note that it occurs at the point in the summary at which there would be expected a reference to the sources for further information. Even his burial showed that he could not be regarded as a true king.

ATHALIAH – THE TRUE KINGDOM IN PERIL

22.1-23.21

These two chapters cover the reign of Jehoram's son and successor Ahaziah (Jehoahaz), his death and the interregnum under Athaliah his mother, and the overthrow of Athaliah and establishment of Ahaziah's surviving son Joash as king. The material is to be found in II Kings 8.24-29, in 9 – though this chapter is hardly used by the Chronicler – and in 11.1-20. The differences of treatment are due very largely to the Chronicler's particular emphases.

22.1. The new king was put on the throne by THE INHABITANTS OF JERUSALEM. The significance of this statement is not clear. Elsewhere (e.g. 33.25) we find the 'people of the land' – probably meaning 'the ordinary people' – acting to set a king on the throne. It is perhaps to be supposed that those who acted in Jerusalem were men concerned about the well-being of the kingdom, but if so they were to be sadly disappointed in their nominee. The disasters of 21.16f. are recalled; AHAZIAH – this name represents a reversal of the two elements of the other name used in 21.17, 'Jehoahaz' – was the sole surviving son of Jehoram.

2a. forty-two His age presents obvious problems. II Kings has twenty-two; the Septuagint has twenty. The figure here might derive from the conflating of the two figures, but since there is a reference to his brothers' sons as his attendants in v.8, the lower figures are no more satisfactory than the higher one which makes Ahaziah older than his father. There are evidently unresolved discrepancies in the text.

2b-4. The significant point about Ahaziah now appears. The queen mother was ATHALIAH, THE GRANDDAUGHTER OF OMRI: it was she who was HIS COUNSELLOR, so that he inevitably followed THE WAYS OF THE HOUSE OF AHAB. And it appears that it was members of the evil royal house of the north who acted as his advisers. The influence of the north was here to be seen as even more evil than in the time of Jehoshaphat.

5-9a. Their counsel led him, like his grandfather Jehoshaphat, into dangerous alliance with the north, in a situation comparable with the earlier one and also involving the Syrians. A visit to the wounded king of the north, JEHORAM (Joram), brought Ahaziah into contact with the divinely appointed avenger JEHU, whose story is told in full detail in II Kings 9. Ahaziah's associates were killed by Jehu, and Ahaziah himself was found IN SAMARIA, the evil northern capital, and no fit place for the Davidic king. There he met his death and was buried; he was spared the indignity of being left exposed, because of the memory of the pious Jehoshaphat (v.9a). This sequence of events is described as divinely ordained (v.7). The Hebrew text actually states that 'the downtreading of Ahaziah was from God'; but probably the letters of this word (*tebūsāh*) should be transposed to give a word meaning 'turn-about' (*tesūbāh*), a word like that used in 10.15 and there rendered 'a turn of affairs'.

9b-12. The ruthless action of Athaliah and the hiding of the child in whom the kingdom will be restored is briefly related. The lack of anyone ABLE TO RULE – more literally 'strong enough' – left the way open to the already influential queen-mother. She endeavoured to secure absolute control by wiping out the royal family (v.10). We are not informed what succession she planned, but it is evident that her policy meant in effect that Judah became one in evil with the apostate north.

In the Kings form of the narrative, the full account of the so-called prophetic revolution in II Kings 9 provides a counterpart to the priestly revolution which appears here alone, with only the brief allusion to the anointed Jehu (v.7). The motif of the rescue of the one child who will in due course be the king, is a familiar story element which heightens the tension. The heroine here is the sister of Ahaziah – not included in the royal massacre – and WIFE OF JEHOIADA THE PRIEST. The child remained hidden in the temple for SIX YEARS. The way was then open for action.

23.1-15. The narrative of the overthrow of Athaliah follows fairly closely that of II Kings, but the Chronicler makes it much more of an ecclesiastical action. It is the priestly officers which are involved and not the royal bodyguard. In addition, greater emphasis is laid upon the restoration of the Davidic line. The stress is laid upon the impropriety of any but the proper officials entering the temple; the people are to be obedient to THE CHARGE OF THE LORD (v.6). The new king is under the protection of THE LEVITES. So the new king is crowned and given THE TESTIMONY – its exact nature is not known, though the probability is that it is the royal law or warrant; the proclamation and anointing lead to a shout of welcome to the new ruler (v.11). The story vividly portrays Athaliah's arrival to be confronted by this *coup d'état*, to see THE KING STANDING BY HIS PILLAR – or perhaps more correctly 'on his dais' (literally 'standing place') – in the centre of a great religious celebration. Her action in tearing her clothes – a sign of mourning and distress – and shouting 'TREASON' leads to no response of loyalty to her. Her death in the temple would defile it, so she is to be brought OUT BETWEEN THE RANKS, or probably more correctly 'outside the precincts' (v.14); she is allowed to leave (rendering 'they made room for her' in v.15) instead of THEY LAID HANDS ON HER). So she was killed in the palace gate.

16-21. The sequel is in reformation: A COVENANT made by the priest involving the recommittal of the king and people to be the true people of God, and the destruction of the temple OF

BAAL and all that is connected with it (vv.16f.). To this the
counterpart is an act of reorganization, the restoration of the
order in the shrine as established by David (vv.18f.). The king
is acclaimed and enthroned by the whole community, and thus
well-being is restored; with Athaliah dead, the evil influence
of the alien north is removed, and for a time all is well (vv.20f.).

JOASH – REFORMER AND RENEGADE

24.1-27

The main account of the reign of Joash follows a pattern
already utilized earlier, for example in the case of Asa (chs.
14-16). Established on the throne securely by Jehoiada, Joash
remains loyal so long as the high priest is there; after Jehoiada's death, Joash forsakes the true faith and comes inevitably to judgment. The Chronicler's account differs at
many points from that of II Kings 11-12, though it includes
the two main elements of temple restoration and war with
Syria. The restoration (vv.4-14) is presented in a manner
characteristic of the Chronicler, with the emphasis resting
upon the propriety of religious practices. The war (vv.23f.) is
integrated into the theme of apostasy, and Joash's death in a
conspiracy against him provides the climax to the judgment.

3. Jehoiada His guidance is made clear from the outset,
for he is here shown as providing TWO WIVES for the young
king, and, as befits one who is divinely blessed, the king has
SONS AND DAUGHTERS, a provision for the true succession.

5-6. The restoration of the temple is made possible by the
collecting of the temple TAX, LEVIED according to MOSES' command (cf. Exod. 30.11-5ff.). The injunction to THE LEVITES to
collect this throughout Judah, and the comment on their
dilatoriness, may point to a neglect and revival of the tax
in the period of the Chronicler; an analogy is to be found in
Neh. 10.32, which points to a renewal of the system, a passage
which possibly refers to the period of Ezra, not long before
the time of the Chronicler's writing.

7. It is explained that this restoration was necessitated by the wickedness of ATHALIAH; it was her SONS who HAD BROKEN INTO THE HOUSE OF GOD and had used consecrated objects for alien deities, THE BAALS. The fact that the only sons of Athaliah who have been mentioned were Ahaziah, the previous king, and his brothers who had all been murdered (cf. 21.17), has suggested to some translators and commentators that the word should be understood as 'adherents' (so e.g. NEB). But such an attempt at harmonization is unsatisfactory; we may better see an emphasis on the evil perpetrated by this queen and her whole brood.

8-9. When the tax is brought in and placed in the chest set up at the royal command outside the temple gate (not 'beside the altar', as in II Kings 12.9, for the ordinary people could not, in the Chronicler's stricter view, penetrate so far), the whole community REJOICED at the giving, as has been said of the time of David (I Chron. 29.9).

10-11. Each day when the chest was filled (at the end of v.10 we should render 'until it was full' for UNTIL THEY HAD FINISHED), it was emptied and restored TO ITS PLACE. The work of restoration proceeded, and temple vessels were supplied to renew the worship, a symbol of the re-establishment of the true worship in succession to its ordering by David.

14. Jehoiada The whole period of his influence was marked by the proper carrying out of worship.

15-16. This ideal picture of an age of obedience is then sharply contrasted with the sequel. The high priest, dying at a truly patriarchal age (cf. the death of Aaron at 123 in Num. 33.39), was buried in the royal graves as befitted so loyal an adherent of God. The contrast between this and the burial of Joash (v.25) is sharp indeed. The Davidic king who became apostate was not worthy of such burial; the true priest is accorded royal honours. We may recall that the Chronicler wrote when kingship had ceased and the high priest was occupying a position of substantial power and influence. His work may reflect the move towards the merging of political and religious posi-

tion in the high priesthood which appears clearly in the second
century BC, but probably is to be traced back considerably
further.

17-19. Apostasy in Joash derives from the change of counsellor. No explanation is given of the evil influence of THE
PRINCES OF JUDAH, but it led to apostasy, the worship of alien
gods, including the female divinity Asherah, here mentioned
in the plural form ASHERIM. An attractive alternative ('covenant of the LORD' for HOUSE OF THE LORD) is perhaps to be
preferred in v.18. The result was judgment on Judah, expressed
as the divine wrath at work, and this in spite of prophetic
witness against the apostasy.

20-22. As an illustration of this prophetic witness, the figure of
ZECHARIAH THE SON OF JEHOIADA THE PRIEST appears. Stress is
laid upon his inspiration by THE SPIRIT OF GOD, described (see
RSVmg) as 'clothing itself with Zechariah', the expression
used of Gideon in Judg. 6.34 and also in I Chron. 12.18
(cf. p.55). But as in other instances, notably that of Jeremiah
(cf. Jer. 26), the people were unwilling to hear and CONSPIRED
AGAINST HIM, here in response to royal command. He was
stoned to death in the temple court. The death of Zechariah
the son of Jehoiada is probably that alluded to in Luke 11.51;
Matt. 23.35; that he is in Matthew called 'son of Barachiah'
suggests that he has been confused with the prophet Zechariah
(Zech. 1.1), or possibly, as some have supposed, with a
'Zechariah son of Baruch' mentioned by Josephus as having
been murdered in the temple by the Zealots at a much later
date (cf. *Jewish War* IV, 5, 4). King and people stand together
and condemnation comes upon both. The king's failure is
underlined in that he has forgotten the KINDNESS of JEHOIADA
– the loyalty of the priest, for *hesed* here points to such a
closeness of relationship, as it is so often used for the relationship between God and man.

23-24. Judgment upon the people is at the hands of an invading Syrian army which attacks in the spring, AT THE END
OF THE YEAR – this being the season for campaigning. The

disaster falls upon THE PRINCES OF JUDAH, the evil counsellors, but also upon the whole GREAT ARMY of Judah, which, by reason of the people's disobedience, is delivered into the power of a tiny Syrian force. Thus the theme of God's deliverance by the few (so especially in the Gideon narrative of Judg. 7; cf. also I Sam. 14.6) is here reversed. This judgment is seen finally as the divine judgment on Joash, and a natural transition is made to the completion of this in a conspiracy against him (as the people had conspired against Zechariah, v.21).

25. Joash was murdered ON HIS BED by two men of alien birth, connected with Ammon and Moab; the implication of this point, not found in II Kings, would appear to be that when king (or people) turn to alien gods, their judgment will be at the hands of alien instruments of divine wrath (cf. Jer. 5.19 for a similarly balanced judgment).

27. The final verse of the account is strangely worded and not entirely clear. THE COMMENTARY (literally *midrash*, cf. on 13.22) ON THE BOOK OF THE KINGS is described as containing HIS SONS (should we perhaps read 'his deeds'?) and THE MANY ORACLES AGAINST HIM – perhaps to suggest a much larger body of illustrative prophetic material to be placed alongside the account of Zechariah's activity – and THE REBUILDING OF THE HOUSE OF GOD (literally 'founding' or better 're-establishment'). It has been suggested that the word rendered ORACLES should here be equated with that rendered 'tax' in the narrative of vv.4-14, and that this final comment thus lists the positive aspects of Joash's reign. Such a positive comment is made at the very end of the Asa narrative (16.14); it would not be altogether surprising here. But if ORACLES is correct, then we may note that this so-called COMMENTARY, the *midrash*, contained a considerable amount of prophetic material, and observe that the other mention of such a *midrash* in 13.22 is connected with the prophet Iddo. We have some evidence for expansions of narratives with prophetic material, as witness the Isaiah sections in II Kings 18-20 and even more plainly the alternative account of the fall of Jerusalem and its aftermath in Jer. 37-44 (which contrasts sharply with the account

in II Kings 24-25, where Jeremiah is not mentioned). There is
perhaps here an indication of the existence of expanded forms
of the Kings narratives, or of related writings, in which more
prophetic material was integrated into the narratives. It is at
the very least a reminder that we do not possess the whole
range of Israel's theological literature.

AMAZIAH – FAITHFUL AND FAITHLESS

25.1-28

One might almost suppose the Chronicler at this point to be
engaged in preaching a series of sermons on one topic. The
contrast between the earlier and later periods of Joash (ch.24),
in which it is shown how a good king, wisely guided, can so
easily fall under evil influence and become apostate, is matched
in this chapter by a comparable, though variant, presentation
of Amaziah as alternating between right action in faith and
obedience, and wrong action in lack of trust in God. The
same type of theme is taken further in ch.26 in the contrasting
of faithfulness and pride, though this may also be found here
(see v.19). It is also at this point in the Chronicler's writings
most apparent that he is expounding for his readers – or
hearers – the already familiar narratives of II Kings and
giving them a twist of his own, with elaborations and comments designed to bring out their meaning as he believes it
ought to be appreciated. It must be very doubtful that he
possessed further documentary material, though it is certainly
quite probable that the text of II Kings was known to him
in a somewhat different form.

His narrative here follows the material of II Kings 14.1-20,
but whereas for the opening (vv.1-4) and conclusion (vv.25-28)
he has followed the earlier text closely, his main narrative in
vv.5-16 has a link only in one brief verse in II Kings (14.7),
and his use of the material of II Kings 14.8-14, though close,
shows a marked difference of emphasis.

1-4. The opening emphasizes Amaziah's rightness of policy,

though this is qualified by the anticipatory phrase: YET NOT
WITH A BLAMELESS HEART (v.2). His execution of his father's
murderers – instruments of divine judgment but yet to be
condemned – is qualified by the insistence that he obeyed the
law found in Deut. 24.16 (and cf. its development in Jer.
31.29f.; Ezek. 18.1, 19f.) that sons should not be punished
for their father's crime. This appears also in II Kings, though
it is possible that it is there an addition made on the basis of
the Chronicler's text.

5-16. The conquest of Edom, so briefly described in II Kings
14.7, is made into a full-scale narrative.

5-6. A military census shows the extent of Judaean power.
The implication may be that the possession of such power
ought to have reminded Amaziah of how richly God had
blessed his people, but the king lacked faith and HIRED mercenaries from the north FOR A HUNDRED TALENTS OF SILVER.

7-8. But reliance on such power will be disastrous. A prophetic
warning reminds Amaziah, and the reader, that THE LORD
IS NOT WITH ISRAEL (the theme of the speech in 13.4ff.); by
implication, too, there is the reminder that victory is of God,
and not dependent on few or many (cf. on 24.23f.). To rely
upon such allies will bring inevitable defeat. The text of v.8
is in some disorder; RSV relies on a reconstruction based on
the early versions, perhaps better to be set out (closer to the
Hebrew text as it stands) as: 'but if with them you are (trying
to) make strength for war....'

9. To the king who complains at the loss of the fees he has
paid to the mercenaries the prophet offers the assurance of a
much greater reward. The anger of the dismissed mercenaries,
who have been paid but who will get no spoil, is a skilful
literary device by which the Chronicler interweaves various
elements in his narrative; it points forward to the sequel in
v.13.

11-12. Amaziah, however, freed of this dangerous encum-
brance of the faithless from the north, wins a tremendous

victory and carries out an appalling massacre of Edomites. The atrocities of the twentieth century make Amaziah's action seem relatively insignificant, but to understand its place here we must note two points. First, the antagonism of Judah to Edom was a frequent theme of Old Testament thought, expressed sometimes in terms of the violence of actions committed by one side or the other (cf. Obadiah) and sometimes, more profoundly, in terms of the mystery of the divine election of Jacob and the passing over of Esau (cf. Gen. 25.29ff., 27; Mal. 1.2ff., and on this latter Rom. 9.13). Second, the Chronicler appears here to be using a tradition hinted at but not explained in II Kings 14.7, by which the name of Sela, the rock, is described as having been changed to Joktheel, which probably means 'God destroys'. The existence of the place-name thus understood may have attracted to itself a tradition of a great disaster brought upon Edom, and it is evident that the figure of ten thousand (twice over) is no more to be regarded as historical than are similar figures in other battle accounts of the Chronicler.

12. the rock This points to the place-name Sela, but the identifying of it with Petra, which also means 'rock', is hardly to be maintained in the light of recent archaeological work (cf. *Palestine Exploration Quarterly*, 1966, pp.123ff.).

13. This verse picks up the theme of the Israelite mercenaries, and strikes the reader as very strange. Amaziah has shown his faith in dismissing them; it is only subsequently that he is shown to have turned to other gods. Why then should Judah have to submit to such a humiliating disaster? The answer may possibly be found in accepting an alternative rendering of the Hebrew, one which is grammatically entirely plausible, demanding a change of subject in the middle of the verse. This is in fact a feature of Hebrew style which may often be recognized. The text will then read: '. . . they (the mercenaries) fell upon the cities of Judah . . . but they (the Judaeans) killed three thousand of them and took great plunder'.

14. Amaziah's victory over Edom, however, is described as

leading him to disaster. We may suppose that THE GODS OF
THE MEN OF SEIR were brought back as part of the spoils of
war, but they formed a snare to the king who proceeded to
offer them worship.

15. The absurdity of this is immediately brought home to him
by a prophet who points out that these supposed gods could
not even protect their own people. This recalls the ironic
comment of Jeremiah on his contemporaries for their apostasy;
they have committed 'a double evil':

> they have forsaken me,
> the fountain of living waters,
> and hewed out cisterns for themselves,

(an absurdity indeed, for who would prefer stale water stored
in cisterns to the fresh water of a living spring?)

> broken cisterns,
> that can hold no water (Jer. 2.13)

(and the absurdity is double, for there is not even any water
in the cisterns they have chosen to prefer!).

16. Amaziah is, however, stubborn in his lack of faith and,
like his father Joash, reacts violently to the prophet, threaten-
ing him with death. The king's refusal to listen is explained as
the result of the decree of God.

17-23. The narrative which follows, only loosely attached in
II Kings, is now integrated into the whole account. The over-
weening pride of Amaziah led him to issue a challenge to
Joash, the king of the north. The latter warned him with a
vivid parable, comparable with the kingship parable of Jotham
(Judg. 9.7-15), but Amaziah would not listen. He is doomed
because of his apostasy. The phrase INTO THE HAND OF THEIR
ENEMIES (v.20) is incomplete in the Hebrew, and may perhaps
be better filled out as 'into the hand of Joash' or 'into his
hand'. The resulting defeat for Judah leads to the breaking
down of the wall of Jerusalem, probably that which lay on
the northern side, the side most vulnerable to attack and

needing a good wall since it lacked the steep escarpments of
east and west which meet at the south of the city. Furthermore, this exposed Jerusalem to control from the north. The
temple and palace treasures were plundered; hostages were
taken to ensure submission by Judah.

24. Obed-edom The reference is a reminder that he was the
ancestor of a family connected with the shrine from the time
of David, and known as gatekeepers, here more clearly as
guardians of the treasury (cf. I Chron. 26.15); the RSV rendering is erroneous, and we should read: ... THE VESSELS
THAT WERE FOUND IN THE HOUSE OF GOD 'in the charge of
Obed-edom'.

25-28. We might have expected immediate and final disaster
upon Amaziah, but the Chronicler preserves the synchronism
of II Kings and mentions his fifteen further years of rule. He
goes on, however, to explain the CONSPIRACY which was formed
against him as resulting from his apostasy. Nevertheless he
was brought from his refuge at LACHISH, where he had been
killed, and BURIED WITH HIS FATHERS IN THE CITY OF DAVID.
The Hebrew text here has 'city of Judah', though some manu-
scripts follow the form 'city of David' found also in II Kings.
Either is a correct term, for Jerusalem is known as the city
of Judah in the Assyrian records.

UZZIAH – PROSPERITY AND PRIDE

26.1-23

The same sermon style continues, based on the relatively
meagre information supplied in II Kings 14.21f.; 15.1-7. New
material is of two kinds. In the first part of the account, the
Chronicler offers an explanation of the prosperity of Uzziah,
perhaps deliberately linked to the length of his reign (fifty-two
years); in the second part, the detail of his leprosy in II Kings
is elaborated into a full narrative, explaining this affliction as
due to the pride of the king. Thus the contrast is drawn
between obedience and prosperity on the one hand, and evil

conduct and disaster on the other. The initial archival material
(vv.1-4) is taken over from II Kings, omitting only the qualifying statement about the high places in his source.

1. Uzziah   The king's name appears here always in this form.
In the main text in II Kings it appears as Azariah, and so too
in the royal list of I Chron. 3.12; elsewhere in II Kings 15 it
appears as Uzziah, as also in the prophetic books. It may be
that the Chronicler preferred this alternative because it avoided
confusion with the high priest named Azariah in vv.17ff. In
contemporary Assyrian texts the mention of a ruler Azriau
of Iaudi, possibly but by no means certainly to be identified
with Azariah, may suggest that this was the throne name, and
Uzziah the 'private' name. But it is also possible that the two
are simple variants, the meaning of the verbal roots underlying them being closely similar ('to help', 'to be strong').

2. Eloth Or Elath.   Its rebuilding points to a further development from the Edomite campaigns of the preceding chapter.
(THE KING mentioned is probably better to be understood as
a king of Edom.) This important port on the Red Sea provided
access to the sea trade with Arabia, Africa and India, and its
control by Judah may be seen as one of the indications of
prosperity in this period. The first half of the eighth century,
during which Assyrian pressure was withdrawn and the kingdom of Aram was relatively weak, was for both the Israelite
kingdoms a time of internal prosperity. Under the long reigns
of Jeroboam II in the north and of Uzziah in the south, the
land enjoyed a time of security and economic growth, reflected
in the prophetic attacks of Amos and Hosea in the north, and
of Isaiah (esp. ch.5) in the south.

5. Zechariah   This man, otherwise unknown, is presented by
the Chronicler as a guide to Uzziah over an unspecified period
of his reign, encouraging his right conduct and his ardour
in seeking God. We may note that the man bears the same
name as the prophet son of Jehoiada (24.20ff.) who warned
Joash in vain. The name is in any case such a common one
that its reappearance need not surprise us. It is possible that

the Chronicler supposed him to be the Zechariah mentioned
as a witness in Isa. 8.2, quite erroneously, since the inference
here is that Uzziah's mentor had died before the end of his
reign. Perhaps the choice of name was simply based on its
meaning: 'Yahweh remembers', very appropriate to such an
adviser.

6-15. We have seen in v.2 that there is a sound historical basis
for the development of Judaean power reflected in the detailed statements which now follow, and some archaeological
support has been found at least in general terms for the civil
and military installations attributed to Uzziah. But the
Chronicler's purpose in recording this material, from whatever
source he derived at least parts of it, is geared to his understanding of the consequences of obedience. The extension of
Judaean control over outlying areas and the establishment of
a greater degree of military security; the paying of tribute and
the thriving of agriculture – these are the marks of divine
favour and of a royal strength which derives from the divine
help (v.15). The theme, seen in ch.11, of the security of the
true people of God, is here too being underlined. The text is
in two parts, marked off by similar refrain-like comments in
vv.8 (HE BECAME VERY STRONG) and 15 (HE WAS MARVELLOUSLY
HELPED, TILL HE WAS STRONG), the latter phrase perhaps being
somewhat mutilated.

6-8. The first part underlines the extension of Judaean control
and may be linked with v.2. Control of the Philistine area
consists in the breaking down of important fortifications of
the cities; JABNEH, later Jamnia, was eventually to be an
important Jewish centre after AD 70. The second half of v.6
looks suspiciously like a duplicate text, for the word translated
HE BUILT could be read as 'Jabneh', and the remainder of the
wording largely overlaps what precedes. Wider military successes against neighbouring groups are noted in v.7; GURBAAL
is unknown, and a better sense is obtained by reading 'in
Gerar and against' (RSV supplies 'and against', though this is
not actually in the text). The MEUNITES (cf. also ch.20) are a
southern group, and it is possible that this name should be

read for AMMONITES in v.8. Uzziah's extension of control appears to be westwards and southwards.

9-15. The second part is concerned almost entirely with military measures; fortifications in Jerusalem and outside (vv.9f.), a newly-organized army (vv.11-12), provided with equipment (v.13) – perhaps there is a change of policy here from the soldiers providing their own arms to government provision; and a detail about a special development in siege warfare at Jerusalem (v.15a). There is some uncertainty about the nature of this special machinery which is not given a name; it may be some kind of protective covers placed on the defences from which the defenders of Jerusalem could shoot and propel stones without being exposed to attack, or it may denote machinery for propelling weapons. The archaeological evidence points strongly against the development of the latter type of machinery at this period.

10. Incorporated in the military details is a brief allusion to agricultural matters. TOWERS and CISTERNS belong together here, for military protection must have adequate support in water supply. But it is linked with HERDS of cattle, and with the numbers of agricultural workers employed. In I Chron. 27.25-31, we have a list of officials concerned with the king's estates, and it is likely that the reference here is to such lands. They are to be found in THE SHEPHELAH, the lower hill-country to the west of Jerusalem; in THE PLAIN, a term which is employed for the area beyond the Jordan north of the river Arnon, a flat table-land, though it is possible that it has some other reference. A more general reference is made to HILLS and FERTILE LANDS (literally 'Carmel', which could refer to a region in the Hebron area in which that name appears.

16-21. The whole tone now changes. We are not told that the adviser Zechariah had died, though this is implied. The divine blessing which made the king strong is forgotten, and he becomes PROUD. Such false pride, as if success depended on merit, is firmly condemned in Deut. 9.4ff. and other passages; the Chronicler applies this teaching to a particular instance.

16. to burn incense This was prohibited to any but priests in the later legislation (cf. Exod. 30.1ff. with Num. 18.1ff.), as indeed were other ritual acts; it is clear, however, that at an earlier date the king was often closely involved in the ritual. II Kings gives no precise explanation of Uzziah's leprosy, though it may be seen as loosely linked with the immediately preceding reference to his failure to abolish the high places. The Chronicler sees in the burning of incense a deliberate offence (RSV WAS FALSE is less appropriate than 'acted improperly').

17. Azariah ... eighty priests ... men of valour The last phrase is perhaps better as 'courageous' (NEB) or as 'men of standing', as it is not really to be supposed that the king would have to be restrained by so large a force. These were ready to resist his wrong action.

18. Uzziah's offence is defined in terms of the law, and he is ordered out of the sanctuary.

it will bring you no honour The condemnation may perhaps be better understood to mean 'God will not reveal his glory to you'.

19. Like his predecessors Joash and Amaziah, Uzziah is shown as a king who resists rebuke, but the moment of resistance is the moment of judgment. The blow falls in a sudden outbreak of LEPROSY, not the disease known from its widespread occurrence in Africa and eastern lands, but a skin disease whose precise nature is uncertain; its sudden appearance and disappearance is noted also in the Mosaic traditions (e.g. Exod. 4.6f.) and in the story of Naaman (II Kings 15).

20. The priests 'turned towards him' – the same word is used as in the exactly similar action by Aaron when Miriam was afflicted in this way (Num. 12.10); it probably denoted the formal designation that the condition is recognized and that the presence of the afflicted person cannot be tolerated in the holy place. He had therefore to be driven out, and is shown also as himself recognizing that he has no right to be there.

21. The condition remains until HIS DEATH; he is separated (though it is possible that the text should be interpreted to mean that he had simply to remain in his own house, relieved of all duties) and EXCLUDED from the temple. The term used of the SEPARATE HOUSE, or this exclusion, appears connected with the realm of the dead in Ps. 88.5, and a similar expression is used in the Ras Shamra texts for that realm. It may perhaps be understood best as the place where men are by definition 'relieved of their duties'. During this period of Uzziah's reign, though we do not know how long it lasted, his son JOTHAM carried out the royal duties.

22-23. This summary contains the interesting note that the account of Uzziah's reign was composed by the prophet ISAIAH; this may be seen alongside the similar references elsewhere in the Chronicler (e.g. II Chron. 12.15) to prophetic authorship of such accounts and as perhaps linked with the references to Uzziah in Isa. 1.1 and 6.1. His burial, because he was a LEPER, was not in the royal graves but in a BURIAL FIELD WHICH BELONGED TO THE KINGS; this suggests that the note WITH HIS FATHERS has been added in error to the text. An Aramaic ossuary text of the Hasmonean period has been found with the words: 'Herein are laid the bones of Uzziah, king of Judah. Do not open.' Such ossuaries were used for bones collected from burial places, though whether the persons responsible for this inscription had reliable evidence as to whose bones they were moving remains doubtful in view of the way in which quite evidently inaccurate traditions grow up associated with tombs.

JOTHAM THE MIGHTY

27.1-9

At this point the Chronicler changes his sermon style. The contrast between belief and unbelief drawn in the preceding

chapters within the reigns of individual rulers is now presented
in this chapter and the next in terms of two different men.
Jotham the good is followed by Ahaz the bad. Such a pattern
was already to be found in the earlier narratives of II Kings
in the alternating of good and bad from Ahaz to Jehoiakim
(Ahaz–bad, Hezekiah–good, Mannasseh–bad, Josiah–good,
Jehoiakim–bad); but the Chronicler does not continue to follow this pattern in quite this way.

1-2. A very short, virtually entirely archival statement in II
Kings 15.33-35 has been expanded, though only slightly, into
the account we have here. Jotham is depicted as a good king,
as in II Kings; but the nature of his obedience is clarified and
its consequences drawn out. It may be that the Chronicler,
rightly or wrongly, identified his mother's father ZADOK with
the high priest of that name who appears in the list at I Chron.
6.12. Since the queen mother is more than once shown as
wielding great influence, it could well be supposed that with
such a mother Jotham must be well advised.

In obedience, Jotham is said to follow his father Uzziah's
pattern, but – and here there is a marked contrast – HE DID
NOT INVADE THE TEMPLE. RSV has translated very freely,
for the text actually has simply 'he did not enter'; but quite
clearly the intention is to point out that Jotham was strict in
his religious observance and did not infringe priestly preroga-
tives. The obedient king is further contrasted with a corrupt
people.

3-4. To the II Kings note of his building of THE UPPER GATE
of the temple – that would be the northern entrance – the
Chronicler adds a reference to fortifications on the OPHEL,
the southern hill, and to cities and fortifications in the HILLS,
a further example of a good king ensuring the protection of
the true kingdom.

5-9. The consequence of obedience is measured in military
success. We might have expected the general comment of v.6
to precede the example of the overthrow of THE AMMONITES in
v.5; this would be the more natural order, and perhaps the

text has been disarranged. Doubt has been expressed about an Ammonite campaign, since it would appear that Judah and Ammon had no common frontier at this time; a very simple rearrangement of the letters would give a reference to the Meunites (cf. 26.7), but we need not press historical verisimilitude so far. For three years the Ammonites made payments to Jotham. This does not necessarily mean that they were then able to reassert their independence, for the payment may equally be interpreted as a war-indemnity (cf. 36.3). A COR is a grain measure probably equivalent to a homer, an ass-load, about eleven bushels. The final summary (in which v.8 appears to be a duplicate either of v.1 or, more probably, a variant text of 28.1) adds to the II Kings summary a reference to other military successes and to HIS WAYS, his right style of life; it significantly omits any reference to the beginning of the Syro-Ephraimite war, seeing this as more appropriate to the deserved discomfiture of his son Ahaz (cf. 28.5-15).

The discovery of a signet ring at Elath with the inscription '(Belonging) to Jotham' has suggested that he might, during his father's life, have been in charge of trade there; but it is dangerous to identify names and persons, even though the date of the ring is probably about right.

C. From Reform to Disaster

II Chronicles 28-36

The differing narratives of the kings of Judah continue, and it is arbitrary to make a break in the series, particularly since we may appropriately see a neatly-drawn contrast between the presentation of Jotham in ch.27 and that of Ahaz in ch.28. The picture of the disastrous reign of Ahaz, in which the Chronicler builds on the earlier condemnatory account in II Kings 16, serves also, however, to introduce one of the two final high points in the narrative in II Chronicles, that of the reign of Hezekiah, the reformer. This in its turn is followed by the story of yet another bad king, Manasseh, whose reign leads on into that of the other great reformer,

Josiah. These pairs of reigns in chs.28-32 and 33-35 pave the
way for the final act of judgment in ch.36. Yet the patterning
is not identical. Ahaz is all bad. The account of the reform
of Hezekiah which follows shows a very substantial elaborat-
ing of the very brief account of reform in II Kings 18. But
this Hezekiah, good though he is and successful in the support
of divine blessing, has his moments of danger and failure, as
the group of brief narratives of ch.32 reveals. Manasseh looks
like being another Ahaz – and so he was and worse in the
II Kings account – but judgment brings repentance and reform, so that Manasseh fits more to the style of the kings
whose reigns show a sharp contrast between belief and unbelief. Josiah, the reformer, is again the example of the loyal
ruler, but even such a one can fail, and his disastrous end is
the result of a failure to perceive the divine will. At the end
the pace quickens, and a few verses only in ch.36 serve to
dismiss the last rulers and lead into the Chronicler's interpretation of the exilic age.

THE DISASTROUS REIGN OF AHAZ

28.1-27

The Chronicler's account of Ahaz provides a very illuminating example of his methods of rehandling earlier material.
No substantial change in emphasis has been made in the
delineation of Ahaz himself, though his evil ways have been
underlined and in some degree extended. What is remarkable
is the use of this context for an unusual depiction of the
apostate north, containing themes to be observed elsewhere
but here drawn out to a clearer degree (vv.8-15).

1-4. The opening verses correspond closely enough to the
opening of II Kings 16; the detail is somewhat amplified,
with a plural SONS in v.3 where the earlier text has the more
natural singular form. Where II Kings contains a reference to
what may perhaps be regarded as an exceptional rite undertaken in a particular emergency (cf. the action of the king

of Moab in II Kings 3.27), the Chronicler implies that Ahaz, and perhaps his people too, made a practice of engaging in this ritual. It is not in fact clear precisely what the ritual was; it is alluded to also in II Kings 23.10 and in Jer. 7.31; 19.5, and appears to be particularly associated with the Tophet (probably meaning 'burning place') in the Hinnom valley to the south-west of Jerusalem. This valley – Ge-hinnom (also called THE VALLEY OF THE SON (as here) or sons OF HINNOM) – was to provide one of the names for the place of torment after death, Gehenna. Its association with rites regarded as particularly loathsome made the extension of the name an appropriate one. It may also have been a place for burning refuse.

5-7. The II Kings narrative (like its counterpart in Isa. 7, where some part of the same material is presented with an indication of Isaiah's involvement in the events, entirely unmentioned in Kings and Chronicles) rightly depicts an alliance between Syria and Israel designed to force Ahaz into collaboration in their common resistance to the advance of Assyria. The Chronicler, perhaps with a view to underlining the judgment theme (he adds further elements of this nature in vv.17ff.), separates the two attackers. First (v.5a) Ahaz is defeated by SYRIA and captives are taken TO DAMASCUS; it is as if a foretaste of the major deportation of the exile is being presented. Then (vv.5b-7) the attack is delivered by PEKAH of Israel; a massive defeat is inflicted on Judah, and the point is emphasized that those slaughtered were ALL OF THEM MEN OF VALOUR. But such military ability is of no avail when men have FORSAKEN THE LORD, THE GOD OF THEIR FATHERS. The detail of individual deaths in v.7 stresses the degree of the threat to Ahaz. The office of ELKANAH, described as 'second' TO THE KING, is mentioned elsewhere only in Esther 10.3, and perhaps reflects a terminology later than that of the period of the monarchy.

8-11. The defeat of Ahaz is interpreted as an act of divine judgment on the apostasy of the kingdom. But it is now used to reveal the Chronicler's interpretation further. The northern army is described as returning with captives and SPOIL TO

SAMARIA. Yet even in that faithless place there is to be found a true prophet, ODED – not mentioned elsewhere, though the same name occurs for the father of a prophetic figure Azariah in 15.1. The suggestion is implicit that even in the apostate north there can be such faithful men, as indeed the mention of Elijah in 21.12 has indicated. Oded preaches a short sermon to the returning army, emphasizing that only divine wrath against Judah could have brought about their defeat. There is here a sharp contrast with the bold affirmations of Abijah in 13.4ff. But Israel, granted this moment of victory, has over-stepped the mark (v.9*b*). This point is found also in the judgment on the nations which went beyond the limits of divine anger in Zech. 1.12, 15ff., and in Isa. 10.15, where the Assyrians, instruments of judgment, are themselves to be brought under judgment in their pride. The north is reminded of its own SINS AGAINST THE LORD, and called upon to SEND BACK THE CAPTIVES.

12-13. The prophetic utterance is underlined by a comparable statement made by leading men, whose names are listed – and we may note that three out of the four have names clearly compounded with the divine name Yahweh, just as we may see that the sons of Sanballat, the governor of Samaria who opposed Nehemiah, have names of this kind (cf. p.272). Their words underline the GUILT of the north – a guilt already indicated clearly in ch.13; to bring captives from the true kingdom would add to this guilt. This second statement is presented as if it were a response to the prophetic word. RSV has included the word ALSO in v.12 by way of implying this. But in fact the two statements, that of the prophet and that of the leaders, could equally well be regarded as alternatives; perhaps we have here an indication of a combining of different elements in the present form of the text.

14-15. The result is as remarkable as the appeal. THE ARMED MEN relinquished their claims, and THE CAPTIVES were cared for and restored TO THEIR KINSFOLK AT JERICHO. This was done by officials designated for the purpose (this being the more probable meaning of v.15*a* rather than THE MEN WHO HAVE

BEEN MENTIONED BY NAME). It has often been observed that the
detail of v.15 – particularly the anointing (of the wounded, by
implication), the carrying ON ASSES, the journey to JERICHO –
finds its counterpart in the parable of the Good Samaritan in
Luke 10.25ff. One might go further and suggest that, just as
the Chronicler is here in effect offering an exposition of the
story of Ahaz in II Kings, so the parable offers an exposition
of this narrative.

The unexpectedness of the account in vv.8-15 naturally
raises questions about the source of the material. It must be
recognized that, quite apart from the immensity of the numbers claimed to be involved (vv.6, 8), the narrative has little
historical probability as it stands. What historical basis it
might have could only be supposed to lie in the circumstances
of the so-called Syro-Ephraimite crisis, for it is evident, particularly in II Kings 16 and rather less so in Isa. 7, that Ahaz
was under great pressure and indeed that Jerusalem was
actually besieged by the northern allies. The detail of the
names in v.7 might itself be one element which attaches to a
genuine historical tradition, for it is clear that the attack on
Judah had as one aim the removal of the king himself and his
replacement by a more amenable character (the Ben-Tabeel of
Isa. 7.6), and the death of two high officials, loyal supporters
of Ahaz, would be a suitable part of that action. One must
admit, however, that the Chronicler could well have included
this detail from some other context. Similarly, the advance
of an army into Judah would mean death and despoiling, and
captives too. Border warfare between Israel and Judah was
not infrequent during the co-existence of the two kingdoms,
and it has been suggested that Hosea (5.8-7.16) is commenting
on the maltreatment of Judaeans by Israelites in this period.
Stories of the atrocities of war and of the treatment of captives, both harsh and lenient, may have been handed down
from this and other times of hostility. The question of sources
and of historicity is, however, a much less important one than
the recognition of the theological significance of the narrative.
The Chronicler is prepared here to make use of a theological

motif, to be found for example in Jer. 3.6-11, in which Judah,
which ought to have been the faithful people, fails to learn
wisdom from the example of Israel's judgment, and so falls
to be even more greatly condemned than the apostate north.
What Amos says (3.2) of the requirements of God from his
chosen people, what Jesus says of the leniency appropriate
to Sodom and Gomorrah (Matt. 10.15), are further examples
of the same comparative judgment. Implicit too is the recognition, to be picked up in the next section, that there are
those in the north who have remained faithful and who can,
if they will, be restored to the true community.

16-18. It is in the context of disaster that Ahaz appeals to
Assyria, and the Chronicler underlines the danger even more
by references to Edomite and Philistine invasions. The first
may be seen as an elaboration of II Kings 16.6; the places
mentioned in v.18 all belong to the border country between
Judah and Philistia, though GIMZO, if correctly identified, lies
in Israelite territory.

19. The nature of the judgment is again underlined.

20-21. The Assyrian response is the reverse of that desired,
in spite of Ahaz' attempt at bribing the Assyrians. It may
be that here the Chronicler is making use of the Isaianic
material concerning this situation, itself already developed
with interpretative comment, for in Isa. 7 we find references
to the 'king of Assyria' (vv.17, 20), probably to be seen as
glosses to the text designed to bring home the idea that the
appeal to Assyria (cf. also v.27) could bring nothing but evil
to Judah. Ahaz is erroneously described as KING OF ISRAEL in
v.19, perhaps because of the use of 'Israel' to denote the true
people. In v.20 the words rendered AFFLICTED HIM could well
be rendered 'laid siege to him'. Since Tilgath-pil(n)eser (cf. on
I Chron. 5.26) did not besiege Jerusalem, we may see the
Chronicler transferring to Ahaz a theme known to him from
the following reign (cf. ch.32). This underlines the danger
brought upon Judah by Ahaz.

22-25. This passage, only very loosely linked to the com-

parable material in II Kings 16.10-18, shows Ahaz as behav-
ing even more evilly. He SACRIFICED TO THE GODS OF DAMASCUS
(v.23 – perhaps to be seen as a re-interpretation of the note
on a copying of an altar at Damascus in II Kings) WHICH HAD
DEFEATED HIM. The view that the defeat of Judah was by the
authorization of the gods of Damascus is being accepted by
Ahaz. Apostasy can only bring disaster, and Ahaz' destructive
action against the temple and his other idolatrous practices
are noted by way of indicating how great a disaster must come.
The final phrase of v.23: THEY WERE THE RUIN OF HIM, AND
OF ALL ISRAEL, may well point the reader forward to the
disaster of the exile, interpreted as the result of the whole
community's failure (cf. ch.36).

26-27. The final summary excludes Ahaz from burial with
the other kings of the line; his apostasy denies him that privilege.

HEZEKIAH THE REFORMER

29.1-31.21

The account of Hezekiah's reign covers four chapters; three
of these are devoted to his reforming activities, one to other
matters, partly of a political nature. The account thus contrasts
very sharply with that of II Kings, where one verse (18.4) is
devoted to reform, and nearly three chapters to the more
political aspects. It is clear that the Chronicler is offering a
new interpretation of Hezekiah as part of his total presentation. Having shown Ahaz as so evil a king (ch.28), he now
presents a contrasting picture of his son and successor. We
may see the Chronicler's description of Hezekiah as influenced
both by the Isaiah tradition – though Isaiah is alluded to only
briefly in 32.20, 32 – and perhaps also by the Micah tradition
of Jer. 26.17-19, which attributes Hezekiah's response to the
latter's preaching.

The three chapters devoted to the reform present three
different aspects of it: first, the restoration of the temple and

the reinauguration of worship (ch.29); second, the passover celebration (ch.30); third, other elements of the reform (ch.31). Incorporated in these sections are many points which illuminate both the Chronicler's own emphasis in interpretation and in all probability also the particular conditions and problems of his own time.

29.1-2. The opening summary is as in II Kings 18.1-3. The remainder of the chapter is devoted to the first stage of reform, viewed as a complete reversing of the evil policies of Ahaz, and a recovery of the situation as it was under David. Here, as in what follows, we may detect that the Chronicler is taking account of his own and his readers' awareness that it was in this period that the northern kingdom had come to an end. Judgment had fallen on the apostate north, and its position as a rival and as a temptation had gone. Within the Ahaz narrative, we have seen an indication of the existence there of some who were aware of their shortcomings and of the place of true allegiance (cf. on 28.8-15); this theme is to be picked up in the next stage of the reform in ch.30. But at this point, the removal of the north makes it possible for the king in Judah to be a true successor to David.

3. This provides the counterpart to 28.24; THE DOORS OF THE HOUSE OF THE LORD shut by the evil Ahaz are reopened AND REPAIRED. We may perhaps best regard this verse as a summarizing heading to what follows; it emphasizes the immediacy of Hezekiah's action to bring the temple back into proper use. Subsequently we are told that the purification actually began ON THE FIRST DAY OF THE FIRST MONTH (v.17). There has been debate as to whether the new king began to reign on that day – a possible but not very probable chance – or whether we should suppose that this is intended to denote the beginning of the first full year of his reign. Such chronological speculation appears somewhat out of place. The Chronicler's emphasis would appear to be rather upon the appropriateness of the king beginning his reform on the first day of the new year, and this would appear by implication to be regarded by the writer as being the very first day of his reign, whether it really was so or not.

4. The king summons an assembly of PRIESTS and LEVITES in an open place, THE SQUARE ON THE EAST of the temple – clearly outside the precincts, since the temple has not yet been made fit for use.

5-11. The king's address asks for the total purification of the shrine. The reason for the present situation is set out at length, not, as we might expect, in terms of the evil deeds of Ahaz, but as stemming from a general failure of the whole community over the years. There is a possible allusion to Ahaz' actions in v.7, but they have been completely generalized, and the comment on THE WRATH OF THE LORD as having brought disaster upon JUDAH AND JERUSALEM is in terms which are used particularly in Jeremiah (e.g. 19.8) for the disaster of the exile. Prophetic judgment themes underlie this sermonic address. The point is made even clearer in the emphasis on the people actually seeing WITH THEIR OWN EYES (v.8) the present condition of the land and city, explained in terms of slaughter in battle and captivity in v.9. The terms are so explicit as to make it clear that the Chronicler is here commenting on the exilic situation, anticipating the themes of subsequent chapters (cf. also below on ch.33). The appeal to the Levites in v.11 – here addressed by the king almost affectionately as MY SONS – is that they should not show complacency in their office. The words underlying DO NOT BE NEGLIGENT (rather freely paraphrased in NEB as 'let no time be lost') are used in the sense of 'do not be at ease'.

12-19. The response of the Levites, whose zeal is subsequently to be contrasted with the less satisfactory conduct of the priests (v.34), is now set out. Two named individuals from each of the levitical orders lead in the gathering of THEIR BRETHREN (v.15). The different stages of carrying out the sanctification and purification and the removal of unclean objects TO THE BROOK KIDRON (as also in 15.16, see note on p.139) are described, with a careful note that only the priests, whose special office fitted them for this duty, carried out the cleansing of the inner shrine (v.16). The complete operation was carried out in sixteen days (v.17). The full extent of the work was reported to the king. In the report, we may note the stress laid upon the proper recovery and ordering of the vessels of the temple (vv.18f.), a theme intimately connected with the restoration after the exile; the vessels represent the continuity of the worship of the temple with the past, for it was at the building of the temple by Solomon that proper provision was made for them (on this theme, which appears a number of times in the Chronicler's work, cf. P. R. Ackroyd, 'The Temple Vessels – A Continuity Theme', in P. A. H. de Boer [ed.], *Studies in the Religion of Ancient Israel, Vetus Testamentum Supplement* 23, 1972, pp.166-81).

20-24. In the first stage of religious celebration the emphasis – as in similar but not identical rituals described in Lev. 4 (and also in the Day of Atonement rituals of Lev. 16) – rests upon the removal of sin. It is to be for THE KINGDOM (better 'for the royal house') AND FOR THE SANCTUARY AND FOR JUDAH (v.21). In that same verse the words 'for the whole (or burnt) offering' should be added after the word LAMBS; we may observe in the subsequent description a distinction drawn between the first groups of sacrifices and the offering of the goats. The laying of hands on these last (v.23) suggests a comparison with the transfer to the scapegoat in Lev. 16 of the sins of the community, but in that ritual that goat is driven away and only the second goat is sacrified.

24. all Israel The final words underline that the concern is with the whole true people of God.

25-30. A further stage in the rehabilitation of worship is now reached. Hezekiah is here seen as a new David, re-establishing the music of the shrine. Emphasis rests upon what David had commanded, and upon David's musical INSTRUMENTS. This is further described as being in accordance with the prophetic words of GAD and NATHAN (v.25), and of ASAPH THE SEER (v.30). The Chronicler thus underlines continuity with that worship which he has already described so fully in the Davidic sections, and which is to be echoed again in subsequent narratives (cf. 34.12; 35.12; Ezra 3.10ff.; Neh. 12.42). The detail of the celebration probably points to elements of ritual familiar to the Chronicler from his own situation.

31-36. Finally the whole community is united in further acts of worship, the expression of the joy of the people at the re-establishment of the temple. Again we may suspect echoes of the later restoration after the exile in these verses, and not least in the reference here to the fact that there were TOO FEW PRIESTS – a problem in part reflected in the complex priestly lists to be found in I Chron. 24. The approval of THE LEVITES as compared with THE PRIESTS in v.34 perhaps suggests a situation contemporary with the Chronicler; his awareness of the special position of the priesthood (cf. v.16) is matched by his apparent recognition that in his own day all is not well. This will be seen in his account of the period of Ezra. The rejoicing at WHAT GOD HAS DONE (v.36) evidently refers to the complete restoration of the temple and its worship, and the reason for the rejoicing appears to be the speed with which, under God's hand, this had been accomplished. Although SUDDENLY is often an appropriate rendering for the word used here, it is more properly understood here as 'speedily'.

30.1-31.1. (This makes a better division.) Now comes the celebration of a great united PASSOVER. The king's intention, here again linked to the overthrow of the northern kingdom (cf. v.6), is to re-establish the unity of the people of God, and, as the end of the section shows (v.26), to demonstrate that here he is a new SOLOMON, the ruler before the kingdom was broken.

1. letters So the appeal is made to the north, as also by the sending of COURIERS (vv.6, 10).

2-4. This parenthetic passage explains that THE PASSOVER, instead of being held in the first month of the year, is delayed until THE SECOND. This is stated as due to two causes: the dilatory behaviour of the priests, and the lack of time for the people to assemble in Jerusalem (v.3). The postponement to the second month appears to be an application to the whole community of a special provision laid down in Num. 9.6ff., by which an individual could defer celebration. (The case there envisages defilement from contact with a dead body, or being on a distant journey, as sufficient causes.)

5. all Israel from Beersheba to Dan   The descriptive phrase for the whole land is used by the Chronicler (so also I Chron. 21.2) in the reverse of the more normal order, presumably because he naturally thinks from south to north. The explanation here added is that the passover had not been kept IN GREAT NUMBERS, i.e. as a total united assembly at the temple. The passover ritual as described in Exod. 12 is a family festival, held in the house; in the account here and in that of Josiah's reform (cf. also Deut. 16.5ff.) it appears as a great central celebration. Elements of these divergent approaches are held together in later practice, where we find a family festival held in Jerusalem (cf. the descriptions in the New Testament).

6-9. The appeal to the northern tribes is to the remnant surviving the disaster from Assyria to return to their true allegiance. They are invited to be different from their stubborn forefathers (cf. ch.13), and to respond. (The sermon style here is similar to that in Zech. 1.1-6.) The assurance is given that their response will be not for themselves alone but also for their exiled compatriots, for thus they will FIND COMPASSION WITH THEIR CAPTORS, AND RETURN (v.9). Here the Chronicler picks up a theme from the prayer of Solomon, found in I Kings 8 but not in his own version in ch.6 (cf. I Kings 8.50). The point is being underlined that 'return to God means return to Jerusalem'. The passage makes considerable play on the word variously meaning 'turn, return restore', much used in these various senses in Jeremiah. The whole approach here is expressive of the concern of the Chronicler and his contemporaries for the gathering from the dispersion of all true members of the community.

10-12. The couriers These meet with mockery, but there is some response in humility from the north. The tribal names which appear in vv.10f. and differently in v.18 and 31.1 are evidently rather loosely used, suggesting that tribal boundaries and areas were no longer clear in the Chronicler's time. Significant also for that period is the lack of reference to the area east of the Jordan. The response of JUDAH (v.12) is described as one of total loyalty.

13-22. This is a description of the great assembly for the feast, here named UNLEAVENED BREAD. Two originally separate celebrations – passover and unleavened bread – had come to be so combined that they could not now be distinguished. (For an earlier stage, cf. Deut. 16.1ff., where the two are partially combined.)

14. This verse is perhaps intrusive, belonging either with the purifications of the preceding chapter or more probably with those mentioned as the culmination of the celebration in 31.1.

15. It would appear that the zeal and unity of the people put THE PRIESTS and LEVITES TO SHAME, though there is some uncertainty about the text here and the reference to 'shame' may be intrusive.

16-17. What we find in the succeeding verses is that the priests and Levites equally are carrying out their full duties, THE LEVITES in particular being mentioned as acting for those who had not carried out the full purificatory rituals.

18-20. These explanatory verses make an important statement. The presence of many who were not ritually clean – for what reason is not precisely explained, perhaps for lack of time – meant that they were eating the passover in an unfit condition. But this problem was met by the intercession of Hezekiah – a function which reminds us of Solomon – in which he asked that genuineness of approach to God should enable them to receive pardon from God. The prayer was heard and God HEALED THE PEOPLE, that is, he did not bring upon them the disaster which was held to be inevitable in a case where men approached the deity in an unfit state. The Chronicler is here voicing a principle of fundamental importance. He is not in any sense underestimating the importance of proper ritual – for with this he is much concerned; he is indicating that God himself has the power to override the normal requirements of ritual, and that the genuineness and wholeheartedness of man's response is acceptable to God.

21. A typical description of the celebration emphasizes rejoicing and singing.

22. the Levites These are commended for their part. The latter half of the verse is probably better rendered, with a very slight emendation to the text: 'So the people completed the festival, namely seven days ...'

23. This leads on into another theme suggestive of Hezekiah's resemblance to Solomon. Just as there had been a double period of seven days in the dedication of the temple (7.8f.), so too the assembly now resolves on another such double period.

24a, 25. The theme of rejoicing is reiterated (v.24*b* is perhaps out of place, being in reality an earlier part of the narrative). The assembly includes JUDAH, AND THE PRIESTS AND LEVITES and those from the north, and in addition what are described as SOJOURNERS from Judah and Israel. This term (Hebrew *gēr*) is used in earlier narratives to denote members of other communities who have settled in Israel, accepting protection and involvement in its life, as distinct from visiting foreigners such as traders (cf. Exod. 12.43-49, though RSV confuses the issue by using the word 'sojourner' in v.45 for a quite different word, and by rendering *gēr* as 'stranger' in vv.48f.). Here it seems to be suggesting the presence of those who will later be called proselytes, who are accepting membership of the community.

26. The final emphasis is on the JOY of the occasion, such as had not been known SINCE THE TIME OF SOLOMON. (The RSV text is not quite clear, and could be misunderstood to mean that there had been no passover celebration since that time.)

27. The priestly blessing (pronounced by the 'levitical priests' so the Hebrew – not by PRIESTS and LEVITES) is spoken and heard, and the last words echo the refrain of the prayer of Solomon in ch.6.

31.1. An immediate result of the celebration is an action by ALL ISRAEL against alien religious objects throughout Judah and the north, after which the whole assembly returns home.

When we think of this description in relation to the time of the Chronicler, we may not improperly see here some allusion to the contemporary situation. It has often been thought that there is a particular reference to the division between the Jerusalem and Samaritan communities, and, though the chronology of that division is very unclear, it is not impossible that such a reference is to be found. But perhaps we should see also a wider concern for unity. Later Jewish experience – as witness the last centuries BC and the first century AD – shows many groupings, with divisions sometimes very sharp indeed. The critical attitude of the Qumran community towards Jerusalem is indicative of the kind of division which existed. It seems not improbable that earlier periods too had such groups, perhaps less closely defined. And we may best understand some aspects of the Chronicler's thought, his insistence on Jerusalem and its worship, his conconcern for a true religious succession, his appeals for unity, if he is looking not at one divisive situation alone but at the whole life of what he believes ought to be a single people of God.

2-19. Further details are added to the picture of Hezekiah, emphasizing even more clearly that he is to be seen both as a second David and as a second Solomon.

2. A considerable place is given to the reordering of the PRIESTS and LEVITES (cf. also vv.12-19), which echoes the activities of David, particularly in I Chron. 23-26. The degree

of idealization in this reordering is also expressed in the somewhat unexpected use of the term CAMP OF THE LORD; this has
also been used in I Chron. 9.18f., and provides a reminiscence
of that conception of the ordering of the whole people of
God which is set out in Num. 2, where, in the context of
the wilderness wanderings, the community is organized for
marching in battle order, with the tribes ranged in their
proper place on each side of the tent, regarded as the fore-
runner of the temple. Similar concepts underlie the idealized
geography of Ezek. 47-48.

3. The royal contributions for sacrifices are underlined, an
echo of 8.12f., which attributes similar functioning to Solomon.
The full details of such provisions are set out in Num. 28-29,
and we may also note the part played in Ezekiel's ideal
organization by the prince who there replaces the king (cf.
Ezek. 45.17).

4-10. These verses are concerned with the provision of tithes
for the support of priests and Levites, a concern also set out
in Neh. 13. It would appear likely that in this and other points
the Chronicler is commenting upon his own period and perhaps enjoining on his contemporaries a better response. The
stress here lies upon the willing and generous response of
the whole community, which thus provides an example for
later generations. The tithes are gathered from the THIRD to
the SEVENTH MONTH (v.7), from the beginning of harvest to the
time of the feast of tabernacles. When the king inspects and
discovers the immense supplies brought in, the high priest
Azariah points out to him that obedience to the law has
brought immediate prosperity, the result of divine blessing
(v.10).

11-19. This leads into the ordering of proper storage and
supervision, with the levitical officials listed. Particular stress
is laid upon the KEEPER OF THE EAST GATE, who is put in
overall charge. Some of the detail of vv.16ff. is not entirely
clear; the opening of v.16 appears to exclude THOSE ENROLLED
BY GENEALOGY, but perhaps means 'irrespective of registration'.

Reference to three-year-olds in the same verse is unexpected, and some commentators suggest a simple emendation to 'thirty', but it appears in v.18 that the children were also involved in this distribution of provisions. Verse 17 appears to suggest that LEVITES entered upon full office at the age of TWENTY. In Num. 4.3 the age is thirty; in Num. 8.24 twenty-five. We may have here a reflection of differing custom at different periods, perhaps occasioned by a shortage of officials of proper family. (Cf. also on I Chron. 23.3.)

20-21. The whole section is drawn together by a concluding comment which echoes 29.2 and which may be seen to pick up the favourable comment on Hezekiah in II Kings 18.5-7a, following the single verse relating his reforming activities. The prosperity of the obedient king points to a preparedness in king and people for the dangers which are to be indicated in the following chapter.

HEZEKIAH – THE REWARD OF FAITHFULNESS

32.1-33

The complex questions of the relationship between the narrative presented by the Chronicler here and that to be found in II Kings 18-19 (Isa. 36-37) are carefully discussed by B. S. Childs, *Isaiah and the Assyrian Crisis*, SCM Press, London 1967, pp.104-11. He designates this as an example of *midrash*, that none too easily defined type of exposition which involves both the endeavour to resolve the difficulties presented by an already existing text and the application to it of the particular viewpoint of the expositor (cf. also on 13.22; 24.27). Both features can be found clearly in that part of the narrative here which deals with Sennacherib, which alone is the subject of Childs' study. The same principles must, however, also be applied to the other elements to be found here, namely the handling of two themes in II Kings 20 (Isa. 38-39) – the illness and recovery of the king and the visit of ambassadors from Merodach-baladan of Babylon. It must be observed that this chapter in the Chronicler would be very difficult to understand satisfactorily if we did not possess the Kings text. Such difficulty confronts the biblical scholar whenever, for example in the Pentateuch or in the Deuteronomic History, he is endeavouring to understand the nature of the existing text without having available to him the actual forms of the sources utilized by the compilers.

Here we are fortunate in being able to make the comparison. Furthermore, we may most naturally suppose that the Chronicler's readers were also aware of the earlier form of the material, and that his exposition was designed to help them in their reading and understanding. The chapter therefore provides an excellent example of one aspect of the Chronicler's technique.

1. The tone is set by the opening phrases which link the events of SENNACHERIB's invasion of Judah with the reform. Such a link was already being undertaken in II Kings 18.7f., but here it is made explicit that the removal of the Assyrian threat is to be seen as the direct result of the FAITHFULNESS of Hezekiah; his reform, his obedience to the divine law, described so fully in the preceding chapters, make the events now to be set out into an illuminating example of the reward of true loyalty. That such a reform should be followed by so dire a threat would appear at first sight to be surprising; but its meaning is drawn out by this particular presentation.

Sennacherib's invasion is well-attested in both the biblical and Assyrian records, though there are many problems of historical interpretation. Here we may note that for the Chronicler the attack remains in some measure at least still only at the level of a projected overthrow of the cities of Judah. No mention is made of their actual capture, so well attested elsewhere.

2-5. The second stage of the threat is to Jerusalem itself. Here the Chronicler skilfully combines the archival information (which he repeats in the summary in v.30) concerning the water supply (cf. also II Kings 20.20) with a characteristic element of his presentation of good kings, namely that they

provide protection by military works at Jerusalem (and elsewhere), thus ensuring the safety of the people of God (for
this theme, cf. e.g. Uzziah in 26.9). In addition, we may observe
that he emphasizes by the allusion to THE MILLO in v.5 (cf.
I Chron. 11.8) the parallel between Hezekiah and David which
has already been suggested in the preceding chapters. In
handling the theme of the water supply, however, the emphasis
is shifted. Whereas it is presented in the archival note in v.30
quite properly as directed towards the ensuring of water for
a besieged city – and as such this and other undertakings find
a sharp word of criticism for wrong priorities in the prophetic
comment of Isa. 22.8-11 – here it is designed to prevent the
invading Assyrians from enjoying the benefits of the waters
which are to be found in Judah and which are quite properly
regarded as the divine gift (for this emphasis cf. e.g. Deut.
6.11; 11.11). It is possible too that in making this point the
Chronicler is alluding to the theme of the taunt-song against
the king of Assyria (II Kings 19.21ff.), in which the claim is
made by the Assyrian that 'I dug wells and drank foreign
waters, and I dried up with sole of my foot all the streams
of Egypt' (v.24). What the Assyrian so arrogantly claims for
himself is here frustrated by the wise counsel of the faithful
king.

The text of vv.3-4 presents some difficulties, and attempts
have understandably been made to conform it more closely
to that of II Kings and to the evidence of archaeology. The
water conduit which brings the waters of the spring Gihon
to the pool of Siloam is well-known, and it appears most
probable that originally the building of the tunnel was
designed to supply an underground and therefore well-pro-
tected pool of which the upper part has long since been
broken away (cf. K. Kenyon, *Royal Cities of the Old Testament*, Barrie and Jenkins, London 1971, pp.137ff.). The reference to SPRINGS in the plural has been thought to include
reference to other sources of water in the vicinity, or to be
due to characteristic exaggeration on the part of the
Chronicler. Furthermore, the phrase THE BROOK THAT FLOWED
THROUGH THE LAND was already corrected by the Greek trans-

lators to 'through the city'; some modern commentators have preferred to render the text 'through the earth'. But this attempt at harmonization does not do justice to the Chronicler's purpose. He has changed the emphasis, and the wider reference to the sealing up of all the water supplies is simply an extension of this change. The Assyrian's boast is totally ineffective.

The building of new fortifications and the repair of old ones are of course normal procedures in times of military urgency, but here they equally characterize the proper conduct of the good king. No indication is given of the reason for the city wall being BROKEN DOWN, but it may naturally be linked to the evil policies of Ahaz. A second wall would most probably be built to the north, since on that side the city lacked the protection of steep valleys. Improvement of weaponry and reorganization of military command (vv.5-6) are other aspects of this same characteristic concern.

6-8. The assembly of the military leaders provides a neat counterpart to that of the religious leaders in 29.4; the meeting is similarly held in an open SQUARE AT THE GATE OF THE CITY (a possible alternative here would appropriately be 'at the gate of the spring', i.e. the water gate, cf. Isaiah's meeting with Ahaz, Isa. 7.3). Here the king addresses them with an exhortation to faith and the people respond. Like other such sermon passages in the Chronicler, this is a skilful construction full of allusions. Its opening is identical with the exhortations of Moses (Deut. 31.6) and Joshua (Josh. 10.25). The phrase FOR THERE IS ONE GREATER WITH US THAN WITH HIM combines an allusion to the Immanuel passage of Isa. 7.14 (Immanuel=God is with us) with one to the story of Elisha in II Kings 6.16: 'Fear not, for those who are with us are more than those who are with them.' The contrast between the enemy's reliance on human power (AN ARM OF FLESH) and Judah's reliance upon God corresponds closely with Jer. 17.5, and may also allude to the contrast between flesh and spirit in Isa. 31.3. That God fights his people's battles is a frequent theme in the Old Testament (e.g. Exod. 14.14). In such a passage we may see the Chronicler's preaching skill, and no doubt in this he reflects the expository method of his time, so strongly to be recovered in the great biblical preachers of Christian tradition.

9-23. These verses provide the Chronicler's exposition of the threats and overthrow of the Assyrians. The word 'exposition' is used deliberately rather than 'account', since the Chronicler here offers a selection and an interweaving and interpretation of the earlier material. The account in II Kings 18.17-19.37 contains two parallel versions of the incident. The Chronicler has dovetailed elements from these with considerable skill.

9-15. These verses are rather repetitive in style, and pick up various elements from II Kings 18. The messengers of Senna-cherib are depicted as coming to Jerusalem, carrying a message. The themes used are: Hezekiah's deceptive conduct (vv.10f.); the interpretation of Hezekiah's reform as an insult to Judah's God (v.12); the example of history in which no god has been able to deliver his own nation, from which it follows that Judah's God can do no better (vv.13-14, and repeated with a combination with the deception theme in v.15).

16-17. This first stage is followed by an allusion to the second narrative in II Kings 19, in which the ambassadors of Senna-cherib are replaced by a letter. The Chronicler explains this as a second stage in the one propaganda campaign, and reiterates the theme of the supposed inability of Judah's God to deliver his people.

against the LORD God and against his servant The latter is a term particularly associated with royalty and hence able to carry messianic overtones. The clause is markedly reminis-cent of Ps. 2.2, which speaks of the kings and rulers taking counsel 'against the LORD and his anointed'.

18. the language of Judah This is the term for the particular local form of what we normally describe as Hebrew (cf. Neh. 13.24). The Chronicler picks up this theme from II Kings

18.26, 28; it is used, not as in the earlier narrative to persuade the ordinary people to disregard the advice of their rulers, but TO FRIGHTEN AND TERRIFY THEM, to lower their morale, so that the Assyrians MIGHT TAKE THE CITY.

19. To this whole passage the Chronicler then adds his own comment, itself an exposition of the theme in II Kings 19.18 which speaks of the impotence of the gods of the other nations which are merely THE WORK OF MEN'S HANDS (cf. vv.13ff.).

20-21. The outcome is expressed succinctly. There is no mention here of anxiety in Judah, nor of the king's lack of faith. THE KING himself AND ISAIAH THE PROPHET offer prayer; so two separate moments of the earlier narrative are combined. Without delay an angelic being brings total destruction on the Assyrian camp, here still thought of as being at Lachish, whereas in the earlier account the disaster is quite evidently thought to have taken place outside Jerusalem (II Kings 19.35). The withdrawal of the Assyrian king is depicted more vividly with its portrait of his shamefaced state, and his death is briefly noted. (Uncertainty about the death of Sennacherib is evident in the variety of Assyrian and Babylonian records, which may be seen conveniently set out in DOTT, pp.70-73).

22-23. The Chronicler then concludes the narrative with his own interpretative comments on the whole episode. Verse 22 not only recapitulates the deliverance from SENNACHERIB, but points to a total condition of peace. The Hebrew text is defective: it has only FROM THE HAND OF SENNACHERIB ... AND FROM THE HAND OF ALL. Some MSS add 'his enemies' (followed by RSV), but this would appear to be an interpretative addition, dictated by the last clause of the verse. A more probable, though conjectural text, would give 'from the hand of all his army'. Then the final clause, which actually reads 'and he led them on every side', but which is better very slightly emended to the RSV form HE GAVE THEM REST, universalizes the deliverance theme. This is then developed (v.23) in the exaltation of Hezekiah over many nations which send tribute to him (cf. the similar theme for Jehoshaphat in 20.29f.).

In the final section of the chapter, the Chronicler ultilizes various other Hezekiah themes.

24. The illness of the king is here very briefly summarized (cf. II Kings 20.1-11; Isa. 38). The SIGN mentioned is quite evidently that of the movement of the sun's shadow described in the longer account. RSV AND HE ANSWERED HIM is a loose translation of a text which has 'and he said', the words spoken being lost – perhaps as NEB reconstructs: 'I will heal you'.

25-26. But the Chronicler offers an exposition of his own, which appears to be linked not to the illness narrative but to the one immediately following, that of the ambassadors from Babylon (II Kings 20.12-19; Isa. 39), though this is not precisely alluded to and is in fact to be used quite differently in v.31. In the Chronicler's interpretation, the result of the saving of the king from death was to produce not gratitude but pride. This results in divine WRATH against king and people, averted only by an act of penitence by both. As a result, the full judgment is deferred till a later day. This deferment of judgment is the theme of the last verses of the Kings narrative.

27-29. These verses elaborate the success and prosperity of Hezekiah (cf. for this the Uzziah passage in 26.10). For SHIELDS in v.27 it may be better to read 'precious objects', and for CITIES in v.29 a very small emendation would give either 'donkeys' or 'herds', though the word may be due to accidental recopying of part of the preceding phrase which is in any case out of order in the Hebrew (NEB omits 'cities'). To this is added the archival note about the water supply already dealt with.

30-31. The last clause of v.30 and v.31 again stress Hezekiah's loyalty and success. The theme of the ambassadors from Babylon (II Kings 20.12-19), from which the negative element has been used already in v.26, now appears as a moment of divine testing of Hezekiah's faith, in which the king shows himself to be truly loyal and therefore in no danger of disaster – again a remarkable restructuring of the earlier material. The visit of these PRINCES OF BABYLON is in fact explained as due to their astrological interest in the SIGN. The Chronicler is evidently using his knowledge of the reputation of Babylon for astronomy and astrology to link together the various elements in a manner quite different from that to be found in II Kings 20.

32. The final summary refers to the king's GOOD DEEDS – his pious acts (cf. also 35.26; Neh. 13.14). We have another reference to a prophetic writing (cf. e.g. 13.22), here not unexpectedly linked with the name of ISAIAH.

33. The somewhat obscure reference to the burial place of Hezekiah seems to suggest, as the following clause indicates, that this good king was accorded special burial honours. The last clause introduces the name of MANASSEH, whose very different reign follows.

MANASSEH – THE RENEGADE WHO REPENTED

33.1-20

1-9. Manasseh The first part of the account follows very closely indeed the parallel text in II Kings 21.1-9. The differences are only in quite small details: for example, the Chronicler makes no comparative reference to the evil ways of Ahab of Israel; he omits the name of the queen mother in v.1 as in a number of other cases. The evils of Manasseh are accentuated by plural forms in vv.3 (BAALS, ASHERAHS) and 6 (SONS).

10-13. Now, however, a totally new presentation is given. A general word of warning, where II Kings has a hortatory passage built upon words of prophetic judgment, finds no response in king and PEOPLE. So divine judgment falls, and Manasseh is taken captive TO BABYLON. The reference to

HOOKS and FETTERS may be illustrated by the portrayal of captive kings with rings in their mouths to which ropes are attached and held by Esarhaddon of Assyria (ANEP, no. 447). The expressions are strongly reminiscent of the words of judgment upon a king of Judah (Jehoiachin) in Ezek. 19.9, and it may be that we should see here the influence of that prophetic passage. The sequel is in the repentance and humility of Manasseh whose prayer is heard and who is then restored to his royal position. The significant comment is added: THEN MANASSEH KNEW THAT THE LORD WAS GOD (v.13), a formula strongly reminiscent of Ezekiel (e.g. 6.7), though also found elsewhere.

14-17. Such a recognition of the true God is appropriately followed by the carrying out of reform. Like good predecessors, Manasseh engages in protective measures for the city, and military measures for the safety of the people of God. The OUTER WALL here described would presumably represent a strengthening of the wall of the city which, as recent excavations have shown, was low down on the Kidron side of mount Ophel. All the improper objects which Manasseh had put in the temple were removed, and proper worship was re-established. The high places continued, but at least worship there is described as restricted to the true God of Judah. This reform, totally unparalleled in the Kings account, makes Manasseh after his repentance into something like another Hezekiah or Josiah, though not quite as highly praised. A remarkable reversal has been achieved by the Chronicler.

18-20. The concluding summary refers to prophetic words (cf. II Kings 21.10ff.), and to HIS PRAYER, which was later to be identified and appears in the Apocrypha as the Prayer of Manasseh, though actually it is a psalm which could be applied to almost any situation. Its reference to 'many an iron fetter' (v.10) and its emphasis upon the many sins of the speaker and upon his repentance, presumably made it seem appropriate for this particular identification of authorship. The evil deeds of Manasseh are said to have been recorded in another writing, connected with THE SEERS (perhaps 'his seers'; the Hebrew

word in fact means 'my seers'). He was properly buried as
befitted a king whose repentance put him among the good
ones, a veritable example of the graciousness of God towards
the repentant sinner.

There has been much discussion about the Chronicler's
narrative of Manasseh. The Assyrian records of Esarhaddon
and Ashurbanipal mention him as among the vassals, at one
point contributing to materials for building at Nineveh, at
another sharing in an Assyrian campaign against Egypt (cf.
ANET, pp.291, 294). It is not impossible that he went to
Nineveh to submit to his Assyrian overlord; perhaps more
likely that his submission would be accepted in some more
westerly place (Ahaz went to Damascus for a comparable
purpose, II Kings 16.10; Zedekiah to Riblah, II Kings 25.6).
It is pure supposition to suggest that he rebelled against
Assyria and was taken captive, for no such suggestion appears
in the Assyrian records, and our knowledge of the Chronicler's
methods forbids the mere acceptance of his statement as historical without support. Nor does there appear to be any
reason for his being found at Babylon. Here we may see in
part the influence of the passage in Ezek. 19.9 to which reference has been made, for there it is said: 'With hooks they
put him in a cage, and brought him to the king of Babylon.'
Babylon is there appropriate to the exilic period. The
Chronicler, perhaps building on this passage, has depicted
the fortunes of Manasseh as a type of the exile of all Judah.
In effect he is pointing out to his readers that just as such a
wicked king was taken captive, repented and was restored,
so the same was to happen to Judah; and in this he may
have seen a further message for his contemporaries of the
total restoration of the scattered people of God. That the
Chronicler was also influenced in his construction of this
narrative by the fact that Manasseh's reign was a very long
one is quite possible; for him, as for other Old Testament
writers, long life was one of the clearest blessings for the
righteous man. But he is not merely applying a rigid retribu-
tive theory and making history fit; he is concerned rather
with expounding the meaning of his people's experience.

AMON THE WICKED

33.21-25

21-25. Amon In his brief account the Chronicler modifies the text of II Kings 21.19-23 so as to depict this king as having, in his short reign, undone everything that the repentant Manasseh had achieved. Like his father in evil, he was unlike him in not repenting. Whereas the earlier account saw in the evil actions of Manasseh the final cause of total disaster, after which no going back was possible (cf. II Kings 21.10-15; 23.26f.), the Chronicler saw the mounting towards the climax as taking place in repeated failures, even in some instances failures of kings otherwise regarded as good. The conspiracy which brought Amon's reign to an end was evidently a matter of court intrigue. Action against the conspirators is ascribed to THE PEOPLE OF THE LAND, a phrase often thought to have a precise technical significance, but more probably denoting simply the ordinary members of the population. The precise significance of the events is not clear.

JOSIAH – THE REFORMER WHO FAILED AT THE
END

34.1-35.27

The reform carried out by JOSIAH, linked to the finding of the law-book in the temple, is very clearly one of the most important of the matters described in the narratives of II Kings. Its relationship to the whole purpose of the Deuteronomic history is evident. The Chronicler, utilizing the earlier material, creates a new structure in which the chronology and interpretation of the period are different. There has been much discussion about the relative value of the historical presentations in the two works. The Chronicler's known tendency to reconstruct and re-order may be held to suggest very strongly that his ordering is due rather to his own viewpoint.

But equally we may recognize that the particular form of the
presentation in II Kings owes not a little to the compilers'
purposes. As so often in the discussion of such variant forms
of the same material, commentators tend either to accept
one or to adopt some kind of harmonizing process. Neither
method is sound. We need to recognize just as clearly that
II Kings, like the whole of the longer work to which it
belongs, represents a particular kind of theological presentation, exalting here the place of the law-book as the basis for
life, an emphasis which is designed to point to the need for
the community, in the exilic age, to re-order its life in
accordance with that same law – quite plainly regarded as
none other than Deuteronomy. And we must see that the
Chronicler has his own reasons, bound up with his particular
kind of interpretation, for re-ordering the material. The reconstruction of an underlying historical sequence can only
be undertaken if the present theological structures are taken
with full seriousness.

34.1-2. The opening is almost identical with the corresponding summary in II Kings 22.1-2. The existing emphasis on
Josiah's adherence to THE WAYS OF DAVID HIS FATHER – a
reminder of the interpretation of this king, as already Hezekiah, as particularly marking the revival of the Davidic ideal
– is picked up immediately by the Chronicler in a new construction.

3-7. These verses are not to be found in this position in II
Kings. In fact, some part of the material underlying them
appears there in 23.4-20, and has been utilized by the Chronicler to indicate the carrying through of a reform before there
is any mention of the finding of the law book. It is evident
that for the Chronicler the law-book of Josiah's time is of
less significance; his outlook may be influenced by the fact
that for him the true climax of the whole history is to be
found not here but in the reading and acceptance of the law
under Ezra (Neh. 8). He provides the basis for reform in
the rightness of Josiah's own attitudes. Josiah is a true descendant of David. Already in THE EIGHTH YEAR OF HIS REIGN

– at the age of sixteen – WHILE HE WAS YET A BOY, HE BEGAN
TO SEEK THE GOD OF DAVID HIS FATHER (v.3). He is shown,
even while still a minor – the word used (na'ar) denotes one
who is inexperienced (cf. Jer. 1.6 and significantly I Kings
3.7 of Solomon, though not in II Chron. 1.8-10; but cf.
I Chron. 22.5) – committing himself to that obedience which
will lead to right action. In his TWELFTH YEAR – at the age of
twenty – he reaches maturity (cf. the age for Levites in 31.17).
Perhaps the Chronicler intends us to see him taking up the
full kingship and acting now in his own right as he knows a
true Davidic king must act. Now the purifying of the land
and city begins. The alien religious objects are destroyed and
defiled (vv.3-5). Reform and purification in the south is followed by action in the north; the whole land is restored
(vv.6-7). We shall see a comparable rearrangement in the
account of Ezra's reforms; the reading and acceptance of
the law and the consequent covenant (Neh. 8-10) are so set
out as to follow the purification of the people by the expul-
sion of foreign wives with their alien influence (Ezra 9-10),
though it is evident that this is not the natural chronological
sequence. The Chronicler is more concerned with theological
than with chronological order. It is a purified land in which
the law will be found and a new order of worship be established.

8-18. The account of the finding of the law follows fairly
closely the corresponding account in II Kings 22.23. The
details of the repairs are reduced – perhaps the account
known to the Chronicler differed, since it seems probable
that the narrative of II Kings 22 has been influenced by that
of II Kings 12. But the number of officials sent to the temple
(v.8) is enlarged, and we find a characteristic emphasis on
THE LEVITES and their functioning in the gathering of the
people's contributions. These contributions are underlined,
for they come, as is natural after the reform, from the north
too – FROM ALL THE REMNANT OF ISRAEL – as well as from
the south (v.9). When attention is devoted to the repair work
(vv.10-13), there is more interest in THE LEVITES who are

listed and in their functions as MUSICIANS, as SCRIBES, OFFI-
CIALS and GATEKEEPERS. It is in this connection that the LAW
is found, linked to the bringing out of the contributions (v.14),
and we may observe that the strongly formalized account in
II Kings, very strongly suggestive of a liturgical procedure,
has become much more prosaic.

18. Shaphan read it This expression differs from that used
in II Kings. Many commentators think the two expressions
should be distinguished. So in II Kings the meaning would be
that the scribe 'read the book', i.e. read it right through,
whereas in the Chronicler the meaning would be 'read in
(from) the book', i.e. read selections from it. Then it is
argued that since the book mentioned in II Kings could
apparently be read right through twice in one day, it must
be relatively short, and could therefore be Deuteronomy (or
an earlier form of Deuteronomy); the fact that in Chronicles
only selections were read suggests that the Chronicler thought
that it was the whole Pentateuch, the Law of Judaism (also
thought to be intended in the Ezra story). This kind of argument is unconvincing on two grounds. In the first place it is
very doubtful if the detail of a narrative which is stylized
should be understood in this very literal manner. In the
second place the usage of the verb 'to read' (*qārā'*) in Hebrew
with a direct accusative or with a preposition does not seem
to admit of the distinction here imposed upon it. (We may
observe that in Jer. 36 Baruch reads 'in' the book of prophecies dictated by Jeremiah, but the natural sense is that
he actually read them through.)

19-28. The consultation of HULDAH THE PROPHETESS follows
almost exactly the II Kings text; in v.21 the Chronicler has
introduced a reference to the 'remnant of Israel', as also in v.9.

29-32. So too the gathering of the community for a covenant
ceremonial shows only a few changes, most notably the substitution in v.30 of LEVITES for the 'prophets' of II Kings
23.2; this expresses the Chronicler's conviction that the proclamation of the prophetic word, especially in homiletic form,

is a prime function of the Levites. The reference to IN BEN-
JAMIN in v.32 is probably due to textual corruption; the text
should read: ... HE MADE ALL WHO WERE PRESENT IN JERU-
SALEM STAND (i.e. adhere) 'to the covenant'.

33. This is a strange verse, picking up again the theme of
vv.6-7. But in fact it takes the point further. The purification
of the north there described is followed by the share in the
temple repairs of the remnant of Israel. Now Josiah is depicted as purifying (literally) 'all the lands belonging to
Israelites', and bringing into the true worship of God ALL
WHO WERE IN ISRAEL. Is there perhaps here a reflection of a
situation known to us from the second century BC – and perhaps not in fact entirely new then – in which the Jewish
community centred on Jerusalem and Judah, recognizing the
existence of religious associates in other parts of the Palestinian area, brings them within its orbit? In the Ezra narrative
we are to find the law imposed on all adherents of the true
faith in the whole province of Beyond the River (cf. comments on Ezra 7.25f.). Under Hasmonean rulers there was
forcible inclusion in the Jewish community of other inhabitants of the land. Here we have perhaps a recognition of a
problem already acute in the Chronicler's own time. What is
to be the relationship between the tiny district of Judah,
administratively separate and religiously unified, and those
who adhere to the faith but who live elsewhere in the Palestinian area? It was to be a problem which exercised later
politicians, not least the Roman generals and administrators
of the last century BC and the first century AD; they were to
find it particularly intractable.

35.1-19. This passage recounts the keeping of the PASSOVER
and represents a substantially expanded form of II Kings
23.21-23. The additions are largely concerned with matters
such as the ordering of the religious officials and the regulat-
ing of the details of the ritual. It is notable that the celebration is not directly linked to the law-book, but rather more
generally to the Mosaic command (vv.6, 12), and emphasis
rests more on Davidic and Solomonic prescriptions for the

ordering of the officials (vv.4, 15). We may note also THE
LEVITES as teachers (v.3), for whom the duty of carrying THE
ARK is now described as no longer necessary. They will be
concerned more with worship, and indeed in the descriptions
of the ritual (vv.11ff.) the Levites perform important duties.
Verses 7-9, in which king and princes are responsible for
sacrificial victims, may be compared with the similar material
for Hezekiah in 30.24. The passover ritual as described in
vv.10-17, somewhat repetitively, appears to be much more
elaborate than elsewhere, including other types of sacrifice
beyond the passover lambs. The element of haste (cf. Exod.
12.11) is transferred to the Levites distributing to the lay
people (v.13).

The uniqueness of the celebration is stated in v.18 with a
reference to THE DAYS OF SAMUEL THE PROPHET; throughout
the monarchy no such PASSOVER ... HAD BEEN KEPT. (II Kings
has 'since the days of the judges'). The account is resumed
in a final note in v.19, to which the Greek text adds the
eulogy of Josiah and the judgment words from II Kings
23.24-27, not very appropriately in view of the Chronicler's
transformation of Manasseh.

20. II Kings summarizes the reign of Josiah at this point
and adds a note on the circumstances of his death almost
as an afterthought. The Chronicler has integrated the theme,
and offers a characteristic explanation. Josiah met his death
because of his failure to hear the word of God, mediated to
him by the Egyptian pharaoh NECO. The brief phrase: AFTER
ALL THIS passes over twelve years to the year 609 BC. Neco
of Egypt, as we know from other sources, was in fact moving
to bolster up the last remnants of Assyrian power as a defence
against the westward pressure of the new Babylonian rulers
who were to bring final disaster to Judah. The Chronicler,
however, appears to have identified the Egyptian campaign
with that of 605 when Nebuchadnezzar as crown prince defeated Egypt at CARCHEMISH; possibly the Chronicler was
influenced by the reference to the place in Jer. 46.2.

21. Cease opposing God, who is with me, lest he destroy you.

Neco is here depicted as sending a strong warning to Josiah
not to interfere with him since he is acting at God's command.
Such a divine word, though coming through a strange mediator, ought to have been enough for a king like Josiah. But
Josiah was blind to it.

22-24. The translation of v.22 is uncertain. The verb rendered DISGUISED HIMSELF may perhaps be understood in the
sense of 'be determined, obstinate'; the idea of disguise recalls
the story of Jehoshaphat and Ahab (II Chron. 18), and the
same story may have influenced other details of the narrative
in which Josiah is wounded by archers and then, badly
wounded, is placed in a chariot to be taken to Jerusalem (cf.
18.33). In II Kings, Josiah is killed by Neco, though the
circumstances are obscure; here he dies after reaching Jerusalem and thus is buried with proper honour. The prophetess
Huldah (34.28) had foretold that he would be buried 'in
peace', not seeing the total disaster which was to come.

25. The mourning for Josiah is elaborated with a reference
to A LAMENT by the prophet JEREMIAH, and lamentation was
to be carried out regularly TO THIS DAY – a phrase which
should be taken rather to mean 'in perpetuity' than necessarily to indicate the actual existence in the author's time of
a regular celebration. It is possible that the Chronicler was
here influenced by Zech. 12.9-14, which appears to allude to
Josiah's death at Megiddo; that the latter part of the book
of Zechariah (quite separate from Zech. 1-8) was sometimes
associated with Jeremiah we know from the attribution to
him of a quotation from this section in Matt. 27.9. The passage contrasts with Jeremiah's injunction not to weep for
Josiah in Jer. 22.10.

The reference to a book of LAMENTS naturally suggests
the book of Lamentations, in some but not all traditions
associated with Jeremiah; but such an identification is not
necessary.

26-27. The final summary stresses, as in the case of Hezekiah,
his 'pious acts'.

(It is to be noted that I Esdras in the Apocrypha begins here and I Esd. 1.1-33 corresponds very closely to II Chron. 35. We shall note some variants in this alternative form of part of the Chronicler's work, though a full discussion would be out of place here.)

THE FINAL ACT OF JUDGMENT

36.1-23

The last years of the kingdom of Judah move rapidly in the narrative of II Kings 23.31-25.30; but they are given an even quicker pace in the Chronicler's interpretation. Not only does he leave out of account a considerable amount of the material in II Kings; he in fact contrives to include quite substantial interpretative comment of his own. For this is the final moment for the kingdom; the true people of God living under a Davidic king now comes to an end, and the emergence of that true people again after the disaster will be on a different basis.

1-4. Jehoahaz He is appointed king by the ordinary people after Josiah's death; the passage corresponds to II Kings 23.30*b*-34. Since none of the kings after Josiah appears to be allowed any claim to right rule, it is not surprising that any mention of 'anointing' has been omitted. Nor is there here any judgment, perhaps because of the extreme brevity of the reign, perhaps because the Chronicler has been influenced by the favourable words of Jer. 22.10-12. Jehoahaz, according to the Chronicler, was not 'bound at Riblah' as in II Kings, but simply DEPOSED, though the statement that this took place IN JERUSALEM may result from an omission in the text of the words 'from ruling'.

5-8. Jehoiakim These verses correspond to part only of II Kings 23.36-24.6. He is an evil king, though the Chronicler, no doubt because of his presentation of the predecessors, does not speak of the evil done by his fathers in v.5. An invasion by NEBUCHADNEZZAR (v.6*a*) is here made the occasion for Jehoiakim being taken TO BABYLON. Though the text can be held to mean that it was only Nebuchadnezzar's intention to take him away, it is more natural to understand it as a reference to actual deportation. There is no parallel to this in II Kings, and indeed the tradition there which simply mentions his death – and not his burial – is perhaps supported also by the judgment words of Jer. 22.18f. and 36.30, which refer to his not being buried, a clear mark of dishonour. In addition v.7 relates that temple VESSELS were taken and placed in the royal PALACE IN BABYLON; the word rendered PALACE may, however, mean 'temple', and this would correspond to Ezra 1.7: 'house of his gods'. The king's reign is summarized in v.8. The question of the historicity of the Babylonian action in regard to king and temple vessels has been much discussed. Dan. 1.1f. has a captivity and removal of vessels in Jehoiakim's third year; here no year is given and the inference is that it happened at the end of his reign. The Chronicler appears to be offering his own picture of an appropriate judgment on Jehoiakim; the Daniel text, much later, offers a midrashic harmonizing of the various elements in the different accounts.

9-10. Jehoiachin This is a very brief account indeed (cf. II Kings 24.8-17). Probably erroneously, he is said to have been EIGHT YEARS OLD at his accession; II Kings has 'eighteen' and the indications that the king was married and had children by 595 point to this. (For the Weidner tablets which shed light on Jehoiachin in Babylon, cf. DOTT, pp.84-86; ANET, p.308.) It is possible that the length of reign (THREE MONTHS AND TEN DAYS, turned in some later versions into 'one hundred days' – II Kings has 'three months') has resulted from a misplacing of the numerical ten from the king's age. There is curiously no mention of the Babylonian advance against Jerusalem, but only of the deportation of the king and of more temple VESSELS, though the mention of THE SPRING OF THE YEAR suggests an allusion to a campaign assumed to be known to the readers. II Kings here has a much fuller statement of the taking of the city – attested in the Babylonian records as happening in March 597 (DOTT, pp.80f.; ANET, pp.563f.) – and of substantial deportations. For the Chronicler it is the final disaster which is determinative.

11-21. Zedekiah Though it picks up a few odd phrases from II Kings, this section is largely a construction by the Chronicler.

11. The opening statement (with v.10b) describes him as BROTHER of his predecessor, where II Kings more correctly indicates him as 'uncle'. I Chronicles 3.15f. may provide either the source of the confusion – a second Zedekiah appears there – or may itself be the result of the statement here (perhaps due to the omission of the word for 'father' in the phrase 'father's brother', equivalent to the word 'uncle').

12. The failure of Zedekiah is stated first in general terms and then as an unwillingness to HUMBLE HIMSELF at the divine word spoken by Jeremiah. The Chronicler here appears to be dependent on the very full traditions of Jer. 37ff., in which an account of the last years of the city is given in a form in which the prophet is shown playing an active part. Jeremiah's appeal to Zedekiah to submit to Babylon appears several times in the book in different forms (cf. e.g. 38.14ff.).

13. That this is the point in mind is indicated by the immediately following reference to Zedekiah's rebellion, interpreted as the infringement of an oath. Here the Chronicler appears to be making use of another prophetic oracle, this time one from Ezekiel (17.18f.).

14. The king's failure is matched by the total apostasy of the people; the 'princes of Judah' (so, by a necessary correction of the text), THE PRIESTS AND THE PEOPLE, all follow the ways of the nations, and they defile the temple.

15-16. This total failure is underlined in a comment which stresses the mercy of God in sending the long line of PROPHETS to warn; but the prophets were mocked, and in the end divine judgment was inevitable.

there was no remedy Perhaps 'none to heal' or 'no appeasing of wrath'.

The comments from vv.14-16 owe not a little to the main lines of prophetic teaching, and particularly to the kind of statements to be found repeatedly in the opening chapters of both Jeremiah and Ezekiel.

17. The judgment falls in terms of Babylonian invasion. It is God himself who uses Babylon as his instrument (cf. e.g. Jer. 27.6; Ezek. 21.19ff.); and we may in fact translate the verbs all with God as subject: 'he' SLEW THEIR YOUNG MEN ... 'he' HAD NO COMPASSION ... HE GAVE THEM ALL INTO HIS (Nebuchadnezzar's) HAND.

18-19. The order of the judgment is significant. First the temple VESSELS – a theme already twice used – are removed, GREAT AND SMALL, i.e. every single one; then THE TREASURES. Temple and city are destroyed. The survivors of warfare (literally 'the remnant of the sword') are taken into exile. The Chronicler sees in the taking of the temple vessels the primary moment of judgment; for without these there will be no worship of God. But he is using this theme to point forward, for restoration will be established by the bringing back of these same vessels (Ezra 1.7ff.).

20. Everything and everyone surviving is taken to Babylon. This is not as in II Kings, where the poorest of the land are left and where a governor, Gedaliah, was appointed, to whom Jeremiah joined himself and in whom he evidently saw a real token of hope. For the Chronicler, nothing was to be left in Judah at all, and here he may well be developing the theme set out in II Kings 20.12-19, where the future judgment is expressed in terms of an oracle of Isaiah in just such a fashion. The servitude in Babylon is also indicated there, though with reference to the descendants of Hezekiah. But the word of judgment issues at once in a word of hope. Servitude is to be until the advent of Persian rule.

21. It is to be linked to the fulfilment of another aspect of the prophecy of JEREMIAH, who is seen as proclaiming both judgment and promise. The period will be of SEVENTY YEARS (cf. Jer. 25.11; 29.10; cf. also the echo in Zech. 1.12; 7.5), a period of recovery for the land. In fact the Chronicler here combines two passages, the reference in Jeremiah to SEVENTY YEARS and one in a long sermonic passage in Lev. 26 (v.34) to the keeping of sabbath. As the disobedience of the people has brought disaster upon the land, expressed in terms of its not enjoying the sabbath rest, the seventh year period of recovery laid down in the law (cf. e.g. Lev. 25.1ff.), so now for seventy years sabbath will be kept. Much later the writer of Daniel was to expound this passage in such a way as to understand the period as indicating not seventy years but seventy sabbaths of years, i.e. 490 years (Dan. 9); for him the exile was not truly to end until the time of deliverance at the end of the age, which he associated with the momentous events of the second century BC.

22-23. The final verses are repeated in Ezra 1.1-3, though they are not in the continuous text of I Esdras. They emphasize the moment of restoration, and serve to round off the books of Chronicles with a hopeful word. They also serve to direct the reader's attention to the sequel. In the Hebrew Bible, the books of Chronicles stand last, and it was appropriate that the scriptures themselves should end not in gloom but in hope. At the same time, these words could provide a cross-reference to the books of Ezra and Nehemiah, which stand before Chronicles in the Hebrew.

THE BOOKS OF EZRA AND
NEHEMIAH

The continuation of the Chronicler's work is in a very complex state. It consists of what are described in the English Bible as two separate books, named somewhat misleadingly after the two most prominent characters. The Hebrew Bible treated the two as one book – there are no notes at the end of Ezra such as are normally found at the end of separate books in the Hebrew text. The Greek version has a much more complex situation. Esdras A is the I Esdras of the Apocrypha; Esdras B contains our books of Ezra and Nehemiah. This latter was then sub-divided to correspond with the two books, and sometimes called Esdras B and Esdras C. In the Apocrypha there is another book named after Ezra; there it is called II Esdras, but elsewhere, to fit in with the numbering already indicated, it is known as IV Ezra (Esdras). For our purpose, the last of these is not relevant; it reflects later developments of the Ezra theme in a largely apocalyptic writing. We are concerned with the two books which appear in the Old Testament, Ezra and Nehemiah, and also, in view of its divergent presentation of the same material, with I Esdras in the Apocrypha, to which some reference will be made.

The naming of the two books is misleading, as already noted. Ezra in fact does not appear until ch.7 of the book named after him, and chs.7-10 are devoted to his activity. Nehemiah appears in chs.1-7 of the book named after him; but then Ezra reappears in ch.8 and, though here a problem exists, Nehemiah disappears until ch.11. Chapters 11-13 are again concerned with Nehemiah. It is most convenient for the reader if we follow the biblical order of chapters, but divide the material as follows: Ezra 1-6, the first period of restoration; Ezra 7-10, Ezra, Part I; Nehemiah 1-7, Nehemiah, Part I; Nehemiah 8-10, Ezra, Part II; Nehemiah 11-13, Nehemiah, Part II. Even for this division, some assumptions have to be made, in particular regarding the assigning of Neh. 10 to the Ezra material. But again the detail can wait for the closer discussion.

THE BOOK OF EZRA

THE FIRST PERIOD OF RESTORATION

Ezra 1-6

RESTORATION

1.1-11

We have already noted that the first three verses of this chapter appear at the end of II Chron. as 36.22-23, providing a hopeful ending to the book as it now stands. We may now see these verses in the fuller context of restoration to which they belong.

1. Just as the final judgment is depicted in terms of the fulfilment of the prophecy of Jeremiah (II Chron. 36.15f., 21), so too restoration is linked to the words of the same prophet. In the first instance we may quite properly see this as a picking up of the prophecy of 'seventy years' used to describe the sabbath period which is the Chronicler's view of the exile. We do not need to look for a precise period for this; it is conceivable that the Chronicler included in the period the time of Jehoiakim's exile (II Chron. 36.6), as well as the main period after the fall of Jerusalem in 587 BC. THE FIRST YEAR OF CYRUS – that is, his first year as ruler of what had been the Babylonian empire – was 538 BC. The fact that

Ezekiel speaks of a forty-year period (4.6) makes it clear that
significant numbers rather than exact chronology are in question. We may also observe that not only has there been the
much later reinterpretation of this period offered by Dan. 9
(cf. p.210), but that in Zech. 1.12; 7.5 a more precise application appears to be made to the period of the destruction
of the temple which lasted from 587 BC to 515 BC (cf. Ezra
6.15 – sixth year of Darius).

But to this particular Jeremiah prophecy a second consideration may be added. The fulfilment of prophecy is here
linked to the statement that THE LORD STIRRED UP THE SPIRIT
OF CYRUS KING OF PERSIA. Such a stirring of men to action
by God is mentioned also in I Chron. 5.26 of Pul, king of
Assyria – for judgment upon Israel; and in II Chron. 21.16
of the Philistines and Arabs – for judgment upon Judah. In
Jer. 51.1 it is used of the destroyer who is to bring Babylon
to disaster, and this is clarified by what may be a later explanatory comment in 51.11 as indicating 'the kings of the
Medes'. Furthermore, we may note that the same word for
'stirring up' is used a number of times in the Second Isaiah
(Isa. 40-55), and most relevantly in 41.25 with reference to
Cyrus: 'I stirred up one from the north, and he has come,
from the rising of the sun, and he shall call on my name.'
Cyrus is not named here, but in related material in 44.28-45.7
he is named and actually described as God's anointed, chosen
for just this purpose. We have already noted that the Chronicler attributes to Jeremiah a saying which in fact represents
a conflation of Jeremianic words with a phrase from Lev.
26 (cf. on II Chron. 36.21). It seems very probable that he is
here utilizing a wider range of prophetic material, some of
which – in Jer. 51 – was to become part of the Jeremiah
tradition (though quite probably not originally belonging to
that prophet), other parts of which were eventually to form
the collection known as the Second Isaiah and quite properly
to be associated with the prophet Isaiah because of certain
linkages of thought. A similar theme, representing a similar
interpretative tendency, is to be found in Hag. 1.14, where
the leaders of Judah, moved by prophetic words, are 'stirred

up' to undertake the rebuilding of the temple. There the words form part of the narrative framework of the prophecies, and quite probably represent the interpretative activity of an editor not far removed in time and outlook from the Chronicler.

a proclamation The reference to this and also to a written edict reminds us that an important parallel to what is said of Cyrus here may be found in a document known as the 'Cyrus Cylinder' (cf. ANET, pp.315f.; DOTT, pp.92-4). This is quite evidently a piece of propaganda directed to the people of Babylonia, claiming that Cyrus' conquest of Babylon was the result of divine action undertaken by the supreme Babylonian deity Marduk. 'He called Cyrus, king of Anshan. He nominated him to be ruler over all ... Marduk the great lord, compassionate to his people, looked with gladness on (his) good deeds and his upright intentions. He gave orders that he go against his city Babylon' (DOTT, p.92). We can suppose the existence of other propaganda statements directed to other communities. More relevant still is the further claim in the Cylinder, with reference to a wider range of places where there were holy cities, 'whose sanctuaries had been in ruins over a long period, the gods whose abode is in the midst of them, I returned to their places, and housed them in lasting abodes. I gathered together all their inhabitants and restored (to them) their dwellings.'

2-4. It is just this kind of claim which is attributed to Cyrus here, in a statement which reappears in a different form in 6.3-5. The wording owes something to the Chronicler's own view. But its essential point is in line with Persian policy, a policy directed towards conciliation and peace, and towards the evoking of loyalty from subject peoples. A further aspect of that policy appears in the Cylinder in its last clauses: 'May all the gods whom I have placed within their sanctuaries address a daily prayer in my favour before Bel and Nabu, that my days be long, and may they say to Marduk my lord, "May Cyrus the king who reveres thee, and Cambyses his son...."' (the text breaks off). Such an extension is to be

found in 6.10, though worded in such a way as to suit the
theological outlook of the Chronicler.

In the form in which the edict is given here, the God of
Judah is described as THE GOD OF HEAVEN, the supreme deity.
It is he and he alone – and here we may compare the passages
noted in the Second Isaiah – who is regarded as giving to Cyrus
ALL THE KINGDOMS OF THE EARTH and who HAS CHARGED ME TO
BUILD HIM A HOUSE AT JERUSALEM. Permission to return is an
element not found in ch.6; what is envisaged there, as in the
Cylinder, is the restoration of temples by the local community, whose life is to be fully re-established. For the
Chronicler the extension was a proper one, for he saw in the
exile the place where the hope of the future lay, and indeed,
from his point of view (cf. II Chron. 36.20), nothing was left
in Judah during the exilic period. A return of exiles was
therefore an inevitable part of the re-establishment of life.
Furthermore, he saw that this return was comparable to the
Exodus from Egypt, and in this he shows a viewpoint linked
with that of the Second Isaiah and other prophets of the
exilic age. There was to be a 'Second Exodus', and for him
it is expressed in the injunction that the exiles as they return
are to be richly supported by those around them. This matches
the theme of the 'despoiling of the Egyptians' in Exod. 11.2;
12.35f. We may note the concept of the members of the
exiled community as being a 'remnant' (RSV refers to EACH
SURVIVOR, which renders the same Hebrew root).

5. A divinely ordered edict is immediately obeyed by a community responsive to the divine spirit stirring it to REBUILD.
As we might expect, those who go include PRIESTS and
LEVITES, without whom a re-establishing of worship would
not be possible; the expression JUDAH AND BENJAMIN recalls
the Chronicler's view that the true people is regarded as
consisting of the two loyal tribes (cf. II Chron. 11.3).

6. The support is forthcoming; a better rendering here
would be: AIDED THEM WITH 'everything, with' SILVER, WITH
GOLD ... WITH COSTLY WARES 'in abundance, as well as' ALL
THAT WAS FREELY OFFERED.

7. Even more important is the firm link with the past which is established by the restoration of the temple VESSELS; these mark continuity with the destroyed temple, and continuity therefore with the ordering of that temple by David and its building by Solomon (cf. pp.91f. on I Chron. 28.18f.). We may observe that the restoring of vessels forms a counterpart here to the claim of the Cyrus Cylinder that the gods of other communities have been returned to their places. No such statement could be made for the God of Judah, for not only was he not represented by any large image, he was also seen as the one real deity beside whom all others were without power or indeed any reality at all (cf. II Chron. 32.19).

8-11. The formal committal of the vessels to MITHREDATH (a Persian name) the TREASURER, and his precise enumeration of them to SHESHBAZZAR (a Babylonian name), THE PRINCE OF JUDAH, guarantees that not one is missing. And this would seem to be the purpose of the listing of the vessels which follows, not without its problems of interpretation and of enumeration. It is not just *some* of the vessels which are returned; there is an emphasis here on the completeness of restoration without which the true continuity of worship might be in doubt. It seems quite likely that the Chronicler here made use of an actually existing inventory of vessels available to him, though this does not mean that it necessarily originally applied to this situation. In fact there is clear evidence in II Kings for the destruction of the temple vessels, and the historicity of their preservation and restoration must be considerably in doubt. RSV has accepted some variant readings, partly to ease the enumeration problems; the footnotes to the text indicate some of the uncertainties. The word translated CENSERS (v.9) is very uncertain of meaning; it has been thought to mean 'duplicates' or 'of various kinds'. Similarly the word rendered in RSVmg as 'of a second sort' may mean 'of various kinds'. It has even been suggested that both words were originally marginal notes meaning 'to be corrected', designed to point out that the numbers did not add up. This suggestion, though ingenious, is weakened by the fact that two different words are used. The detail is, however, much less important than the main point being made about total restoration. (On this theme, cf. also p.182.)

Sheshbazzar He appears here and is mentioned again in
ƺ 5.14-16. The latter passage equally presents him as receiving the vessels and instructions, and claims that he actually laid the foundations of the temple. Strangely, however, in the actual narrative (continued in ch.3) he disappears and his place is taken by Zerubbabel and Jeshua the high priest. The Chronicler's account is quite evidently confused, and perhaps results from his utilizing more than one source and endeavouring to conflate different evidence. It seems most likely that we should see the activity of Sheshbazzar as marking the first stage, in the early years of Cyrus, and suppose that Zerubbabel was active some years later. We have no knowledge of who Sheshbazzar was. Like other Jews of the period, e.g. Zerubbabel, he had a Babylonian name; he is described as THE PRINCE OF JUDAH but is not given any ancestry. This suggests that the proposal that he be identified with Shenazzar, of the royal house (cf. I Chron. 3.18), is unsatisfactory. Quite apart from the difference of name, the fact that no Davidic ancestry is claimed, whereas it is claimed for Zerubbabel, makes it most unlikely that he had such a status. He was, we may assume, a prominent member of the Jewish community, whose position made him an acceptable commissioner both to the Persian authorities and to those with whom he was to work. It is possible (cf. Neh. 2.6) that he was appointed for a fixed term of office and that his disappearance from the narrative is simply due to the expiry of that term.

THE RETURNED EXILES

2.1-70

It is not surprising to find the Chronicler providing at this point a list of names of those who came back from the exile in Babylonia. But the fact that this list is duplicated in Neh. 7 immediately raises questions about it, and a closer examination of the list in its various forms (I Esdras 5.7-46 has a somewhat deviant form) makes it clear that it does not really belong to this particular context. A fairly close parallel to it, though very different in detail, is provided by the list in I Chron. 9 which occurs also in a variant form in Neh. 11 (see comments at both points). That too purports to be a list of those who were 'the first to dwell again in their possessions', and we may note that the classification there too is in terms of 'Israel, the priests, the Levites, and the temple servants' (I Chron. 9.2). Doubt about the originality of the list in Ezra 2 is further raised by the list of names in v.2. At this point, with Sheshbazzar appointed as royal commissioner, we should surely have expected to find his name. Instead, the list of the leaders begins with ZERUBBABEL, and the historical evidence points strongly to his work belonging some years later than the first return.

On the other hand, the presence of such a list and a number of its points of detail are fully intelligible in the light of the Chronicler's view of the return.

1. The opening emphasizes the return of exiles to their own places in the PROVINCE – the Aramaic term *medīnā* is used quite frequently in the later Old Testament literature and denotes an administrative area, here that of the small sub-province of Judah, limited in area, as may be seen from the place-names of this chapter and of the narrative of Nehemiah. It is a true restoration of the people of God to its own land, a re-establishing of that people in its proper possession of the land.

2a. The list of leaders here probably lacks one name – Nahamani – which is to be found in the corresponding passage in Neh. 7.7. This would make a total of twelve, and while there is no open suggestion that these men are representatives of the twelve tribes, we may see the number as indicating that the whole of the true people is regarded as restored. Following on the hints of a new exodus in ch.1

(cf. p.215), such a picturing of the whole of the twelve-tribe Israel is appropriate. The leaders, however, bear some remarkable names. ZERUBBABEL as governor and JESHUA as high priest are known to us as contemporaries, joint leaders of the community in the first years of Darius I (522-486). NEHEMIAH could be the governor of the mid-fifth century BC, though it is of course quite possible that a totally different person is intended. The name SERAIAH appears in Neh. 7 as 'Azariah'; is it pure chance that this name is virtually identical with Ezra? BIGVAI is a name known to us from the Elephantine Papyri of Egypt as governor of Judah in about 410 BC; Josephus has a story about one Bagoses, a general of Artaxerxes, which may relate to the same person. While it would be quite wrong to suppose that we can firmly identify these personages with the names in the list, it would seem not impossible that there is here some reflection of the whole period after the exile.

2b-58. The list itself falls into clearly defined sections. First, ISRAEL, the lay people (vv.2b-35), a list which falls into two main parts: vv.3-19 list families, vv.20-35 mainly, though not entirely, localities. It may be that the mention of the family name points to people of higher status than those connected only with particular centres. The latter provide some indication of the area belonging to the 'province'. Second, PRIESTS (vv.36-39). Third, LEVITES (vv.40-42), within which THE SINGERS and GATEKEEPERS are included; the numbers here are very small, which suggests that this particular list reflects one particular moment. Fourth, TEMPLE SERVANTS (vv.43-54), the NETHINIM (see note on I Chron. 9.2). Fifth, but evidently connected with the preceding, a group described as THE SONS OF SOLOMON'S SERVANTS (vv.55-57). We have no knowledge of who these are, but since in v.58 they are counted together with the temple servants, it would appear that we have a note of another related group whose origin was traced, no doubt by themselves as a matter of status, back to the Solomonic period (cf. on these points, J. Blenkinsopp, *Gibeon and Israel*, esp. pp.106ff.). At every point in this list there are small differences of numbers and names (orthographic or more substantial) as compared with the other forms of the text, though it is quite clear that it is the same list in each case.

59-63. These verses present a very important qualification within the list. Those so far mentioned are the members of the community whose status and ancestry were clearly established. Now a note is given of certain members of the community whose position was in doubt. They came from particular localities in Babylonia; the names TEL-MELAH, TEL-HARSHA may be compared with Tel-abib in Ezek. 3.15 (Tel means 'mound', and is used for an area of raised land, also for a 'ruin mound' from an ancient city). The lay members in this position are noted first. More serious is the position of certain priestly groups. Of these, the second, THE SONS OF HAKKOZ, appear in the priestly list in I Chron. 24.10 and also among Nehemiah's helpers in Neh. 3.4, 21; if these are correctly identified, then it would appear that this group was subsequently able to establish its ancestry, whereas the first name, HABAIAH, does not appear elsewhere. The third name BARZILLAI recalls the story of the man from Gilead who gave assistance to the fugitive David (II Sam. 17.27-29; 19.31-39; I Kings 2.7); is the problem here perhaps uncertainty about a claim to descent which appears to come through the female line? Failure to prove an adequate genealogy led to exclusion from the priesthood. We may note that it is the political officer, the GOVERNOR (*tirshāthā*, a Persian term equivalent to 'Your excellency'), who rules that they must not partake of the most holy food (cf. Nehemiah's ordering of religious matters in Neh. 13). The governor is not named, and we have no basis on which to identify him with any particular personage. The decision about their position is to wait for the proper consultation of the sacred lot, URIM AND THUMMIM, of which the real nature is obscure; such a consultation is shown in I Sam. 14.41. The injunction to wait for a true priest who can get a proper decision suggests the working out of a procedure for decision-making. In I Macc. 14.41 a similar provision is made at the appointment of Simon Maccabaeus as 'leader and high priest, until a trustworthy prophet should arise', i.e. until a more final decision could be made. The importance of this passage lies in its revealing of that concern about true membership of the community which seems to be a great interest of the Chronicler and no doubt of some of his contemporaries in the post-exilic period. The securing of the proper membership is a matter of urgency if the people is to be the true people of God.

64-67. The final summaries give figures which do not correspond to the numbers which precede (nor can they be readily adjusted, since the alternative forms give some differences of enumeration). The details here about servants, MALE AND FEMALE SINGERS – not for the cult but for entertainment (cf. e.g. II Sam. 19.35) – and transport animals, perhaps suggest that the list may be connected with some census or taxation purpose.

68-69. These verses, which appear in a very different form in Neh. 7, could possibly be part of the original narrative context into which the list has been inserted – a note linked with the arrival of Sheshbazzar and the temple vessels designed to point to the degree of co-operation of the returned exiles with the temple rebuilding. The mention of DARICS – the coin in use from the time of Darius I – is an anachronism for the period before that. The support for the rebuilding recalls the giving for the tabernacle in Exod. 25.2ff., and for David's planned temple in I Chron. 29. But the appearance of similar material in Neh. 7 shows that the list had already been combined with such material before its use here. The literary relationships are very uncertain.

70. This now provides a link to what follows in 3.1, but the repetitions suggest that originally the two were distinct.

Any decision about the origin and purpose of the list – or indeed whether it is a single list or itself the product of a combining of older material – remains very tentative. For the Chronicler its purpose is to provide a picture of the community; it may be seen as linked also to the provision of a register of builders for the Persian authorities (5.3ff.). Perhaps originally, certainly in its present place, it served to emphasize who were and who were not the true members of the community. It is possible, therefore, that it reflects a moment of particular urgency – it could be in relation to the Samaritan community – in the life of the post-exilic people. For the true understanding of Judah, the people of God, the determining of proper ancestry, full membership, must be of significance.

THE RESTORATION OF WORSHIP

3.1-13

The narrative of ch.1 is now resumed. The emphasis there on the restoration of the temple vessels, and hence the possibility of a full renewal of worship, is picked up in a narrative which lays stress upon the full sacrificial order, as ordained by THE LAW OF MOSES (vv.2, 4) and upon the music of worship, as ordained by DAVID (v.10). It is the old worship which is being recovered, and the new community is thereby shown to be in continuity with the past.

To the Chronicler, such a restoration of worship must have been the first stage of the community's new life. But it would appear that his sources provided very little clear evidence of the first stage, and much more concerning the full temple rebuilding programme of the early years of Darius I. (For this, we may compare the prophecies of Haggai and Zechariah, where the point is clear that real revival came only then.) It is evident, though we do not know the precise causes or the order of events, that an initial stimulus (so ch.1 and cf. 5.14-16) under Sheshbazzar did not lead to full recovery. The Chronicler has his own way of presenting the reasons for the delay, and these we shall see in chs. 4 and 5. But to bridge the gap, he appears to have transposed the activity of Zerubbabel and Jeshua from the early years of Darius I, where it clearly belongs, to provide for the early years of

Cyrus, where he believed that theologically it must belong. The exact process of this transfer cannot be described, but we may see certain hints and possible lines of interpretation. This chapter is of particular importance.

1. The opening verse is identical with Neh. 7.73b-8.1; there as here it forms the conclusion to the list which also stands here in ch.2. It also there forms the introduction to Ezra's reading of the law. As we have seen, the literary aspects of the list are not easy to unravel.

2. The wording here strongly suggests a quite new beginning, originally not dated; the first verse may therefore be seen as a link verse, providing an appropriate date for the events which are now to be described. But we may also observe that the dedication of the first temple under Solomon took place IN THE SEVENTH MONTH (II Chron. 5.3), and that there may be a deliberate cross-reference both to that and to Ezra's activity. The great moments of recovery have points of correspondence.

2-7. This self-contained narrative is concentrated on the re-establishment of worship, even before the restoration of the temple. The natural expectation would be to find Sheshbazzar engaged in this activity, as indeed he is said to have been in 5.16. Has the Chronicler here substituted JESHUA, the priest of the true line of Zadok, and ZERUBBABEL, THE SON OF SHEALTIEL (his genealogy is differently given in I Chron. 3.19, but his ancestry is clear in either case), the true descendant of David? Or did he perhaps inherit already confused accounts of this period which admitted of various interpretations? (We may note that the opening of II Macc. [1.18ff.] quite erroneously attributes the building of the temple and the re-establishment of worship to Nehemiah. It is clear that there were many different ways of relating the story of restoration.) Sheshbazzar the unknown has disappeared, to give place to men whose ancestry and status is impeccable. The first stage is the building (better 'rebuilding') of THE ALTAR (v.2); it is set up in ITS PLACE, that is, restored in its statutory form (for the law, cf. Exod. 20.25) to the holy spot to which it belonged. It is not relevant to the Chronicler's understanding of the period to speculate what had happened between 587 and this moment; there is evidence to suggest that worship of some kind continued (cf. Jer. 41.5). For the Chronicler (cf. II Chron. 36.17-21), there was nothing in the land during that time; there could not have been any worship at all. Now all the regular sacrifices are re-instituted (vv.4-5, a list from which the mention of sabbath offerings has been accidentally omitted, cf. I Esd. 5.52), and the autumnal feast which fell just at this period of the year is properly reconstituted.

3. for fear was upon them because of the peoples of the lands
A difficult problem of interpretation appears here. As the text stands (possibly better read as 'fear had come upon them'), it would appear that the re-establishment of worship is understood as a protection against the outside world, the opposition which is soon to be shown in action against the true people (cf. chs.4-5). The text of I Esdras (5.50) offers a different view: 'And some joined them from the other peoples of the land. And they erected the altar in its place, for all the peoples of the land were hostile to them and were stronger than they.' It would appear probable that this text represents more than one rendering of the original, conflating alternative interpretations. If the text originally read: 'fear came upon them, and they were joined by some from the peoples of the land', the sense would be quite clear. The theme of awe at the wonder of God's action and the response to this of the outside world appears elsewhere in the Chronicler's work (cf. I Chron. 14.17; II Chron. 20.29); and the same point is to be echoed in 6.21. Such a text fits well with the overall outlook; worship of God is for the true people, but to that true people those who are faithful may be joined. It would also help to explain the present form of the text, for the theme of opposition is shortly to be introduced, and the attitude towards the outside world which is expressed in Nehemiah's and Ezra's foreign marriage policy, together with the drawing in upon itself of the Jewish community con-

fronted as it was in the second century BC and after by a
hostile world, would make such a re-interpretation intelligible.
But it cannot be regarded as certain that this is the right
view, for the I Esdras text could reflect the presence at a
later date of non-Jewish proselytes, associating themselves with
the life of the Jewish community.

6. This verse points to the moment of the beginning of
worship, but contains the reminder that THE FOUNDATION OF
THE TEMPLE OF THE LORD WAS NOT YET LAID; this is a misleading rendering, for it suggests that total rebuilding was
to be undertaken. Better would be the translation: 'the temple
was not yet re-established'.

7. Provision for the restoration is described, echoing the
preparations for the first temple (I Chron. 22.2-5; II Chron.
2), and recalling the 'permission' (better than GRANT) from
Cyrus (cf. ch.1). The mention of this latter serves also to
anticipate the opposition and its successful countering in
chs.5-6.

8. Yet another new narrative begins here, and the close resemblance between this and chapter 5 and also Hag. 1 strongly
suggests that, in fact, as at other points in the narrative, the
Chronicler is in reality passing over nearly twenty years to
give the fuller account of the rebuilding work.

8b-10. We may note the characteristic stress on THE LEVITES
as overseers of the work and again in the music to accompany
the act of worship, and the co-operation of ALL WHO HAD
COME TO JERUSALEM FROM THE CAPTIVITY. It is the returned
exiles who form the real people of God. The re-establishment
of the temple was begun, accompanied by appropriate worship.

11. The same psalm refrain is introduced as elsewhere in
the Chronicler's writing (e.g. I Chron. 16.34; cf. Ps. 136.1,
etc.). The RSV rendering: THEY SANG RESPONSIVELY is probably wrong; it should simply be 'they sang' or possibly 'they
began to sing praise'. The act of praise is accompanied by

the GREAT cultic SHOUT, associated with the theophany (cf.
I Sam. 4.5); the presence of God is to be hailed by such a
joyous noise (cf. Ps. 95.1f.).

12-13. The text of v.12 is not entirely clear. We might render
'... old men who had seen with their own eyes the first
temple when it was established (i.e. in its fully established
state) wept with a loud voice.' A glossator appears then
to have added the words 'this is the temple', presumably
to clarify the reference. Such a rendering may suggest
that the weeping is not to be seen as a sign of mourning at the contrast between the old temple and the new,
an interpretation picked up from Hag. 2.3 (cf. Zech.
4.10) which lays stress on this difference. It is rather part
of the ritual, a vivid expression of the intensity of the prayers
being offered (cf. Hos. 12.4, interpreting Jacob's wrestling with
the angel, Gen. 32.24-32, in such terms). Weeping and rejoicing combine to produce a noise to be HEARD AFAR. A Babylonian cornerstone carries the words: 'I started the work
weeping, finished it rejoicing' (quoted by R. North, *Jerome
Bibl. Comm.*, p.430). It is all part of the great act of worship which marks this new beginning.

OPPOSITION

4.1-24

The material grouped in this chapter is clearly out of
order, with Darius (522-486) at the end following Artaxerxes
(465-424). What has happened is that the Chronicler has
brought together into one section a number of pieces of
information about opposition to the activities of the Jewish
community. The matter is complicated further by the fact
that 4.8-6.18 is in Aramaic, a Semitic language of a different
branch from Hebrew, though with many points of close contact, a language already very widely used in the pre-exilic
period (cf. II Kings 18.26) and now in the Persian period
established as the language of diplomacy and trade in the
western part of the empire. It was to become the vernacular

of Palestine and the normal language of everyday life, while Hebrew came to be the language of religion and learning. Its script was derived from the old alphabet of Canaan, as was the old Hebrew script found in inscriptions and preserved in some Qumran texts, particularly for the sacred divine name; it was the Aramaic script which was in due course to be used as the normal vehicle for writing the Hebrew scriptures, the so-called 'square script'. A further Aramaic section appears in Ezra 7. It seems likely that the Chronicler made use of an Aramaic document, preserving it perhaps partly because it added a flavour of officialdom and authority to the narrative. But the order within the Aramaic document is now wrong, and presumably 4.8-23 ought to follow 5.1-6.18 (4.24 is a link verse). In part, in chs.5-6, this material runs parallel to the account of restoration to be found in 1-3 and 6.19-22; but it includes some important further and different information.

The various opposition themes have been gathered together, thereby producing a greater effect. That the order is not the only possible one is indicated by I Esdras; here the first part (4.1-5; I Esd. 5.66-73) follows on the material corresponding to ch.3 (I Esd. 5.47-65); the second part (4.6-24) is placed so as to follow immediately on the commission of Sheshbazzar (I Esd. 2.16-30). This solves none of the historical problems, but it enables that account to lead straight on into the account of Darius' reign and does this by incorporating a long story about a contest of wits at the royal court in which, surprisingly – for the name is introduced without explanation (4.13) – Zerubbabel is the hero and is granted permission to rebuild the temple (so I Esd. 3.1-5.3). This in its turn leads on through the list of returned exiles (cf. Ezra 2: I Esd. 5.4-46) into the restoration of the worship and rebuilding (I Esd. 5.47-7.15, corresponding to Ezra 3.1-4.5 and 5.1-6.22). This arrangement represents an alternative; it cannot be regarded as historically better, but it reveals another way in which the different elements can be related.

We may best examine the different elements and consider the Chronicler's purpose.

1-5. This report tells of opposition to the temple building and to the delaying or halting of its progress until the reign of Darius. In some measure it runs parallel to the much fuller and more elaborate account of opposition in 5.3-6.13, where opposition is prevented by royal action. It is very difficult to interpret.

1-3. the adversaries of Judah and Benjamin The opponents are not clearly designated; they offer to share in the rebuilding but are rejected (vv.2-3). They claim to be true worshippers, ever since they were settled in the land by the Assyrian ruler ESARHADDON (681-669). We know of the Assyrian policy of bringing settlers from outside from the account of the fall of Samaria in II Kings 17. There is no reason why another such settlement should not have taken place at a later date; yet another may be intended in 4.10 (see below). Such a settlement could be connected with Esarhaddon's Egyptian campaign of 671, and may be alluded to in the obscure reference to 'sixty-five years' (i.e. after *c.* 735 BC) in Isa. 7.8. That the settlers would adopt the local religion is indicated by II Kings 17.25ff. But their claim to share in the building is not allowed by the Jewish community, which claims the sole privilege of building in accordance with Cyrus' decree. We are not given any more information about these opponents. Most often they have been identified with the Samaritan community, but this would be an anachronism, for the division between Jews and Samaritans belongs to a later time, and in any case there is no good reason to believe that the Samaritans were an alien group. Their claim to an ancient religious tradition and to firm adherence to it was a sound one. We must not read back what the later Jewish and Samaritan communities said about one another into an earlier situation (cf. John 4.9), though it is possible that the Chronicler was making such an identification himself, faced as he may have been by the early stages of the division.

The name 'Jeshua' has accidentally fallen out of v.2. The adversaries' words may be rendered 'we have not sacrificed ...' This may be the result of a deliberate alteration of the word for 'to him' to the similarly sounding negative; it is also possible to translate this form of the text: 'and have we not been sacrificing ...?'

4-5. the people of the land A new term is used for the opponents. Is this the same group, or are two pieces of information put together? The expression most naturally means 'the ordinary people' or 'the native population'; it is perhaps expressive of the Chronicler's belief in the true community having returned from Babylonia and finding itself confronted by some who were in the land, who did not share their faith or who pretended to share it for their own purposes. These verses describe a rather different type of attack, by discouragement – literally, 'the weakening of the hands' (cf. Jer. 38.4) – inducing fear, perhaps by threats, and by hiring COUNSELLORS, presumably, as in the other opposition material, by undermining the Jewish position *vis-à-vis* the Persian authorities.

Whether there is really one narrative here or two, it is clear that the Chronicler's interest is twofold. He is offering a comment on the dangers which threaten the true people of God. In the pre-exilic period, when the northern kingdom existed, the risk lay in becoming entangled with this apostate people. The successors to the old northern kingdom are to be found in these adversaries and others of a later day. He is also bridging for the reader the gap between the first stage of rebuilding – described in ch.3 – and its continuance and completion, according to his view of the events, nearly twenty years later in the reign of Darius.

6. We appear to have here an isolated note of opposition during the reign of Xerxes I. It is linked by idea to the immediately preceding verses in that it speaks of a written ACCUSATION, just the kind of thing we might expect from the hired counsellors. There is no information whatever about the situation to which this belongs.

7. We now have the beginning of a new section, but probably this verse too contains a single element, an allusion to A LETTER to ARTAXERXES; since the names of the persons

involved are not the same as those in the material in vv.8-23,
it would appear to be separate from that incident. The name
BISHLAM is doubtful; it could be a misunderstanding of the
word of greeting 'in peace', or it could be a corruption of 'in
Jerusalem', i.e. they wrote there or they wrote with reference
to the city. If we knew who MITHREDATH and TABEEL were, we
might get a clearer understanding; it has been suggested that
they were in fact members of the Jewish community writing
a favourable note, an apology; but the context suggests that
we should probably see another opposition element here. The
last clause is not clear, as RSVmg indicates. The final 'in
Aramaic' simply serves (as also in Dan. 2.4) to mark the
beginning of the Aramaic section.

8-23. This section begins with a somewhat repetitive and
perhaps overloaded introduction which links this group of
opponents too with Assyrian deportation and settlement policy.

8-10. Osnappar This may be intended to denote Ashurbanipal (669-633?), the last great Assyrian ruler.

REHUM THE COMMANDER (perhaps better 'commissioner'
or 'chancellor') could be the governor in Samaria, since this
area is singled out for mention (vv.10, 17) within the whole
PROVINCE BEYOND THE RIVER, the correct administrative description for the area lying to the west of the Euphrates, within
which Judah lay. It is very likely, indeed, that at this time
Judah was administratively under the control of the governor
in Samaria, and that the authority of the commissioners sent
to Jerusalem was limited. The Nehemiah narrative indicates
a different stage in the relationship between Jerusalem/Judah
and Samaria. But here again we must not confuse this with
the Samaritan question; these are the political leaders, and
there is no religious issue involved.

The letter follows a normal epistolary style, with its separate
sections introduced by the word NOW (vv.12, 13, 14).

12. The reference to Jews from the east who have come up
to Jerusalem may be to a recent further movement (within
the reign of Artaxerxes) or to the original returned exiles of

the restoration period. The description of Jerusalem as REBELLIOUS and WICKED echoes prophetic judgment, a neat reversal of terms as they are now put into the mouth of opponents. In fact, as the broader context shows, the true people at Jerusalem can now be seen as obedient to the divine will.

14. eat the salt of the palace. This means 'on the royal payroll', part of the imperial establishment. The complainants are government officers. The argument follows lines familiar from such diplomatic correspondence (cf. the fourteenth-century BC Tel el-Amarna letters, DOTT, pp.38ff.; ANET, pp.483ff.); one subject group or one local official seeks to gain favour and perhaps to divert attention from any misdeeds of his own by pointing to the activities of another.

15. was laid waste Jerusalem came under judgment because of its rebellious activities, an interpretation which can be seen to be related to the Chronicler's own judgment in II Chron. 36, though there it is rebellion against God and here it is rebellion against an imperial overlord.

16. There is a nice irony in the claim that once Jerusalem is rebuilt and fully walled, the whole PROVINCE BEYOND THE RIVER will be lost; the opponents of the Jewish community cannot fail to acknowledge the superior power which belongs to it if it is obedient.

17-22. The Persian ruler's reply confirms the rightness of the complaint and orders the cessation of building. It takes even further the theme of v.16 by recalling the MIGHTY KINGS who RULED OVER THE WHOLE PROVINCE (v.20), an allusion to the Davidic tradition of a kingdom stretching from the River (i.e. Euphrates) to the Sea, hardly fully historical but nevertheless expressive of an ideal (cf. Ps. 72.8).

23. The result is the stopping of the work. However, the work here complained of and brought to a halt is nothing to do with the building of the temple. It belongs to a much later date, probably in the mid-fifth century BC, and it is entirely concerned with walls and fortifications.

force and power Its use may imply that parts of the walls were destroyed, and it has often been thought that this passage could fit well as a prelude to the activity of Nehemiah. For in just about this period – 445 BC – he learnt of the destruction of walls and gates (Neh. 1.1f.).

24. This reference back to the temple is perhaps best seen as the link verse which introduces the narrative of chs. 5.6.

Whatever the true explanation of the material gathered in this chapter, and whether it already combined elements belonging to temple building and to wall building before the Chronicler took it over, it is clear that he has made skilful use of it. The result of this rather sombre passage is that the achievement of the community in re-establishing itself is made all the more remarkable – and the next narrative explains this more fully – and it may serve therefore to inculcate faith in a later generation. A similar recall to the faith of this community of the days after the exile is made in Zech. 8.9, which equally looks back to the time of the temple building as a moment of great confidence amid difficulties. Indeed the whole prophetic collection in Haggai, Zechariah 1-8 provides just such a recall, and perhaps should be set alongside the Chronicler's writings as another example of the interpretation of older material in a new situation.

THE REBUILDING OF THE TEMPLE

5.1-6.22

The main part of this section continues in Aramaic, presenting a coherent account of the rebuilding of the temple in the early years of Darius' reign. A close linkage may be seen with the prophetic books of Haggai and Zechariah (1-8), particularly the former, which indeed reads almost like an extract from an alternative form of the narrative. We may observe too that the character of this Aramaic material is markedly theological, with its emphasis (5.1-2; 6.14) on the support provided by prophetic word, with its assurance of divine favour (5.5), and with its concern for the details of religious observance and order, a point in which it clearly stands very close to the Chronicler himself. The last verses of ch.6 (vv.19-22) are in Hebrew, and we may see them as forming the conclusion to the alternative account of the temple building which is to be found, perhaps incomplete, in ch.3.

5.1-2. The account may be said to begin with the link verse 4.24, and the prophetic message and the response of the leaders and people in these next two verses then reflect the reluctance to build, the lack of faith, and the response which may also be seen in Hag. 1. The two prophets, who belong so closely together in the tradition, saw the temple as central to the life of the community; without that centre, with its relationship to the presence of the deity at the heart of the people (cf. also Ezek. 40-48), a full and prosperous life was impossible. Zechariah appears here as SON OF IDDO, whereas in Zech. 1.1 he is grandson; the importance of the genealogy lies in its establishment of his priestly ancestry (cf. Neh. 12.16).

3-5. In the context of the opposition material of ch.4, the inquiry by Tattenai THE GOVERNOR OF THE PROVINCE BEYOND THE RIVER – an official known from a Babylonian record of 502 BC – is very naturally interpreted as hostile. But it is not necessarily to be so regarded, and we may observe that the questions concerning authority for building and the request for the names of the builders are followed not by a halt to the work but by its continuance. The narrator interprets this as the result of divine favour to the elders of the Jews, the leaders of the community; the authorities themselves would presumably have halted the work had they had reason to think that there was something politically amiss. The supposition that the governor had been prompted to investigate the situation by the officials in Samaria is a reasonable one, but it could equally be recognized that the function of the superior governor was, through his agents, to keep an eye on signi-

ficant activities throughout the province over which he exercised authority. The word translated STRUCTURE in v.3 is of
uncertain meaning, perhaps 'sanctuary'.

6-17. These verses record a letter sent to Darius, reporting
on what has been found at Jerusalem. It is evident that the
form of this letter owes a good deal to Jewish views. The
temple at Jerusalem is THE HOUSE OF THE GREAT GOD (better
'the supreme God', v.8); its building is described in terms
which suggest rather the view of the pious Jew than the sober
official. That the work PROSPERS is strongly suggestive of the
experience of divine favour. The reply to the inquiries not
only stresses the supremacy of the God of the Jewish community (v.11), but also traces significant moments of the history of the people – a temple built by A GREAT KING (Solomon),
the angering of their God, the judgment at the hands of
Babylon and the captivity (v.12). The assurance of favour at
the hands of Cyrus and the restoration of the temple vessels
are themes found also in ch.1, and it may be that the narrative there is dependent on this source. The appearance of
SHESHBAZZAR as GOVERNOR (a term used for various types of
official) also provides a link with that account. The statement
of v.16 appears to conflict with the evidence of a long period
of cessation in the building, though the wording does not
necessarily mean IT HAS BEEN IN BUILDING 'continuously', but
perhaps only that no completion point has yet been reached.

6.1-2. The search for the original DECREE of CYRUS requested
by Tattenai's letter (5.17) is now related. It is found at
ECBATANA in Media, the summer capital of the empire, in the
form of A SCROLL, suited to Aramaic, rather than a tablet
suited to cuneiform script.

3-5. The decree itself corresponds in some measure to the
more elaborate statement of it in ch.1, though there we have
observed the inclusion of elements of interpretation. That
the Persian authorities took concern for such supporting of
religious buildings and rituals is known to us from various
pieces of evidence – an Egyptian shrine purified at the orders

of Cambyses, the respecting of a holy place in Asia Minor. The detail of the building would be appropriate in view of the financial support to be provided; the dimensions are incomplete, and such as are given point to a much larger shrine than that of Solomon where we might have expected close correspondence. The note about the building method – THREE COURSES OF GREAT STONES (the term is uncertain of meaning) AND ONE COURSE OF TIMBER – points to a system of using the two types of material together, perhaps with a view to enabling the building to withstand earthquake tremors (cf. H. C. Thomson, *Palestine Exploration Quarterly*, 1960, pp.57-63); the same system is described in I Kings 6.36. It is evident here again in this form of Cyrus' edict that the primary emphasis is on the re-establishing of the former temple, a rehabilitation of worship which provides continuity with the past.

6. Somewhat abruptly the text moves over to Darius' instructions; it is possible that a phrase has dropped out introducing these, e.g. 'Then Darius issued this order' (so NEB). Or we may see the compiler of this section setting out the various elements side by side, with only the minimum of narrative; thus at 5.6 the letter to Darius is introduced only by 'THE COPY OF THE LETTER'; at 6.1-2 narrative is needed and hence it is given. At 6.6, we might assume: 'Copy of Darius' order'.

7-9. Darius' reply is that there should be no interference, and it is clear that this will extend to any subordinate officials such as those at Samaria who might be endeavouring to impede the work. Darius further authorizes what appears to be fuller financial provision, not simply for building but also for the establishment of the ritual.

10. The purpose of this support is to placate THE GOD OF HEAVEN, the interruption of whose worship might bring disaster upon the king, and that prayer may be offered FOR THE LIFE OF THE KING AND HIS SONS, a theme already noted as appearing in the Cyrus Cylinder (see p.214). For this we may also compare Jer. 29.7.

11. The unchangeable nature of the decree is underlined in a curse upon anyone who alters it; the unalterability of law is an ancient principle (cf. the Code of Lipit-Ishtar, probably belonging to the nineteenth century BC, which invokes curses upon anyone who damages the inscription, ANET, p.161. Cf. also Deut. 4.2; 12.32 and the somewhat fanciful development of the idea in Esther and Dan. 6).

12. The invocation of the deity is markedly influenced by the Deuteronomic concept of the presence of the NAME of God at Jerusalem (cf. e.g. Deut. 12.5 and the prayer of Solomon in I Kings 8.29; II Chron. 6.20).

13-15. The result is shown in a picture of the completion of the temple, in which the support of the prophets is again emphasized, by THE SIXTH YEAR of Darius, in THE MONTH ADAR, the twelfth month, i.e. February to March 515 – the day given here (THIRD DAY, v.15) differs from that given in I Esd. 7.5 (twenty-third day); the latter is more probable, since a word or abbreviation for a numeral may more easily fall out than be inserted, though it is conceivable that there were two alternative traditions of this significant moment. It has been noted that the names of Jeshua and Zerubbabel, which appear in 5.2, do not occur in this last part of the account. There are various possible explanations. It may be simply that the writer did not consider it necessary to mention them again, though we may note that he did repeat the names of the prophets. It could be that Zerubbabel's term of office came to an end – was he perhaps a special commissioner on a limited assignment (cf. Neh. 2.7)? But what then became of Jeshua? Had he died in the meantime? It has been suggested that they were removed by the Persian authorities for political pretensions; Hag. 2.23 and Zech. 6.9-14 – a problematic text – might point to this. But then we might ask whether the Persians would have permitted the continuing of the temple building in such circumstances. Yet another possibility is that originally this Aramaic account did not mention these two leaders at all, but presented the rebuilding as the action of the Jewish community, urged on by the words of the two prophets; the names were then

added at 5.2 to conform this account both with ch.3 and with
the prophetic books in which the leaders' names are mentioned. There is a further oddity in v.14 in the mention of
ARTAXERXES, who does not belong to this time at all; here we
may see the compiler reflecting upon the longer history of the
post-exilic period, and seeing a further example of divine
protection in the favour shown by this later ruler to
Nehemiah and to Ezra (on these points, cf. the commentary
below).

16-18. dedication The term for this, 'Hanukkah', was to become the technical name of the feast commemorating the
rededication after the desecration of the temple by Antiochus
Epiphanes in the second century BC, and celebrated in Decem-
ber (cf. I Macc. 4.52ff.; John 10.22). But it is likely that that
celebration marked a renewal of older practice, and the
Chronicler uses the term also for one aspect of Solomon's
ritual (II Chron. 7.9), namely that of the altar, a point governed
by legal prescription in Num. 7.10f., 84, 88. The emphasis in
v.17 on THE TRIBES OF ISRAEL is again a reminder that the
contemporary community is to be seen as the true successor
of all Israel (cf. on 2.2). Priestly and levitical orders are reconstituted, according to Mosaic prescription, though actually this
is to be linked with the setting out of the arrangement
particularly in I Chron. 23ff.

19-22. The text now returns to Hebrew. The preceding verse
marks an appropriate end to a celebration which takes place
at the end of the sixth year. The final section fits neatly after
this with its description of a PASSOVER celebration in THE FIRST
MONTH of the new year. If this is really the end of the Hebrew
narrative of ch.3, then we may see it as providing a climax to
that account of the rebuilding, culminating in the passover
in the same way that the reforms and renewals undertaken by
Hezekiah and Josiah lead up to great passover celebrations
(cf. II Chron. 30; 35). It is significant as an expression of the
Chronicler's theology that the celebration is undertaken by
THE RETURNED EXILES, the primary part of the true people,
but also by those who were willing to separate themselves

FROM THE POLLUTIONS OF THE PEOPLES OF THE LAND, an expression which points strongly to the concept of faithful members of the northern tribes being able to join the true people, and indeed the Chronicler has revealed a marked tradition that they had done so (e.g. II Chron. 30). As an appeal to his own contemporaries, the Chronicler is perhaps calling on dissident groups – or what he regards as dissident groups – such as the Samaritan community to see where the true centre of faith lies.

22. the king of Assyria A puzzling reference. In the context this can only mean the king of Persia, who could be viewed in this way as the successor to the more ancient imperial power, just as he could be considered as king of Babylon. But the change of term is odd. Is it perhaps due to the inadvertence of a scribe? And if so, was he thinking of the position under Greek rule when the term KING OF ASSYRIA could perhaps be used to refer to the Seleucid rulers of Syria? Or should we suppose that there has been a deliberate updating of the text to meet the needs of that much later situation, an awareness that God can turn the heart of even hostile rulers to show favour to his own people (cf. Dan. 2-4; 6). At all events, the final phrases point the theological moral; the rebuilding of the temple, so essential a part of the recovery of the life of the true people of God, is possible only because God himself moved the hearts of rulers, from Cyrus onwards (cf. 1.1), to bring about this work. The theme of divine protection through alien rulers is taken further in the narratives of Ezra and Nehemiah.

THE WORK OF EZRA - I

Ezra 7-10

EZRA'S COMMISSION

7.1-28

1. Now after this The opening phrase conceals a lapse of many years. Even if the older view that the ARTAXERXES here mentioned is the first ruler of that name is maintained, the gap covers nearly sixty years (515 to 458). If, as is assumed here (see pp.24ff.), it refers to Artaxerxes II (404-358), then the gap is over a hundred years (515 to 398). We have no means of knowing why the Chronicler should consider that nothing within that period was of consequence for the work which he was composing. It is true that if the Nehemiah material was included by the Chronicler in the original work, one important gap in the period would be filled (445-433 and later – Neh. 1.1; 13.6); but it has been argued that a better understanding is obtained if we recognize in the Nehemiah narrative an independent work later incorporated in the Chronicler's writings (see p.24). Such a telescoping of events is, however, to be understood as revealing something of the writer's purpose. It becomes evident that Ezra is to him a great hero, and it is in his work that the climax is reached. Furthermore it is clear, in the light of the earlier narratives of the books of Kings, that the Chronicler is offering a new and more comprehensive interpretation of his people's history, and in particular of the place within that history of the experience of judgment and restoration. The pattern is written through the whole work; in particular it is exemplified in the final disaster to Judah, the true people of God, and in the restoration of that true people in the early years of Persian rule. The work of Ezra is then seen as confirming that moment of restoration, and the contemporaries of the Chronicler, living not long after the work

of Ezra as they probably did, are being reminded of the
perspective of divine purpose within which his activity is to
be seen. The Chronicler appears as an apologist for Ezra, as
one to whom his contemporaries must look if they are to see
how they are to respond and be, as they ought to be, the true
people of God.

In making the leap over the intervening years, the Chronicler
may presumably be aware that there is a considerable gap;
yet for him – as we may see from his use of the 'seventy year'
prophecy of Jeremiah (II Chron. 36.21) – chronology is less
significant as a record of the passage of time than as a meaningful comment on events. So it may not be accident that he
conveniently places next to one another narratives which refer
the one to the 'sixth year' (of Darius, 6.15) and the other to
THE SEVENTH YEAR (of Artaxerxes, 7.7f.). The interrelationship
of these year numbers may, of course, have been further
assisted by the reference to Artaxerxes in 6.14, though this is
perhaps a later addition to the text.

The significance of Ezra for the Chronicler may be seen
generally in the fact that the final stages of his work are
concentrated upon this particular figure. That he should end
his narrative here could, of course, be explained on the assumption that this was the latest event and that the experience of
the law-reading and covenant described in Neh. 8-10 had only
just passed. But the evidence of rearrangement even in the
Ezra narrative (see below) would suggest rather that some
space should be set between Ezra and the Chronicler, though,
since no evidence appears of the change over to Greek rule,
a date around 350 BC seems to fit the evidence most readily
(cf. pp.25ff.). But Ezra's significance may be gauged at the
outset in the details which are given in 7.1-10, which forms
the Chronicler's introduction to a narrative which appears to
make use of various source materials.

1-5. Here Ezra is given a substantial priestly genealogy,
though not a complete list of ancestors back to Aaron (cf. I
Chron. 6.3-15); such is the status which he enjoys.

6. a scribe skilled in the law of Moses This further description is taken up in the comment in v.10 which elaborates that aspect of his activity which is concentrated upon the STUDY of THE LAW and obedience to it and instruction in it. The interpretation of the title SCRIBE given to Ezra is not easy. The same phrase for SKILLED SCRIBE is used also in Ps. 45.2, where the psalmist describes his tongue as 'like the pen of a skilled scribe'. And the word rendered 'skilled' is used in Prov. 22.29 of a 'man skilled in his work'. Ahikar, a hero of ancient legend whose story has influenced the narrative of Tobit, is described in an Aramaic text from Elephantine with a corresponding expression in which the word 'skilled' is placed side by side with 'wise'. But none of this gives us a precise indication of the function in relation to the law of Moses, though it would point most naturally to wisdom and skill in handling that law and not merely skill in writing. The scribe is known to us as an important government functionary in Israel as elsewhere. This has suggested seeing Ezra as himself such a functionary, and the further consideration of the nature of the commission recorded in vv.12-26 has suggested that he might have been a functionary at the Persian court, one whose particular concern was the affairs of the Jewish community, whether generally or with particular reference to Judah. Of this we may say that it is not impossible, though it may be doubted if it is proper to draw conclusions by conflating the evidence of two rather different types of source material. Whatever may underlie the wording of the commission, we should look here rather at the way in which the Chronicler has depicted Ezra, and for this the further evidence of the narratives in chs.9-10 and in Neh. 8 is important; for there we find Ezra clearly indicated as an expounder of the law, an interpreter of its requirements, and also as demanding obedience from the whole community.

The work of Ezra, briefly indicated in these opening verses of the account, is stressed as being under the blessing of God (vv.6, 9). Divine favour shows through the king's willingness to grant HIM ALL THAT HE ASKED, and further in protection to bring him safely to Jerusalem. The latter point is to be elaborated in ch.8.

7. The fuller nature of his work is also indicated by the statement that he was accompanied on his journey to Jerusalem
by some lay members of the community, but more particularly
by all the essential classes of temple officials, from the PRIESTS
to the 'Nethinim' (see pp.44f.).

9. The text is not entirely clear; a word may have dropped out,
and we should perhaps read: '... THE FIRST MONTH, that is
Nisan, he instituted (initiated) the going up ...'

The opening section is continued in two different ways, in
passages now set side by side: first the text, in Aramaic, of
Ezra's commission from the Persian king (vv.12-26, with an
introductory formula in v.11); and second an extract from a
first-person account of Ezra's activity, of which the first stage
is the account of the journey to Jerusalem (7.27-8.36).

12-26. The commission is quoted in Aramaic. The purpose of
using this language, as in the passage in chs.4-6, may be to
give a clearer indication of authenticity and authority. Here,
it would appear, is the actual document connected with this
event. The fact that in some respects its wording is such as
one might expect from a Jewish writer rather than from a
Persian administrator is not necessarily an argument against
authenticity, though our recognition of the way in which the
Chronicler handles his sources – as witness the two different
forms of the Cyrus edict in chs.1 and 6 – must leave open the
possibility, even the likelihood, that some embellishments have
been made. A good government, however, and one which takes
account of the susceptibilities of subject peoples, may be
expected to endeavour to word its communications so as to
meet the needs of a particular situation, and to avoid offend-
ing, particularly in such a delicate area as that of religion.
A commission of this kind would therefore be drawn up either
by a Persian official who had knowledge of the community
in question or who took advice from its members or by a
member of that community himself; even such a scribe as
Ezra might, in the political sense, be thought to be. The
occasion for the commission may have been a request from

the Jewish leaders for action in view of some internal concerns
of their own, and the commission be then a rewording and
perhaps modifying of their request. Or it may have arisen
from some particular need of Persian policy. Or perhaps a
judicious combining of the two. We should hardly suppose
that the Persian government would respond to a request for
the sending of Ezra and his company without considering
whether it would be advantageous to their own position, or
at the very least not harmful. If Ezra was being sent in the
seventh year of Artaxerxes II (398 BC), then we know that,
whatever internal needs there may have been, this was certainly
a moment when it would be to the advantage of the Persians
to have an orderly and contented community in Judah. For
this was the point at which Egypt had just claimed its independence and Artaxerxes had only recently established
himself at home after the attempt at a coup by his younger
brother Cyrus, in whose support Greek mercenaries had been
used (cf. the *Anabasis* of Xenophon).

At the same time, we may observe that the wording of the
commission does not precisely correspond to other evidence
about the activity of Ezra, and we should therefore keep open
the possibility that it expresses an alternative tradition and
interpretation of the nature of his activity.

11. This simply provides a Hebrew introduction, which makes
use of wording similar to that of vv.6 and 10. The commission
itself covers a considerable range of points.

13. First, it authorizes the return to Jerusalem of PEOPLE,
PRIESTS and LEVITES who so desire. 8.1-14 is to give a list of
the company. Ezra's work is in part seen as the rebuilding of
the community in Jerusalem and Judah.

14. Second, it authorizes a fact-finding mission or investiga-
tion, with the backing of THE KING AND HIS SEVEN COUNSEL-
LORS (cf. Esther 1.14), though the nature of the inquiry is not
disclosed. It may point to some internal dissension which
needed resolving. Josephus' account of the period (*Antiquities*
XI, 7, 1) tells of the murder by the high priest John (Jehohanan)

of his brother in the temple. Josephus' account of the whole
period does not appear to be historically coherent, but such
an upheaval might well call for strong action. Not a hint of
this appears in the Ezra narrative.

15-16. Third, there is a charge to transport the gifts of the
king and his counsellors – royal support for the temple and
its worship as in the case of Cyrus and Darius; in addition
to this and to freewill offerings by PEOPLE and PRIESTS, for
royal support does not exempt the people from giving, a
remarkable ALL THE SILVER AND GOLD WHICH YOU SHALL FIND
IN THE WHOLE PROVINCE OF BABYLONIA. (We may compare Hag.
2.8: 'The silver is mine, and the gold is mine, says the LORD
of hosts.') In 8.25 such gifts are restricted to the royal gifts and
those of Israel. It would appear that here the theme of 'spoiling
the Egyptians' utilized in Ezra 1 in relation to the first return
(cf. note on 1.4, 6) is extended even further. It may be doubted
if this was really an original element in the commission.

17-18. The gifts so provided are to be allocated for providing
sacrifices and for such other purposes as may fall within THE
WILL OF YOUR GOD. This again represents a broadening of the
concept of Persian support for the re-establishment and em-
bellishment of worship. Such a concern with the detail of
worship and indeed much more specific directives may be
found in one of the Aramaic documents from the Jewish
colony at Elephantine on the Nile in this period. It lays down
precise directives for ritual procedures, perhaps, though not
certainly, connected with the Passover (cf. ANET, p.491;
DOTT, p.259).

19. This introduces the now familiar theme of temple VESSELS,
an essential in any moment of revival in the Chronicler's
work.

20. This is extended to cover any requisite for the temple, to
be met from THE KING'S TREASURY.

21-24. Somewhat strangely, these verses are not a part of the
commission to Ezra but an independent section concerned

with directives to THE TREASURERS IN THE PROVINCE BEYOND
THE RIVER. A copy of these might well be given to Ezra so
that he would know the position, but they would hardly be
incorporated in the actual commission. Furthermore, the un-
limited openness of the royal treasury in v.20 is now followed
by quite evidently exaggerated amounts – A HUNDRED TALENTS
OF SILVER would be a very large sum indeed – which suggests
that the theme of royal support is being given an extension to
underline the respect with which Persian rulers held the temple
at Jerusalem and the supreme deity associated with it.

23. The protection of the empire from the possible WRATH
of this great deity (cf. comment on 6.10) is next introduced.

24. The total exemption of all religious officials from any
taxes is a remarkably wide provision. There are some parallels
to this in tax exemption at a later date, e.g. by Antiochus III
(so Josephus, *Antiquities* XII, 3, 3), and we might perhaps see
here a reading back and idealizing of later practice, resulting
in the extension of a more limited concession in the original
provisions.

25. We now return to the commission to Ezra, and indeed to
the most fundamental and far-reaching point of all. Here there
is given to Ezra the royal authority for the appointment of
MAGISTRATES AND JUDGES for the whole PROVINCE BEYOND THE
RIVER; they are to operate for ALL ... WHO KNOW THE LAWS
OF YOUR GOD. This sets out the very important principle that
in effect all who are adherents of Jewish faith within the
province, no matter where precisely they live, are brought
within the jurisdiction of the Judaean community. Later
generations of Jews, living under the changing political situations of Greek and Roman rule, were to be keenly aware of
the problem of relating political organization to religious
adherence. Different methods of dividing the area were
attempted, and there were times, under Hasmonean rulers,
when the aim was to make the whole area Jewish, even to the
extent of imposing forcible circumcision. We may appreciate
the difficulties faced by administrators, and also see the prob-

lem created for district governors finding that some part of
their population owed another allegiance, that to the Jewish
law regulated from Jerusalem. The last clause of v.25, if taken
at its face value, goes even further; it enjoins that THOSE WHO
DO NOT KNOW THE LAWS are to be taught them. It is quite
possible that the original intention underlying this was the
provision of instruction in the law for younger members of
the community such as is envisaged in the scheme for a seven-
year reading of the law in Deut. 31 (and cf. Neh. 8). There
comes a point at which the young must be incorporated fully
in the community, accepting its obligations. It may be understood in terms of instruction for the ignorant who nevertheless
belong to the Jewish community. But this is not what the text
says. It appears to envisage a situation in which the whole
province becomes one community, all obedient to the law.
We may see in such an idealizing proposal a claim for the
re-establishment on a different basis of the ancient Davidic
kingdom, a claim not unlike that which is put into the letter
to Artaxerxes in 4.20, where it speaks of kings who have
ruled over the whole province. It becomes evident that the
wording of the commission as it now stands has moved a long
way from reality as this would be envisaged by a Persian
ruler.

26. The point is underlined with the indication of the sanctions
to be imposed, allowing the widest rights to the community in
the demand for obedience.

All in all it is a remarkable document. But whatever its
authentic basis, it does not appear to be the original commission as it now stands. It is significant for the claims it
makes in regard to the magnitude of the work of Ezra and the
position which he is believed to occupy. And we may notice
too that, while there is a general correspondence between the
commission and the work of Ezra as it is described in the
narratives, there is no exact cross-reference. There is thus no
suggestion that Ezra attempted to impose the law outside the
area of Jerusalem and Judah. That is a piece of utopianism
which belongs to the commission tradition and not to the other

material in which it is now incorporated. We must give a proper weight to the different elements, but recognize that the traditions concerning Ezra are not all of one piece.

27-28. These verses serve to round off this narrative, but in fact provide the link between the opening verses (7.1-10) and the sequel in ch.8. Furthermore, especially if we add before v.27 words which are found in one form of the Greek text: 'Then Ezra the scribe said', we have a clear introduction to the first-person narrative which runs through to the end of ch.9. The comment on the marvels of the divine ways is an extension of the repeated observation that what Ezra is able to do is possible only by reason of God's favour (cf. vv.6, 9; and again 8.18, 22, 31). It is interesting to observe that this method of punctuating the story finds its counterpart in the narratives of Nehemiah, where there are passages inviting God to remember for good the faithful governor and to remember for ill those who oppose him. It is evident that we have here a particular style of writing.

EZRA'S JOURNEY TO JERUSALEM

8.1-36

The introduction to this section of the narrative lies in 7.28*b*, with its emphasis upon the assurance which comes to Ezra from his knowledge of the power (HAND) OF GOD upon him.

1-14. The narrative proper follows at 8.15, but first there is another of the characteristic lists of names, setting out the composition of the party of returned exiles associated with Ezra. We may observe that the list begins with two priests, members respectively of the two Aaronic lines of PHINEHAS and ITHAMAR (cf. I Chron. 24), and then a member of the Davidic line. The form of priestly and royal leadership is preserved; but the Davidic descendant plays no obvious part in what follows. The Chronicler's interest does not lie in that kind of Davidic restoration. The remainder of the list is

grouped in twelve families, again providing a convenient correspondence with the tribes of Israel, though the point is not
drawn out (cf. 2.2). This band of returning exiles is to be seen
as truly representative of the whole people of God. The names
themselves, here and there somewhat confused, provide a
number of points of correspondence with the first part of the
list in ch.2 (Neh. 7), which suggests some degree of artificiality.

15-20. The first stage of the move to Jerusalem is an assembly
FOR THREE DAYS at an unknown place (and river) named
AHAVA. The next verses are, however, concerned with a major
question regarding the composition of the party. A surprising
absence of Levites leads to immediate moves to remedy this
deficiency. We may suspect a stylistic device here to underline
the point that the true people cannot be such without its
proper complement of Levites and their associated servants.
The whole ordering of worship depends so fully upon them
that existence without them is unthinkable. So we find an
impressive procedure for obtaining an adequate number of
Levites, and this comes about as a result of the wisdom of
those involved (v.16, 18) and the divine guidance which is
afforded (v.18). A group of named officials, none of whose
names appears in the preceding list, is sent to IDDO ... AT THE
PLACE CASIPHIA. More probably we should render: 'he com-
missioned them (to go) to Iddo' – the language is formal. The
curious place name – unidentified – appears twice in the same
form: 'Casiphia the place', and since the word for 'place' is
often used in the sense of 'holy place', it is natural to see here
a reference to a sanctuary at this particular town. Indeed,
where more natural to find Levites and other temple officers?
The information is important since it makes it clear that there
were other holy places for the Jewish community; the ideal
of the one holy place at Jerusalem was not necessarily to be
so narrowly understood. And this is confirmed by our knowledge of the contemporary temple at Elephantine whose worshippers made appeal in the last years of the fifth century for
support in restoration both from the governor in Samaria and
from the authorities in Jerusalem; nor did they meet with any

denial from Jerusalem of the propriety of their temple's existence.

21-23. Preparation for the journey is in the religious observance of A FAST and in prayer for protection. Confidence in divine protection makes it impossible to ask for a royal bodyguard. The confident faith is expressed in the words of a poetic saying:

The hand of our God rests for good upon all who seek him;
His power and his wrath against all who forsake him.

24-30. A further stage of preparation is concerned first to emphasize the colossal treasures being taken to the temple at Jerusalem; the figures for gold and silver are beyond all belief. These represent the royal support from Persia and the offerings made by ALL ISRAEL, and they include temple vessels of silver, and BOWLS OF GOLD, and TWO VESSELS OF FINE BRIGHT BRONZE AS PRECIOUS AS GOLD (v.27). The numeral appears as 'twelve' in I Esdras; the LXX has 'various'. Certainly the very small figure appears rather oddly in so impressive a list. But value is not all. The theme of v.28 is the holiness of the VESSELS and of those appointed to guard them on the way; here the implication may be that it is their holiness, their belonging to God, which is their real protection from danger. Verses 29-30 lay emphasis upon the completeness of the treasures and in particular of the vessels; worship at the temple will depend upon the full provision of the vessels and treasures appointed to be brought.

31-34. By contrast with the extensive emphasis on the preparations, the journey itself is very briefly described. If v.31 is correlated with 7.8, the arrival falls four months after departure, in the fifth month of Artaxerxes' seventh year. The journey is again pronounced to be under divine protection. Another pause of THREE DAYS (v.32, cf. v.15) ushers in the formal handing over of the treasures and VESSELS to the appropriate PRIEST and LEVITES, and the total in number and weight recorded (vv.33f.). Again the emphasis rests upon com-

pleteness, and hence by implication upon the perfection of
worship.

35-36. A celebration by the whole community, described in
terms of THOSE WHO HAD COME FROM CAPTIVITY, THE RETURNED
EXILES, again points to the totality of Israel in the use of the
numerals TWELVE, NINETY-SIX, and probably 'seventy-two' with
I Esdras for the SEVENTY-SEVEN of the Hebrew text. THE
KING'S COMMISSIONS too are delivered throughout the province, and people and temple are given support. Actually these
last two verses mark a change-over again to a third-person
narrative, and this links closely with the logical sequel to this
chapter, namely Neh. 8, which is also in the third person,
whereas Ezra 9 is in the first-person form, followed by Ezra
10 in the third person. This interchange of forms is not necessarily to be regarded as indicating separate sources; it is more
probably to be seen as a difference of style even within the
same narrative material. Examples are to be found in Isa. 6-7;
Hos. 1 and 3; and it may be that the first-person passages in
the Acts of the Apostles – the so-called 'we passages' often
used in relation to the question of authorship – are in reality
only the result of this particular stylistic device.

THE PEOPLE'S FAILURE

9.1-15

A note on the order of the narratives. Both the form of the
text and that to be found in I Esdras follow the same order of
the material, though the absence of the Nehemiah sections in
I Esdras means that Neh. 8 follows immediately on Ezra 10
(cf. I Esd. 9, where vv. 36-37 mark the transition). But the
sequence is not altogether satisfactory, for such chronological
information as is provided points to a rather odd situation.
The journey, as we have seen, is placed in the opening months
of Artaxerxes' seventh year, the party reaching Jerusalem
in the fifth month – in the summer. Ezra 10.9 places the action
of foreign wives as being initiated, after the preliminaries of

prayer and confession in 9.1-10.8, in the ninth month – in the winter – and completed in the period from the tenth month to the first day of the new year (year eight, 10.16f.). In Neh. 8, the reading of the law is placed in the seventh month (7.73*b*, 8.2), and this is followed by fasting later in the same month (9.1). If this order is correct, we have to assume a lapse of over a year after Ezra's arrival before the law is read, though this inculcation of the law is presented as the prime object of his journey. (Of course, the matter is aggravated out of all proportion if the biblical chronology is followed exactly as it stands, for then Ezra, having reached Jerusalem and taken certain action in Artaxerxes' seventh year, appears to have done nothing further until Nehemiah arrived in the twentieth year.) It is arguable that the order as presented is correct. Before the law could be applied, the major problem of foreign marriages must be dealt with. But the more natural order is to see Ezra as waiting only two months after his arrival, until the appropriate moment in the seventh month which was traditionally associated with the reading of the law (cf. Deut. 31.10), and following this up by firm action against a particular abuse. The relationship between the various sections is not, in fact, as simple as this; but this order appears to be the most intelligible. Moreover, it is possible for us to see a good theological reason for the Chronicler's present arrangement of the narrative. If the merely chronological order was followed, the last stage in the work would be the foreign-marriage action, a rather gloomy ending to a work which quite evidently sees the period of Ezra as a high point of hope; the Chronicler's order presents as the culmination of the whole the reading and acceptance of the law (Neh. 8) and the prayer and renewal of covenant described in Neh. 9-10, a fitting climax in worship and obedience to the theme of the true and faithful people of God. It is important in reading the various narratives to see both the probable chronological sequence and also the significance of the Chronicler's arrangement of his material.

1. After these things had been done The loose connecting phrase (cf. II Chron. 31.1 etc.) does not mark any precise relationship with what precedes. The first-person form of the narrative, after its interruption in 8.35-36, also marks a new and not directly connected section.

The officials A general term perhaps or one which indicates the leading laymen. They report on the failure of the community to conform to the laws which forbid intermarriage with other peoples.

The list of peoples is paralleled closely in many occurrences of such a description of the former inhabitants of the land of Israel; lists of six or seven peoples (e.g. Gen. 15.20) are used to stress the action of God in giving this land to his people (so e.g. Neh. 9.8). But the lists are also used, as here, for a negative purpose, as a warning to the people against forming connections with the alien world, and here Deut. 7.1-4 is one of a number of passages in which the point is made that no kind of contact is to be established. Indeed, Deuteronomy (cf. 20.17) enjoins the total destruction of these peoples so that contact with their abominations will be impossible. The recognition that the peoples were not so destroyed is then explained in various ways, and their continued existence is indicated as a source of disobedience and of evil consequences (cf. Judg. 3.5f.). This is the point here.

The lists vary among themselves, though in general the same names are given. Here we may recognize the conventional list, which is almost entirely of peoples whose continued existence in the time of Ezra must be regarded as very doubtful: they have become names symbolic of the alien world. The mention of EGYPTIANS is unusual, and is probably to be seen both as a reflection on the Exodus traditions and also as deriving from prophetic diatribe against alliance with Egypt (cf. e.g. Isa. 30; 31). AMMONITES and MOABITES are the subject of a particularly violent attack in Deut. 23.3-6 (cf. the same theme in Neh. 13.1f.), perhaps deriving from the hostile contacts between these peoples and Israel during the monarchy. The appearance of THE AMORITES is again antiquarian, but an alternative reading of 'Edomites' would point to that antagonism between Israel and Edom which is typified in the

Jacob/Esau traditions in Genesis and expressed also in the numerous prophetic attacks on Edom (cf. esp. Mal. 1.1ff. and comments on II Chron. 25.11f.). There is probably here a combination of historical reminiscence and later experience of conflict with this community (eventually to be associated with the hatred of the Idumaeans and focussed on such a figure as Herod the Great), but also a symbolic use of Edom as the representative of the outside world.

2. The observance of the conventional nature of these names shows how in this passage older themes are being used to express a very deep concern of the post-exilic community. And this is made clear in the second clause: THE HOLY RACE HAS MIXED ITSELF WITH THE PEOPLES OF THE LANDS. The preservation of the true people, in its absolute allegiance to God, is a deeply felt concern. The reading of the older history as this is presented in the Deuteronomic History, and also in the writings of the Chronicler, points to contact with other peoples as a prime cause of religious failure. The obverse of this must be the view that purity of religion can only follow from purity of race. It is a concern for protection, a concern for proper obedience. Its narrowness of view must be understood in the context of a situation in which it appeared all too easy for right faith and life to be dissipated. (Another aspect of this problem is to be seen in Mal. 2.10-12.)

in this faithlessness The prominent part has been played by leading members of the community, and this makes the situation even more serious. It is small wonder that we find Ezra performing a ritual associated with mourning and distress, and that, like Ezekiel (3.15), he SAT APPALLED (v.3). Confronted by such evidence of apostasy, the ardent upholder of the law must feel the deepest distress.

4. The picture of those who are in awe at the divine commands (cf. the reaction of Josiah to the reading of the law in II Chron. 34.19), gathered around the distressed leader, is very reminiscent of the pictures of Ezekiel and the elders who gather around him (cf. Ezek. 8.1). We may note that the faithlessness is that of THE RETURNED EXILES, a term used to describe the true community.

5. After a day of such reaction – RSV mentions FASTING, the meaning given in later Hebrew to a word which only occurs here in the Old Testament but which is better understood as 'humiliation, self-abasement' – Ezra offers prayer at the time of THE EVENING SACRIFICE, an appropriate moment for prayer to be offered and heard.

6-15. The prayer contains various elements and is partly prayer, partly sermon.

6-7. In the opening, Ezra, associating himself fully with the community, makes a statement of GUILT, rooted as it is in history of the people; the resumé alludes rapidly to the events leading up to CAPTIVITY, to a condition which is regarded as still existing. To the Chronicler, the captivity is not yet over.

8-9. We now have a further insight into this understanding of the contemporary situation. There is FAVOUR shown FOR A BRIEF MOMENT, A REMNANT has been left, there is a SECURE HOLD WITHIN HIS HOLY PLACE, relief from BONDAGE. The word for SECURE HOLD actually means a 'peg', a possible allusion to Isa. 22.22-24 where an official is so designated, as one upon whom the whole weight of his father's house can be hung. This seems a more likely point of analogy than to understand it as a 'tent-peg' and to compare the use of this as a theme for the restored Jerusalem in Isa. 54.2. But a very small change, attested in one manuscript, would give another word for 'remnant', and this is clearly also a possible sense. The restoration is here depicted as a signal example of divine favour, and it is further related to the policy of the Persian kings who have been moved by him to bring about the repairing of the temple and PROTECTION (literally 'a wall') IN JUDEA AND JERUSALEM. This idea of a protective wall to the whole community is clearly metaphorical (cf. Ps. 80.12, using the same word, and also Zech. 2.1-4 for the idea), and makes no reference to the rebuilding of the city walls (a quite different word) under Nehemiah. But BONDAGE (slavery), though alleviated, continues. The Chronicler is very conscious of the position of his people as subject to Persian, alien, rule (cf. also Neh. 9.36f.).

10-12. This is a confession of failure in terms of what is described as prophetic command, based on a quotation full of reminiscences of earlier Old Testament passages, though not itself a precise quotation of any one. It picks up phrases particularly from Deut. 7.1-3; 23.6; Ezek. 23.32; Lev. 18.24ff., laying stress upon three words which speak of contamination by contact with the alien world of the nations: POLLUTIONS, ABOMINATIONS, UNCLEANNESS. It goes further than other passages known to us in describing the LAND as UNCLEAN when Israel entered it (v.11), though we may see this as a quite logical development from the thought of the land as previously possessed by nations whose religious practices were regarded as improper. It is notable also that this complex of allusions is regarded as a prophetic word, for this points to a conception of the older writings as having the authority of the divine word mediated through the prophets. We are moving into an understanding of scripture as prophetic word, as divine command.

13-14. The hortatory tone already evident in these verses is now taken further, as the prayer form is left behind. What we really have, even though couched in the form of an address to God, is a strong remonstrance with the people not to respond in further disobedience to God's mercy and judgment – though that is described as LESS THAN OUR INIQUITIES DESERVED. Such a response could only lead to total destruction, with NO REMNANT at all. In the light of the Chronicler's description of the judgment of exile, this is a pointer to the possibility which the people must never forget, that God might in judgment bring his people to a final end. It is a reminder that the very existence of the people depends upon divine favour, a favour not to be lightly assumed as if it would permit disobedience to continue.

15. The final verse draws the themes together in an acknow-

ledgment of the justice of God, the status of the people as a
REMNANT THAT HAS ESCAPED and inevitably therefore in itself
a reminder of judgment. With such GUILT upon them, the
people cannot STAND before God.

This prayer passage is of greater importance than in its
shedding light upon the demand for racial purity which is
here made a central theme of the work of Ezra. It provides
an occasion for showing how the community could see itself
– in the eyes of one of its most distinguished thinkers – as
totally dependent upon God. The Chronicler is not one to
pass lightly over the present condition of his people as a
small subject province (cf. also Neh. 9.32-37). He is aware
of ancient and greater ideals, such as are expressed in the
picture of the empire over which the greatest of her kings
once ruled (cf. 4.20; and comments on 7.25). It may be that
he was also aware of political moves in his own time, hopes
of independence whenever there were changes in the international scene. The threats to Persian security in the time of
Ezra; some indications of rebellion in the mid-fourth century; perhaps even the beginnings of the threat from Greece
which was to overwhelm Persia when Alexander came on the
scene – all these may have moved some in the community to
suppose that success lay in military action, perhaps in the
re-establishment of Davidic rule. For the Chronicler, the
Davidic hope lay not in this, but in the way of true worship
and obedience. He appears as a political quietist, a true
successor of the prophet Isaiah – and of others – who proclaimed that 'in quietness and in trust shall be your strength'
(Isa. 30.15).

THE DISMISSAL OF FOREIGN WIVES

10.1-44

The narrative continues in third-person form, but the closeness of the link makes it clear that this is to be seen simply
as stylistic variation.

1. The prayer of Ezra is now presented as being the occasion for a GREAT assembly to gather, to join with him in the expression of distress in WEEPING.

2-5. The confession of sin already expressed by the leaders in 9.1f. and by Ezra himself is now taken up by a representative of the assembly, perhaps to be assumed as himself one of the leaders referred to earlier. The acknowledgment of failure is accompanied by an expression of HOPE which picks up the exhortation of Ezra in 9.14 and points to the need for A COVENANT, an undertaking to dismiss all the foreign wives and their children. Such a response is in accord with Ezra's own counsel – implicit in his prayer – and that of all THOSE WHO TREMBLE AT THE COMMANDMENT OF OUR GOD, i.e. who are in awe and show proper regard for the law (vv.2-3). In v.4 a summons to Ezra to act in the confidence that he will be supported by the community is underlined with an echo of words of faith like those spoken by Joshua to the Israelites at the beginning of the conquest (Josh. 1.9). The result is a covenanting by OATH by THE LEADING PRIESTS AND LEVITES AND ALL ISRAEL (v.5).

6. The sequel is unexplained. It describes Ezra's withdrawal for a period of MOURNING; the more elaborate parallel here to 9.5 could perhaps suggest that the present form of the narrative actually incorporates more than one element. So notable an occasion as this might well be expected to have been related in more than one manner – in one the summons comes from leaders and Ezra responds with mourning and prayer (9.1-15); in the other the summons comes from a single named leader, SHECANIAH, and issues in a covenant ceremonial and an expression of mourning and prayer by Ezra (10.2-6). In that case 10.1 would be a link verse to bind the two together. The second element has the greater precision of detail, with the naming of Shecaniah and the statement about Ezra's going to a room belonging to JEHOHANAN THE SON OF ELIASHIB. It is tempting to believe that this Eliashib is the one who is known from the Nehemiah narrative as high priest in his time (Neh. 3.1; 13.28), and in that case Jehohanan could be his grand-

son; in Neh. 12.22 a priestly list sets out Eliashib, Joiada,
Johanan, Jaddua, while 12.23 describes Johanan as the son
of Eliashib. There is evidence in the Elephantine papyri for
a Johanan as high priest in about 410 BC (cf. ANET, p.492;
DOTT, p.263). Whether son or grandson, he would fit quite
reasonably into a chronological sequence placing Nehemiah
in 445 and Ezra in 398. Furthermore, there is evidence in
Josephus (*Antiquities*, XI, 7, 1) for the line Eliashib, Judas,
John, and the last of these is said to have murdered his brother
Jesus in the temple apparently because Jesus was trying to
get the high priesthood for himself. This story, if it is
historical and if it really belongs to this time – for Josephus'
account of the whole period raises considerable chronological
problems – would then seem to create a rather odd situation.
Here, it would appear, is Ezra, the faithful upholder of the
law, actually occupying a room belonging to a high priest
who was guilty of fratricide. Perhaps we should accept this
and recognize both that we do not really know anything about
the circumstances and also that it is idle for us to try to apply
to the situation of Ezra's time the kind of ethical criteria which
would be appropriate later. A threat to the high priesthood
was, after all, to be taken as a very serious crime. But there
are so many uncertainties and so many cases where names
coincide but do not refer to the same people that we should
not suppose that we can prove the position one way or the
other.

7-17. The carrying through of the dismissal procedure is now
described.

7-8. The whole community, THE RETURNED EXILES, is sum-
moned on pain of confiscation of property and exclusion from
membership of THE CONGREGATION – a term particularly used
for the religious assembly (so rendered in v.1).

9. The assembly takes place on THE TWENTIETH DAY of THE
NINTH MONTH, in winter, and in HEAVY RAIN. The text expresses
the people's condition in a remarkable example of syllepsis:
we might paraphrase it to bring out the construction as 'the

people trembled with apprehension and in the heavy rain'.

10-11. An address by Ezra, here described as THE PRIEST, pronounces the offence and calls on the assembly to praise God, i.e. to acknowledge him for what he is and hence to make confession, and to do his will by separating themselves from alien contact.

12. The appeal meets with a response by acclamation.

13-14. These verses, evidently not to be taken literally as part of the assembly's reply, represent the working out of a manageable scheme for dealing with the problem. Central officials are to act, and to deal with individual cases in the local communities in consultation with the local ELDERS and JUDGES. A very slight emendation of v.14 would give '... the elders of each city, and let them (i.e. the officials and the elders) decide the cases ...' The point is again underlined that the removal of this cause of offence will serve to avert the divine WRATH. An unfit community, one which has in it that which is regarded as an abomination, something totally unacceptable to the deity, is one which cannot enjoy divine blessing but only divine wrath.

15. A note of opposition appears to be voiced. The fact that I Esdras (9.14), supported by other early translations, reverses the statement: 'Jonathan ... and Jahzeiah ... undertook the matter on these terms, and Meshullam and Levi and Shabbethai served with them as judges' may be explained simply on the assumption that a tradition of opposition was felt to be unacceptable. Ezra could only, on this view, have met with wholehearted support. It must be admitted that the sense of the text is not absolutely clear; the opening word, rendered ONLY, may be adversative, but it may also be used to mean 'in fact', and the words rendered OPPOSED THIS, while probably having this negative sense, are not certainly only so used, and could denote literally 'standing beside' in the sense of supporting. The fact that of the four mentioned, MESHULLAM and SHABBETHAI both appear in the list of active supporters of Ezra in Neh. 8.4, 7, provides additional support

for this interpretation. Another alternative, which fits well
with the text, is to suppose that their opposition is not to
the policy as such but simply to the procedure: were they
perhaps wanting even stricter action to be taken, perhaps having in mind that decisions made in the local communities
might be less firm than those made by central authority alone?
Yet another possibility is that the verse preserves an alternative to v.16 concerning the officials appointed for the inves-
tigation.

16-17. In a three-month period, from THE TENTH MONTH to
THE FIRST MONTH of the next year, the whole matter is dealt
with. The appointment of the officials was either made by
Ezra – so RSV translating an amended text – or we should
read 'and they set apart men ...' The Hebrew text appears
to represent a conflation of two readings offering these two
alternatives; one might well suppose that the more original of
the two contained no mention of Ezra's part, and that it was
subsequently believed that the decisions must have been his.
At this point, as perhaps also at some others in the narrative,
we may detect a tendency on the part of the Chronicler to
give greater prominence and authority to Ezra than the
original traditions indicated; it is a very natural development
in view of the position which he accorded to Ezra.

18-44. The list of those found guilty is now given. First,
PRIESTS, including significantly four members of the high
priestly house (v.18) and then priests of other orders (vv.19-21).
In the case of the priests there is a full statement of the procedure: an undertaking to divorce their wives, and the offering of the appropriate sacrifices. We may assume that a similar
procedure applied to the other groups, unless it is proper to
see in this fuller action for the priesthood the recognition that
without such a ritual it would be impossible for them to continue to function.

A small number of LEVITES, SINGERS and GATEKEEPERS
follow (vv.23-24), and then the longer list of ISRAEL in which
we may observe a number of the same family names as in
2.3-35. The total – of which the exact computation depends

on decisions about some confusions and corruptions in the text – amounts to little over one hundred men, and it has been felt by some commentators that this is so small as to suggest that the list must be incomplete, perhaps including only the prominent persons (cf. 9.2). But, on the view which the whole narrative presupposes about the relationship between God and people, even *one* such case would defile (cf. the Achan narrative in Josh. 7 for a much older counterpart), and in any case some further comments may be made on the significance of the action (see below).

44. The final summary appears to consist of a resumptive statement: ALL THESE HAD MARRIED FOREIGN WOMEN, and then a very evidently corrupted second clause which could perhaps be amended to read 'and they sent away wives and children'. This could also be understood as a mutilated conclusion to the narrative of vv.16-17 into which the list has been inserted; its text is obscure, the Hebrew actually meaning 'and some of them were women, and they had set (?borne) sons (children)'.

Whatever precisely we make of this account of the dismissing of foreign wives – and it is evident that to a modern reader the injustice and the inconsiderateness of the policy loom large – we must understand the underlying purpose, which is the preservation of the life and faith of the community. We should not underestimate the sense of threat to a relatively small religious group, and the urgency with which it was felt proper to deal with the danger. Since the narrative tells us nothing whatever of what became of the divorced wives and of their children, we cannot assume that nothing was done to meet their needs, nor can we supply imaginatively the kind of social and remedial action which a later community might think proper. We have absolutely no means of knowing what, if anything, was done. A divorced wife would presumably again become the responsibility of her own family. The narrative is concerned not with this but with the nature of the community's life.

We may, however, consider more closely the reasons for

the action undertaken, and here there is some evidence, both
in Ezra 2 = Neh. 7 and in somewhat later practice, to suggest
the extent and the reason for what was done. Racial purity,
even where there appear to be very strict rules, is very difficult to preserve, even supposing it to be a good thing, which
is, after all, very doubtful indeed. In any community, inter-
marriage does tend to take place, and the Old Testament
provides evidence both for a stricter view and for a very large
measure of openness of practice. It is evident that the Jewish
community in the post-exilic period was in fact of very mixed
ancestry; the ideal is a relative one. But at one point we can
observe a greater strictness, namely in regard to the priesthood. In many of the Old Testament laws, there is a stricter
code for the priesthood than for ordinary people. Thus much
stricter limits are laid down to the extent to which a priest
may properly come in contact with the dead: such contact
was held to involve defilement and therefore to necessitate
appropriate rituals of cleansing, and for the priests it was
therefore limited to the nearest relatives according to a strictly
regulated code (Lev. 21.1-4). Similarly there are stricter
marriage laws for priests (e.g. Lev. 21.7) and for the high
priest (Lev. 21.13-15). Ezra 2.61ff. = Neh. 7.63ff. (see comments above) are concerned with priests who could not prove
their genealogy, and were therefore excluded from the full
priestly activities. In later Judaism, various schemes were
drawn up to govern the assessment of status in order to ensure
that no priest was unfit for his office as a result of any alien
contact. What we might describe as the top stratum consists
of those, priests, Levites and Israel (i.e. full Israelites), where
it was necessary for a pure descent to be proved if there were
to be marriage into a priestly family. A lower stratum, where
there could be found some impurity, was excluded from
marriage with priestly families, but not excluded from marriage
with Levites or ordinary Israelites, and below this there was
yet a third stratum where there were more serious questions
of ancestry. In other words, we may be able to see in Ezra
9-10 the counterpart to the concern about correct genealogy
for priests in Ezra 2; what is important is that there should

be an absolute assurance of fitness at the centre, for without this the community would be at risk. We may see a
partial counterpart to this in the demand for 'apostolic succession' for Christian priesthood; it is a method, almost at
times a device, for stressing the need to preserve the faith
firmly at the very centre. (For some of the evidence here,
cf. J. Jeremias, *Jerusalem in the Time of Jesus*, SCM Press,
London 1969, Part IV).

THE BOOK OF NEHEMIAH

THE WORK OF NEHEMIAH – I

Nehemiah 1–7

JERUSALEM IN DISTRESS

1.1–11

1. The words of Nehemiah the son of Hacaliah This heading, with which the narrative of Nehemiah begins, can be understood as meaning 'the acts of Nehemiah' and hence 'the history of Nehemiah'. But it is worth noting that the formula is that used at the beginning of the books of Amos and Jeremiah; this is not the only feature of the account which suggests that Nehemiah was being described in certain respects as a prophetic figure. What follows is not, of course, a prophetic call, but it relates an incident which provides the moment for Nehemiah to be shown as inspired to undertake the task to which he is called. The influence of the prophetic books appears not unlikely.

A precise date for his activity is given (cf. also 2.1). The two dates do not accord unless we make the unlikely supposition that the system here used is that in which the new year begins in the autumn. For the winter month CHISLEV, the ninth month, would be later in the year than the spring month Nisan (2.1), the first month with the normal Babylonian system of the new year beginning in the spring. There would appear to be an error here (read 'nineteenth'), since 5.14 sets Nehemiah's governorship from the twentieth to the thirty-second year. The king's name, Artaxerxes, appears only at 2.1. and this must be Artaxerxes I (465–424). This is confirmed by the priest's name Eliashib (3.1) and also by the fact that Sanballat the governor of Samaria, who is active in opposition

264

to Nehemiah, is mentioned in the Elephantine papyri *c.* 410 only by reference to his sons. By then he was evidently elderly.

No indication is given of the political background to the opening of the narrative. But the period around 450 BC was one of considerable upheavals in the western part of the Persian empire, and the commissioning of Nehemiah in 445 could therefore be, from the Persian point of view, a means of establishing a greater degree of security and order in an important area for the control of the lines of communication to Egypt. The opening scene is placed in SUSA THE CAPITAL, or better 'Susa the citadel', the winter residence of the Persian rulers.

2. The occasion is that of a visit – or is it perhaps a delegation? – from Jerusalem of HANANI, brother or kinsman of Nehemiah (the former seems likely from the reference in 7.2), together with others who have been in Jerusalem. The point at issue is immediately raised by questions concerning the state of THE JEWS THAT SURVIVED, WHO HAD ESCAPED EXILE, AND CONCERNING JERUSALEM.

In view of what we have seen of the Chronicler's thought about the exile, with his supposition that nothing was left in Judah at all (cf. II Chron. 36.21), we may see this as referring to the community as the descendants of those who had become the remnant, the survivors of the captivity. It is this community which is the true heir of the past. It must be admitted, however, that an alternative interpretation is possible: the phrase could refer to those who had not actually undergone captivity at all. This would produce a marked difference of understanding from that found in the Chronicler, and it is possible that the Nehemiah narrative originally presented this rather different view, and that it is only in the context of the Chronicler that the narrative has come to be understood as presenting the same view as he does. The main narrative is in any case concerned with the community as separated from alien influences in Palestine rather than with presenting its origin as deriving from the exilic situation.

3. The reply, using the same phraseology, points to distress and specifically to the breaching of the city WALL (better than RSV BROKEN DOWN) and the burning of the GATES. We have already noted (see pp.229ff.) that Ezra 4.7-23, dated in the reign of Artaxerxes (I?), points to an attempt to rebuild the walls which was prevented by a royal decision based on a complaint. Force, we are told, was used to stop the work, and this could have resulted in the condition here described. Certainly we should expect there to be a reference to some event more recent than the destruction of the city in 587, 140 years earlier. But although this is likely enough, we may wonder whether this narrative is really concerned with so precise a point. The walls of Jerusalem appear as a theme of prophecy in Isa. 54.11f.; 60.10ff., and the theme of protection in a visionary prophecy in Zech. 2.4f. The breached walls are a symbol of the distressed condition of the community. We may observe too that in II Macc. 1.18-23 the restoration, including the rebuilding of the temple and the re-establishing of worship, is attributed entirely to Nehemiah, with no mention of any other stage in recovery. That account can hardly be dependent on this, since it makes such very different statements. But it does suggest the existence of a belief that Nehemiah was the one primarily responsible for restoration, and we may note the appearance of his name in great prominence in Ecclus. 49.13, in the listing of the heroes, immediately alongside the mention of Zerubbabel and Jeshua. Is chronology again here being telescoped in the interests of a theological point?

4-11a. Nehemiah's response – like that of Ezra when confronted by a situation of distress (Ezra 9.3f.; 10.1) – is in weeping and mourning, prayer and fasting.

4. God of heaven. We may note the use of the expression both in the narrative and in the prayer itself, as also in Ezra 1 and other passages.

5. The prayer follows a clear liturgical pattern, its wording

being particularly close to Deuteronomy and other material
in style.

the great and terrible, who keeps covenant and steadfast love
For this address, cf. Deut. 7.9, 21.

6-7. The deity is called upon to hear the prayer which is
offered (cf. Ps. 130.2 and the prayer of Solomon in I Kings
8 and II Chron. 6.20, 40; 7.15). In the confession of his people's
sin – not specified but assumed and set out in very general
terms of disobedience to the COMMANDMENTS of God mediated
by MOSES (v.7) – Nehemiah specifically involves himself and
his own family. Like Ezra (9.6) and like the prophets (e.g.
Isa. 6.5), Nehemiah knows that he is bound up in his people's
failure and does not in any way stand over against them in
judgment. The assumption underlying these verses is that the
continued distress of Jerusalem and its ruined state must
derive from the people's sin; the counterpart of this will be
seen in the act of divine grace by which restoration becomes
possible.

8-9. Next, the prayer recalls the divine threat mediated by
Moses, that the people would be scattered AMONG THE PEOPLES
if they were UNFAITHFUL, but that God would GATHER THEM
again in Jerusalem if they repented. These verses may be
compared most closely with Deut. 30.1-5, but also with such
passages as Deut. 4.25-31; Lev. 26.27-45, and it is also a
theme of the prayer of Solomon (II Chron. 6.36-39). The
emphasis on Jerusalem as the place where God has caused
his NAME to DWELL is particularly characteristic of Deuteronomic thought.

10. A theme of appeal is introduced: the people belong to
God and are his SERVANTS, and the basis of this is the Exodus
events in which God's redemptive action was to be seen in
THY GREAT POWER and THY STRONG HAND (cf. e.g. Deut. 9.29);
an allusion could also be intended here to the 'new Exodus'
after the exile (cf. Ezra 1).

11a. A further appeal for hearing (cf. v.6) again unites

Nehemiah as the one who offers the prayer and his people, described again as the SERVANTS of God and as those WHO DELIGHT TO FEAR THY NAME. In the final clause of the prayer comes the application of the whole to the particular situation; a prayer whose wording is entirely general thereby becomes specific. A comparison may be made between the appeal that THIS MAN – i.e. the king – would show favour to Nehemiah and the way in which Esther is depicted as approaching king Ahasuerus on behalf of her people (Esther 4.1-5.2; but much more fully developed with prayers and appropriate rituals in the apocryphal form of the book, where the sections 13.8-15.16 provide material to insert between 4.17 and 5.1 and to replace 5.1-2).

11b. Now I was cupbearer ...   This last clause may be treated as explicative of the preceding passage and also as introductory to ch.2. It makes the point – clear also in the stories told about Daniel and about Mordecai in the book of Esther – that Jews might rise to high office in the alien government. The Joseph stories in Genesis and to a limited extent the Moses traditions make a similar point. In such a position, we may see expressed an ideal of obedience and faithfulness maintained even when it might have been possible for a Jew to gain greater power or honour by disclaiming connection with his own people. It is a theme of popular tales in other contexts too; it also provides a basis for encouragement and exhortation to equal faith and obedience. The fact that Nehemiah is found (2.6) in the presence of THE QUEEN has suggested that he might have been a eunuch, and it has been thought that this would also explain the repeated emphasis on 'remember me, O my God' (e.g. 13.31). That a man's sons and further descendants would be his memorial, keep his memory alive, is a common theme of Old Testament thought, and much attention was devoted to the preserving of a man's name. We may note too that whereas the eunuch was excluded from membership of the people of God (cf. Deut. 23.1), in Isa. 56.3-5 – a passage very difficult to date, but within the section 56-66 probably belonging to the early post-exilic period – the eunuch is promised acceptance. The Greek translation here offers two different renderings. In one form of the text we have cup-bearer (*oinochoos*); in another eunuch (*eunouchos*). The similarity of the words could have led to an error in copying, but the rendering 'eunuch' could hardly have arisen unless the supposition had already existed that Nehemiah was one. On balance, the supposition is unlikely; since the narrative contains considerable evidence of hostility to Nehemiah, we might have expected there to be some more direct hint of this disability which would make him, at least in the view of stricter Jews, unacceptable as a leader and for ordering religious matters (cf. esp. ch.13).

NEHEMIAH'S COMMISSION

2.1-20

1. No explanation is given for the lapse of time between the bringing of the news to Nehemiah and his request to the king in the first month (NISAN) of the new year (spring 445). Since the clause WHEN WINE WAS BEFORE HIM may contain an error for 'before me', i.e. 'when I had charge of the wine' (following some duty system unknown to us), we could surmise that it was only at this point that he was able to approach the king. The difficulty of approaching the Persian king is one of the themes of the book of Esther (cf. chs.4-5). The last clause has been variously interpreted. RSV, without indicating it, really depends on a small emendation, better shown by rendering 'I had not been sad previously'. Other possibilities are 'I was not out of favour with him' or, treating the negative as emphatic, 'I certainly was sad in his presence'.

2-5. The king's recognition of Nehemiah's distress evokes great fear. Since much in the narrative suggests Nehemiah's position as a royal favourite, we may wonder why he was afraid, unless something in the king's tone of voice were to imply displeasure. The phrase might express his sense of awe at the working of the divine purpose, his realization that he is confronted with the opportunity of being the instrument of that purpose. His reply indicates his concern for THE CITY – the name Jerusalem is not mentioned, but we have no reason to suppose that the king was ignorant of Nehemiah's homeland; it is described as the place of MY FATHERS' SEPULCHRES, an expression of a proper piety towards the place with which one's ancestry is connected. A proper respect is shown by concern for burial, and burial places are not to be desecrated.

6. As in the comparable story of Darius and Zerubbabel in I Esd. 4.42ff., the occasion is one for the granting of whatever request is put. Such a fairy-tale element may correspond to the reality of a ruler who acts according to whim, but we may probably believe that the whim was not altogether unconnected with possibilities of political advantage. Renewed prayer by Nehemiah at this point would concern the precise nature of the divine will, since it is already evident that favour is being shown by the king. The request sets out the basic commission as that of being appointed to have charge of the rebuilding of the city: only subsequently in the narrative is Nehemiah described as 'governor' (5.14), though the term *peḥāh* is used so broadly that we cannot precisely define the nature and limits of his function. A term of office is fixed; the language seems to imply reluctance on the king's (and perhaps the queen's) part to let him go, but probably we should see here simply a further indication of the overruling divine will which permits a twelve-year period of office (5.14), a period long enough to ensure total re-establishment of life in Jerusalem.

the queen The term is a rare one, used also in Ps. 45.10 for the royal consort. Her presence may indicate a private occasion, but could also mark a public feast (cf. Dan. 5.2). The implication is that she too was involved in the action, exerting an influence like that of Esther upon her husband; but this aspect of the theme is not developed here.

7-8. Further details of the commission are given: royal pro-

tection with the provincial governors is to be important
support, as is a royal authorization for TIMBER from THE
KING'S FOREST (or 'park'; the word *pardēs* is the origin of
our 'paradise'), either in the Lebanon for cedars or nearer at
hand in some royal domain, apparently under the control of
a Jewish official, ASAPH. The repair is to include THE FORTRESS
OF THE TEMPLE (cf. also 7.2), a reference which has been
thought anachronistic and more appropriate to the second
century BC, when we have clearer evidence (cf. I Macc. 1.33).
But ancient temples were often strong-points, and temple and
royal palace belonged closely together in Jerusalem. Work on
the CITY WALL is expected; the reference to THE HOUSE WHICH
I SHALL OCCUPY seems to point to a new or repaired governor's
residence. The explicit reference to fortification in this makes
it clear that Nehemiah was absolutely trusted by the king
and perhaps also that the king had in mind the re-establishing
of a strong Jerusalem for the protection of the route to Egypt
(cf. p.265). The whole section vv.1-8 is drawn together with
the acknowledgment of divine favour and protection in the
final lines. The words echo those of Ezra 5.5; 7.6, 9, 28.

9. The sequel immediately makes plain the skilfully drawn
contrast between divine (and hence royal) support and opposition. The provincial governors are under royal orders, and
Nehemiah has a military escort.

10. But certain notable figures appear (to whom a third is
added in v.19) who are to constitute the opposition. We can
immediately detect the delicacy of the position both for them
and for Nehemiah. The royal favourite occupies a privileged
place, and those who oppose him may find themselves incurring
royal displeasure. At the same time, royal favour is notoriously
fickle, and Nehemiah would not have been the first royal
favourite to betray his trust if he had in fact been set on
rebellion (cf. v.19). Underlying the opposition there must lie
various motives.

Sanballat A Babylonian name – 'Sin, the moon god, gives
life'; but this tells us nothing of his religion. He is associated

with Horon, presumably the well-known place Beth-horon north-west of Jerusalem. He is known to us from the Elephantine papyri in his official capacity as 'governor of Samaria', though by the last decade of the century his sons, Delaiah and Shelemaiah, were evidently acting for him. But their names indicate him as a Yahwist, and indeed nothing in the Nehemiah narrative suggests anything else.

Tobiah Another Yahwist name. His title THE SERVANT is an honorific one, given to kings, and his designation as THE AMMONITE is unlikely to indicate his origin but rather his position, probably as governor or other high officer in the Transjordan area, and perhaps an ancestor of the later Tobiad family indicated in the third-century Zeno papyri and in the political rivalries of the second century. It was easy for both these terms to be given a derogatory interpretation: 'Tobiah, the Ammonite slave'.

Geshem the Arab The third opponent (Gashmu in 6.6) is likely to be another influential personage, perhaps a leader of southern or south-eastern Arab groups, perhaps a royal officer in that area. All three would then represent the neighbouring authorities, resentful at the prospect of a revival of prosperity and well-being for Jerusalem. We may see here political opposition – resentment at a possible lessening of their own influence, especially if Nehemiah's appointment were to mean that Judah was to be a separate administrative area instead of remaining, as it probably had been for over a century, under the aegis of Samaria. We may suspect economic opposition, for a revived Judah and Jerusalem would take its share of trade profits. We may also, as the narratives develop, suspect some measure of personal opposition, especially because of Nehemiah's privileged position. Of religious opposition there is not a word. But however much we may detect these realities of a particular situation, we may also suspect some interpretation of the position in the light of the concept of the true people of God, and particularly of Jerusalem, as beset by enemies on every side. Such a picture of the attacks of the nations on Jerusalem is found in Pss. 2 and 46, and equally in a passage of prophecy not perhaps very far in date from Nehemiah, Zech. 14.1ff. God, as the true defender of his people, may be seen to reign supreme at the centre of their life and to protect the re-estab- lishment of city and people. We may note such an idea too in Zech. 2.1-5, which uses the city wall theme to stress such divine protection.

11-16. These verses describe a careful examination of the problems of rebuilding the walls and gates, undertaken by Nehemiah secretly BY NIGHT. The precise topographical details, as also in ch.3, must clearly correspond to Jerusalem as it was then known, but there are many uncertainties about the interpretation. The archaeological evidence points on the whole to the city still occupying in the south only the spur between the valleys known as Kidron and the Tyropoeon; the extent of the city north and west is very uncertain. The extent of the devastation at the Babylonian conquest points to the impossibility of rebuilding on the eastern slope of that spur, and perhaps helps to explain why it was impossible for Nehemiah to ride all round. Nor is it clear whether he carried out all the inspection from outside the walls, or completed it on the inside. As yet the fact that Nehemiah had come with royal authorization was clear, but not the precise nature of his commission. Verse 16 indicates that none of the people had been informed: the term THE JEWS should probably be taken as the general term – 'all the people of Judah' – speci- fied more precisely in the list of officials which follows. The last mentioned – THE REST THAT WERE TO DO THE WORK – perhaps indicates 'other administrators', or more generally 'those who were concerned in the matter'.

17-20. The sequel to the inspection is an appeal to all these to recognize the present distress of the city, a cause for DIS- GRACE in that Jerusalem cannot be properly honoured as the city of God in this condition. The relating of the divine favour to Nehemiah in royal support brings a response and a resolve to build. But the author skilfully brings in again a mention of the opposition. Mockery is one form of attack; an accusa-

tion of rebellion another (v.19). Nehemiah's reply is in terms
of divine support, and the refutation of any claim that the
opponents may believe they have in Jerusalem. They have
NO PORTION – a term appropriately used of territorial allocation; NO legal RIGHT – the word used more often to indicate
'righteousness', but here denoting a legal claim; NO MEMORIAL,
in the sense of 'no established rights from the past', no traditional hold (v.20). Set alongside such a passage as Ezra 4.1-5,
there seems to be a suggestion here of total repudiation of
religious opponents; but that is to read into the text more
than is present.

The possibility has been noted (cf. p.232) that the material
of Ezra 4.7-23 describes a situation immediately preceding
the activity of Nehemiah. If that is so, then we may suppose
a change of royal policy, brought about either by the appeal
being made by the royal favourite or by the changed political
situation which pointed to the need to strengthen Jerusalem.
But our knowledge of the period of Persian rule is so limited
that it is hazardous to put forward so precise a sequence.
And we have seen reason for thinking that even if there were
such an immediate cause, the author here is thinking of a
much broader setting for the work of Nehemiah. He is the
one who brings about the restoration of the people from the
disasters of exile, and an intermediate event may really be
irrelevant.

THE REBUILDERS AND THE OPPOSITION

3.1-4.6

Although this section is clearly made up of two quite
separate elements, it is proper to treat them together and
make the division where it is made in the Hebrew text, for
which this forms chapter 3. The first part is of an archival
kind (vv.1-32) and clearly depends on the completion of the
whole work; the completing of the gates here noted is indicated as undertaken by Nehemiah in 6.1 and 7.1. Indeed the

entire absence of any mention of Nehemiah in this list, and the only possible reference to him in v.5 'their Lord' (or 'lords'), using a word not otherwise employed of him, might even tempt one to suppose that here, as in other cases, a piece of archival material belonging to one situation has been applied to another. More probably we should see this as an alternative record of the rebuilding, in which prominence is given to ELIASHIB THE HIGH PRIEST, who heads the work (v.1). The whole constitutes an important documentary witness to the topography of Jerusalem, and to administrative matters for city and province. It has been placed neatly to fit between the confident affirmation of Nehemiah in 2.20 – 'we will arise and build', picked up in the opening phrase of 3.1 – and the recurrence of the opposition theme in 4.1-3 with its response in 4.4-5 and resumé in 4.6. There is evidence here of a skilful dovetailing of different elements within the Nehemiah material.

The archival material provides a wealth of information which is difficult to fit together to produce a coherent picture. It is clear that here, beginning from THE SHEEP GATE in v.1 and following through the sequence of gates mentioned in succeeding verses, a complete circuit of the city is given, ending at the starting point in v.32. But the positions of the gates cannot be defined with certainty, since our knowledge of the area enclosed by the city wall at this period remains very ill-defined, and other passages, notably in ch.12, give lists of gates which only partly correspond. The stretches of wall between the gates are also left unspecified except in one instance (v.13); drawing a plan of the city is not possible on this basis. A whole series of localities appears in the chapter; few of them can be identified with any real satisfaction. We may note, for example, THE POOL OF SHELAH in v.15; the word means probably a 'conduit', and it is probably equivalent to Shiloah (Isa. 8.6); but is it the same as that of Siloam?

Some of the builders are noted by personal names, though in some cases these may in fact denote families. The mention of a man AND HIS DAUGHTERS as builders in v.12 is odd, and more probably there is here an obscured reference to 'daughter villages' associated with builders from a particular locality. Some builders are listed by localities: JERICHO in v.2, TEKOA in vv.5 and 27, and others. GIBEON and MIZPAH in v.7 are described with a phrase which is of very uncertain interpretation: RSV's UNDER THE JURISDICTION OF THE GOVERNOR OF THE PROVINCE BEYOND THE RIVER, if correct, is still of uncertain meaning. Would it indicate that these places lay outside the control of Judah and really came under the direct rule of the provincial governor? An alternative interpretation would see a reference here to the stretch of wall being built 'up to the throne (i.e. residency) of the governor'. The mention of 'districts' connected with JERUSALEM (v.9, 12), BETH-HACCHEREM (v.14), MIZPAH (v.15), BETH-ZUR (v.16), KEILAH (v.18) – places west, north, south and south-east of Jerusalem – may indicate administrative areas. But the phrase used (see RSVmg) may indicate not rulers of areas but foremen of sections of wall-building.

Some builders are linked with guilds (GOLDSMITHS and PERFUMERS in v.8). Some are described as undertaking repairs opposite their own houses (v.23) or sections defined by particular houses (v.24). This becomes marked in the latter part of the list (cf. also vv.28f). If the circuit goes anti-clockwise, then this section would appear to cover a part of the east side, overlooking the Kidron valley. Here the old wall stood well down the hillside, but destruction was so great that it appears that it could not be restored, and the post-exilic wall stood much farther up. It has been suggested that at some points house walls were strengthened to make a replacement for the city wall and that this is reflected in these references.

The information is incomplete – at a number of points only one part of an item is given (cf. e.g. v.11, which refers to a second section repaired by two individuals, but the first section is not mentioned). There are obscure allusions, as in v.5 where the activity of the men of Tekoa is followed by a reference to the unwillingness of THEIR NOBLES (leaders) to condescend to serve their governor (or their God, or their overlords). The absence of expected place names – Bethlehem, for example – invites the question: did whole sections of

Judah not respond at all?

The text – as so often in lists – is at many points difficult and probably corrupt. It is said that the priests CONSECRATED the Sheep Gate (v.1); a small emendation would give (as in v.3): 'they laid its beams'. But perhaps the mentioning of the high priest and his associates first and the reference to consecration are intended to suggest that the whole rebuilding began, as it was to end (12.27ff.), with a religious act. In v.26 there is an ungrammatical reference to 'the temple servants (*Nethinim*) were living on Ophel', which is probably a marginal note, perhaps originally applied to v.27 and derived from 11.21, where it belongs. But the effect is made. The response of the leaders in 2.18 is set out in the activity of a great mass of builders, and the first impression (modified by 4.10) is of great enthusiasm.

4.1-6.* The enthusiasm here receives further emphasis. The opposition, in the person of SANBALLAT, emerges angry and mocking, by ridicule calling down scorn on the puny efforts of the Jews. The reference to THE ARMY OF SAMARIA is perhaps intended to point forward to more material opposition, but words of ill-omen have their own effect. The impossibility of the task of rebuilding is emphasized, and the futility of the work jeered at by the apparently sycophantic TOBIAH (v.3).

The answer to such mockery, directed against the builders but by implication against the God who has brought about the work, is in a prayer form in vv.4-5. It provides a counterpart to other words inviting divine remembrance for the good deeds of Nehemiah and for the evil deeds of his opponents (cf. 5.19; 6.14). The captivity, from which the people of God is being rescued by this re-establishment of its life, is called down upon the enemies (v.4). Their guilt is to remain perpetually (v.5). Such prayer forms may be found in the psalms (e.g. Ps. 109.6-19), and a particularly close parallel is in Jer. 18.23 and in other similar passages in Jeremiah in which the opponents of the prophet appear to be treated with equal vehemence. To understand such violent language, we need

* Heb. 3.33-38.

to appreciate fully the sense of the divine purpose at work, so that opposition is not seen in human terms but as opposition to God himself.

It is in this context of opposition that a confident statement is made, summing up the first stage: the wall reaches HALF ITS HEIGHT (or possibly, 'half its extent', 4.6). The second stage is to be marked by a similar interweaving of opposition and resolute action.

OPPOSITION AND RESOLVE

4.7-23*

7-9. A new phase of opposition introduces not only the two main enemies, SANBALLAT and TOBIAH, but also what is envisaged as whole populations – ARABS to the south, AMMONITES to the east, ASHDODITES to the west. These last represent the administrative area known as Ashdod from Assyrian times, replacing the old Philistine territory. The theme of Jerusalem surrounded by her enemies (cf. pp.272f.) is made even clearer. On this occasion, anger leads to a conspiracy to attack Jerusalem; the text for TO CAUSE CONFUSION IN IT is ungrammatical, and a better suggestion would be to read 'to cause confusion to me', i.e. to undermine Nehemiah's leadership. How far the political situation would have warranted such full military action is doubtful; Persian rule would hardly have permitted it. But the point being made is not to be taken merely at the literal level. Here is another aspect of the attack upon Nehemiah, and hence upon the people of God and God himself. So the solution is found in prayer and in A GUARD ... DAY AND NIGHT. The section is complete in itself, but is now linked with what follows as a further stage of the same threat in the following verses.

10. The sequence of thought is interrupted by a poetic saying expressing the distress of the people at the immensity of the task. It does not really belong in this context, but its placing has the effect of correlating threat from outside with discouragement within.

* Heb. 4.1-17.

11-13. A new narrative begins at v.11, perhaps to be seen as in part a parallel to vv.7-9, since the same point is made with greater elaboration. The ENEMIES are here unspecified, but clearly (if the meaning of v.12 is as RSV gives it) those who are on every side of Judah (cf. above v.7). There is to be a sudden attack by which the builders are killed and the work brought to an end. The news of this threat is apparently brought to Jerusalem by Jews who live in the outlying areas (v.12). Repeated warnings lead to action by Nehemiah to protect the city. The translation of vv.12-13 is, however, very uncertain, and many suggestions for emendation have been made. The Greek translators – whose rendering differs considerably at many points in this section – link the opening of v.13 into the report of the danger. (This is followed in NEB which renders: '... to attack us and that they would station themselves on the lowest levels below the wall'. But this involves a serious reversal of the natural sense of the expression BEHIND THE WALL which can only mean 'inside the city'.) One possibility is that v.13 contains two separate elements of Nehemiah's action: 'I stationed them (the reference is not clear, and there may be a word missing) below the shrine (literally 'the place') inside the wall in the open places, and I stationed the people according to their families (i.e. to guard the sections on which they are working)'; this would indicate a special protection for the holy place alongside the guarding of the wall. The arming of the builders is implied here, and further developed in vv.16ff.

14. This is an important element in the passage. An exhortation, DO NOT BE AFRAID OF THEM, rests upon confidence in the GREAT AND TERRIBLE God (cf. 1.5), the God of the covenant, in whose power the people may fight to protect the life of the community. The phrase links back to such a passage as Hag. 2.5 and to the words of Moses in Exod. 14.13. The opening may lack a word: 'And I saw their fear ...'

15. The consequence of this resolve and the protective action taken by Nehemiah is seen in the enemies' implied withdrawal, and the work continues.

16-21. These verses elaborate the theme further, first by detailing more fully the precautions taken. Here we have a first mention of the personal bodyguard of Nehemiah (MY SERVANTS, literally, 'my young men', a term used, for example, of the warrior band with David, e.g. in I Sam. 25). The fuller list of weapons and armour in v.16 suggests that these formed a well-equipped group, and they were to be significant in other contexts too (cf. 5.10; 13.19). The builders are supported also by their leadership, evidently with their arms to hand. The workmen work with weapons in hand (vv.16-18a). A further precaution is provided by a trumpeter whose duty will be to summon the whole community to the point of danger (vv. 18b-20). Military preparedness is here again closely linked with the awareness of divine protection.

20. Our God will fight for us This echoes the ancient belief in the holy war, that fight to which the deity of the people is believed to send and to lead his own army, with its conviction that the fight is God's and is waged against the enemies of God. We may observe that the Nehemiah narrative in this section is using a theme which we have seen frequently in the writings of the Chronicler. Battles for him are occasions for divine action. The Nehemiah passage does not describe a battle, but it applies the principle of the holy war, of God's protecting action, to the needs of a somewhat different type of situation.

21. and half of them held the spears To be seen as an accidental recopying of the phrase from v.16. The passage is resumed here.

22-23. Yet another detail is added. The implication here is that those builders who came from other localities went home each day, leaving the city inadequately protected. The theme of Jersualem's underpopulation appears subsequently (7.4). By staying overnight, these men can provide both protection and the necessary labour force. The final verses stresses the example set by Nehemiah, his kinsfolk and his own bodyguard. It is perhaps this which has led to the placing of ch.5, a section dealing with the right conduct of Nehemiah and the example he thereby sets to the community at large (cf. 5.16).

SOCIAL INJUSTICE REMEDIED

5.1-19

The problem of the protection of the community, symbolized in the building of the wall and in the countering of external opposition, is now matched by another aspect of protection in the resolving of internal difficulties which affect the life and wholeness of the people. That there should be those in the community who lose their proper status by loss of family and property is a danger which is the concern of both Old Testament legislation and of prophetic injunction. The community has its total being, consisting of its full members. The loss of one such, like the larger-scale loss of a city (cf. II Sam. 20.19) or a tribe (cf. Judg. 21.6), means a deficiency in the community as a whole. Marriage laws, property laws and slavery laws are in part directed towards such preservation of each family unit intact, and a number of Old Testament narratives (Gen. 38; Ruth) turn on the need for such preservation. So we find Nehemiah, here a successor to prophetic teaching and an upholder of the right principles which underlie particular laws, responding to an urgent situation.

The passage is historically out of position, since it is evident that the social problems here indicated are not the result of a moment. The fifty-two days of the wall-building (6.15) could hardly be responsible for so large-scale a problem, however much those engaged in the work left their ordinary occupations on one side. The social problems involved are in fact endemic to a society in which the majority of the population, engaged in simple agricultural activities, lives not very much above the subsistence level. There is a link in that the chapter points to the good example set by Nehemiah (cf. 4.23) and contains an allusion to his refusal to profit by the work on the wall (v.16). The second part of the chapter indeed (vv.14-18) clearly reflects a much longer period and looks back on the whole extent of Nehemiah's first term as governor (v.14).

1. The problems are vividly presented in terms of a complaint by the ordinary PEOPLE and THEIR WIVES against their compatriots. It is the oppression of one member of the community by another which is particularly at issue.

2-4. Three different aspects of the situation are set out. We may see here a stylized presentation, in which three different points, not related to one another nor necessarily expressive of entirely different groups, are made. The first, as the text stands, appears to envisage a population explosion – too many mouths to feed. But the word rendered MANY may be corrupted from the very similar one meaning 'pledging', i.e. 'we are having to pledge our sons and daughters'. The sale of children into slavery is allowed under the law (cf. Exod. 21.7; Lev. 25.39f. presents a similar position). The second envisages the MORTGAGING of property, and this too is covered by the law (cf. Exod. 22.25ff.; Deut. 24.10ff.); the cause here is indicated as FAMINE. (The fact that the Hebrew has the definite article, THE FAMINE, does not mean that a particular occasion is in view, for Hebrew may use the construction to make a general statement.) The third points to the problem of raising MONEY FOR THE (Persian) KING'S TAX; we do not know how this was levied, but it would appear that it was not raised by a special imposition on the wealthy as is indicated in the time of king Menahem of Israel (II Kings 15.20). A more general tax appears to be indicated in II Kings 23.35, where Jehoiakim is said to have exacted money 'from the people of the land, from every one according to his assessment': if this means 'from the ordinary population', as seems most likely, then we may suppose that in Persian times a similar tax could be imposed on all holders of property, rich or poor. The annual raising of such a tax could be a very considerable burden, and we have here one of the few insights in the Old Testament into the degree to which alien rule could be felt as an imposition by a subject people.

5. This may best be taken as a general reflection upon this threefold aspect of financial distress. It emphasizes the common membership in the community of oppressed and oppressor (mortgagee and mortgagor, enslaved and enslaver). In particular, the loss of children to slavery is a matter for distress; the repeated reference to DAUGHTERS suggests enslavement for prostitution (cf. Exod. 21.7ff).

6. Nehemiah's anger is the counterpart of the divine anger expressed in prophetic judgment.

7. brought charges This recalls the use of similar wording in prophetic indictments (e.g. Hos. 4.1: 'controversy'). It is the leadership which appears to be primarily to blame, though the end of v.13 – if correctly rendered in RSV – points to a larger acceptance of blame.

you are exacting interest Better read 'you are imposing a burden'. (The present form of the text, here and in vv.10 and 11, appears to reflect a criticism of the imposing of interest; but in each case it is more probable that we should see a reference to the imposition of burdens, the oppression of some members of the community by others.) In a public ASSEMBLY, like that held by Ezra (Ezra 10.9), the accusation is made.

8. Nehemiah voices his endeavours to deal with the evil of JEWISH BRETHREN sold to the outside world.

9. The people are enjoined to turn from their evil ways and to honour God so that he will be honoured by the nations. A similar sentiment is found in Prov. 14.31: 'He who oppresses a poor man insults his Maker, but he who is kind to the needy honours him (i.e. God).' Again we may see the close link between social justice and THE FEAR OF OUR GOD, one of the Old Testament expressions for what we should call 'religion'.

10. The support being offered by Nehemiah and his entourage contrasts with the burden being imposed by others. It does not seem likely that we should see here any suggestion that

Nehemiah himself was implicated in the wrong conduct, for
this would conflict sharply with both v.6 and v.8.

11. This appears to inaugurate a release of debts as an
immediate emergency measure. Old Testament law (cf. Deut.
15.1ff.) envisages a seven-year release from debt and slavery
(Lev. 25.8ff.: a jubilee year). But an *ad hoc* decision could
also be made (cf. the release of slaves in the siege period in
Jer. 34.8ff.), and this is what appears to be undertaken here.

12-13. The response is a willing one. There is no need to
suppose that the responders were reluctant, or that there is
a contrast between leaders who had to be forced by OATH
and curse and ordinary people who rejoiced because they
were freed from their burdens. It is rather a picture of a community ideally presented, in which there is a glad acceptance
of the obligation, solemnized by OATH in the presence of THE
PRIESTS as the representatives of God, and undergirded by the
symbolic action which Nehemiah, like the prophets, performs
and interprets. The action involves the shaking out of the
fold of the garment in which money or valuables would be
carried. It appears to be given a double interpretation: as
the fold is shaken out, so the man who does not respond will
be shaken out from home and occupation; and as this results
in an emptying of the fold, so that man will be empty, i.e.
propertyless. The whole ASSEMBLY responds in an act of praise
which echoes the refrain: Praise Yahweh, for he is good (cf.
e.g. Ezra 3.11). The last clause of v.13 implies action by the
whole community, and this appears to be the right understanding. An alternative is that the members of the community
copied Nehemiah's action (literally 'they did according to this
thing'); but this would appear to come too late after the assent
and praise.

14-15. The theme of Nehemiah's good action (v.10, cf. 4.23)
is now taken further by a reflection upon his whole conduct
as governor during his twelve-year term. He is contrasted with
FORMER GOVERNORS; the term is the general one which may
allow it to refer either to such special officers or commissioners

as there may have been – a governor is mentioned in Mal.
1.8, which may reflect the period shortly before Nehemiah –
or to the governor in Samaria who, in the absence of an
independent officer in Jerusalem, appears to have controlled
the whole area. We may allow here a little of that rhetoric
by which a ruler contrasts himself to his own advantage with
those who have preceded him, and so not look for too literal
an interpretation. The predecessors LAID HEAVY BURDENS UPON
THE PEOPLE, exacting, as they were entitled to do, a part of
the tax as their own allowance; THEIR SERVANTS LORDED IT
OVER THE PEOPLE. Nehemiah claims that his right religious
attitude prevented his conducting himself in such a manner.

16-18. He claims no profit from the work on the wall, and
he points to the entertainment which he offered to local
OFFICIALS and others, as well as to visitors from outside –
Jews or non-Jews presumably – out of his own resources and
not from the normal allowances provided for the governor.
And this BECAUSE THE SERVITUDE WAS HEAVY UPON THIS
PEOPLE – another slight allusion to the troubles of a subject
people (cf. on v.4).

19. In the final verse there appears the first of the com-
memorative refrains of the narrative in which a prayer is
offered to God to REMEMBER FOR GOOD what Nehemiah has
done (cf. 6.14; 13.14, 22, 29, 31). It is a formula found in
ancient votive inscriptions: 'May N.N. be remembered for
ever for good and prosperity.' In some of the other occurrences
in Nehemiah, the form is extended and suggests an affinity
with royal inscriptions in which the deity – and posterity –
is reminded of the king's deeds. It is also a familiar form in
Old Testament prayers, in psalmody and prophecy. (A negative counterpart has already appeared in 4.4f.) In the preservation of the memory of a great man, such a form may also
serve as an apology, a justification for his actions which may
or may not be viewed with favour by his successors. That
Nehemiah was regarded well by some is clear from Ecclus.
49.13 and II Macc. I.18-36. That he was not viewed so favourably by all is suggested by his sharp action against opponents

in ch.13, and also by the recognition that Ezra, following Nehemiah a generation later, found himself confronted by at least some of the problems which had faced Nehemiah (cf. Ezra 9-10 on foreign marriages, and cf. Neh. 13; and note the more general admissions of failure of Neh. 8).

THE TEMPTING OF NEHEMIAH AND THE COMPLETION OF THE WALL

6.1-19

The completion of the wall and its effect on the enemies and the surrounding nations form only a very small moment in this chapter (vv.15-16). It is embedded in a series of narratives, loosely linked together on the theme of the enemies' endeavours to bring fear into the hearts of Nehemiah and his associates (vv.9, 14, 19), endeavours which are met by steadfastness and true confidence. In effect, the section is divided at v.14, which may be seen in its 'remember' formula to mark the end of a passage, but it is convenient to take the remaining verses with this since the theme of opposition appears there again.

1. I had built the wall and ... there was no breach left in it This statement sets the scene; only THE GATES remained to be put into position, a final task to bring about the community's security. It is the news of this which provokes action. The first narrative extends to v.9 and concerns SANBALLAT and GESHEM and THE REST OF OUR ENEMIES (the mention of TOBIAH in v.1 [not in v.2] appears to be intrusive and is in fact grammatically unconnected, a point which does not appear in the translation).

2-4. The opponents repeatedly endeavour to persuade Nehemiah to come to a conference at ONE OF THE VILLAGES IN THE PLAIN OF ONO, in the plain of Sharon near Lydda; the text might better be rendered with a proper name 'at Kefirim in the plain of Ono'. It is quite possible that this place was in neutral territory under direct Persian rule, between the administrative areas of Samaria and Ashdod. If this is so, then we may perhaps see that there is another side to the case, and remind ourselves that we are reading this account entirely from the viewpoint of Nehemiah.

2. His opponents may have INTENDED TO DO ME HARM; but it is also possible that his suspicions were over-easily aroused and that there was at least some concern for a discussion aimed at easing tension. The other governors in the area could not afford to lose favour with Persian authority.

3-4. Nehemiah, however, interprets the invitation entirely negatively, and refuses to stop the GREAT WORK which he is doing.

5-6. Perhaps a separate narrative begins here, involving SAN-BALLAT alone; GESHEM (here written as Gashmu) appears almost in an aside in v.6. In this narrative a letter is sent by messenger, and this states that there is a report that Nehemiah and the Jewish community are contemplating rebellion – the theme of part of 2.19, which may be an abbreviated allusion to this longer account – and that Nehemiah himself aims at kingship (v.6). That the letter is OPEN may be intended to imply that Sanballat wished the contents to be publicized, but it is also possible that we have here a reflection of a normal procedure, known to us particularly from legal practice, in which an open and a sealed copy of a document guaranteed that the text available for immediate consultation could not be contaminated without detection, since there was a sealed copy which could provide a check (cf. Jer. 32.11 for a legal example, of which others are known from actual documents from Elephantine and from later times).

7. The report about kingship is supported by a reference to PROPHETS whom Nehemiah is alleged to have SET UP. Prophetic support for a claim to rule is well known from narratives in the books of Samuel and Kings. The comments of Haggai (2.20-23) and Zechariah (6.9-14) on Zerubbabel envisage a status for him which is very near to a claim for kingship. It would not be altogether surprising if some in Judah, dreaming of the past greatness of Davidic monarchy, saw in Nehemiah a potential successor, though there is no evidence to suggest that he was a Davidide. Three centuries later, non-Davidic rulers were accepted in the line of the Hasmonean kings. One of the delicate aspects of the position of an influential personage such as Nehemiah must be the risk that over-zealous supporters would go too far. The New Testament provides indications of the nature of this risk in the case of Jesus. Sanballat proposes to use these rumours as a bargaining point in consultation.

8. While Nehemiah's vehement denial of the report as being nothing but inventions of Sanballat's OWN MIND may be entirely genuine, politicians have been known to deny as firmly as this what they do not wish to admit. We can appreciate that the rumour, if it had foundation, could be a considerable embarrassment to Nehemiah who, from all the evidence, was a loyal subject of his Persian overlord.

9. His interpretation of the attempt is that it was designed TO FRIGHTEN US and thereby to hinder the building work. The last clause of this verse may be interpreted as in RSV as a prayer for help, though no word for GOD appears in the text. An alternative is to read a first-person verbal form and render: 'I strengthened my hand' – i.e. 'I set myself with firmer resolve (to the task)'.

10-13. This section contains a new narrative. Here we may suspect that the appearance of SANBALLAT is secondary, since he is added in second place (as nowhere else) after TOBIAH in v.12 (and again in the prayer of v.14). Such an activity as is here described as undertaken by TOBIAH would fit well with what we hear subsequently (vv.17-19) about his close connections in Jerusalem (and cf. also 13.4ff.). Nehemiah is here found visiting a prophet SHEMAIAH in his own house. No explanation of this visit is given other than the difficult phrase WHO WAS SHUT UP, using the same word as is found of Jeremiah in Jer. 36.5. In the latter passage, it would appear that for some

reason, equally unexplained, Jeremiah was unable to go to
the temple. If that is the meaning here, then we must suppose
that Shemaiah's disability (some limited period of uncleanness, perhaps) would soon come to an end, for in the almost
poetic oracle which he pronounces – perhaps rhythmic prose
rather than true poetry – he envisages meeting Nehemiah in
THE TEMPLE. His prophecy enjoins Nehemiah to seek divine
protection by taking refuge in the temple from assassins.
Nehemiah's response and comments in vv.11-13 are somewhat
ambiguous, and it is possible that two separate motifs are
here combined. On the one hand, the theme seems to be one
of courage: SHOULD SUCH A MAN AS I FLEE?, to which the
sequel is his recognition that the words were aimed at inducing fear and so enabling his opponents to give him AN EVIL
NAME and TO TAUNT him. This theme may also be detected in
the rendering of v.11 in RSVmg: '... would go into the
temple to save his life'. On the other hand, there is a theme of
true piety. Verse 11, translated as in RSV, ... GO INTO THE
TEMPLE AND LIVE? implies that Nehemiah is refusing to pre-
sume upon the deity, aware that for one who is not a priest,
to enter the inner shrine would be to court death (cf. the fate
of Uzziah in II Chron. 26.16ff.). This is developed further in
the reference to SIN in v.13. Whichever theme is preferred –
if indeed a choice needs to be made – the main point is that
Nehemiah is able to recognize that this cannot have been a
true prophetic word, and it transpires, though we are not
given the evidence, that Shemaiah had been HIRED to speak
the prophecy. The suborning of a prophet by payment is a
denial of the true prophetic call (cf. Mic. 3.5). It is not that
payment is improper in itself (as witness I Sam. 9.7f.), but the
influencing of what purports to be the divine word by the
payment. The response of Nehemiah provides an example of
that ability to detect true prophecy from false by the knowledge that a true prophetic word cannot override what is
known on other grounds to be right (cf. for this the comment
on prophecy in Deut. 13.1-5).

14. The section so far, or perhaps only this last narrative, is resumed with the second formula REMEMBER, but here it is entirely in the negative form (cf. 4.4f.) of remembering the evil done against Nehemiah. It extends the reference to Shemaiah by an allusion to a PROPHETESS NOADIAH and to THE REST OF THE PROPHETS WHO WANTED TO MAKE ME AFRAID. It appears that the example given in vv.10-13 is only one of a number of attempts made at undermining the position of Nehemiah by invoking the divine word through prophetic agency.

15. A brief statement records the completion of the wall in the short period of FIFTY-TWO DAYS, ending in the sixth month ELUL (autumn 445).

16. More important is the statement of the effect on the ENEMIES and THE NATIONS ROUND ABOUT, though the text is uncertain. That they WERE AFRAID (RSV) would fit well with the indications elsewhere (e.g. I Chron. 14.17) that the great moments of the people's history are moments when the nations feel awe, and this accords here with the recognition that the work is of God. The verb could also be understood in the sense of 'they saw' (RSVmg); this seems a much weaker meaning.

fell greatly in their own esteem is very strange, but virtually without alteration the text could be interpreted as 'and it was marvellous in their eyes' (cf. Ps. 118.23 for an almost identical expression). The word translated 'marvellous' is very closely connected with the great acts of God in the Exodus events, and this awareness of the reality and power of God provides an appropriate basis for the statement of the nations' awe.

17-19. Another aspect of Nehemiah's difficulties now appears in the close relationships established by TOBIAH, by marriage and by an allegiance of OATH, with important personages in Jerusalem. That these SPOKE OF Tobiah's GOOD DEEDS and REPORTED Nehemiah's WORDS TO HIM indicates both that there were those who viewed Tobiah's activities differently from the suspicion which was characteristic of Nehemiah, and also that there were 'spies' in Jerusalem. Tobiah is further accused of sending LETTERS TO MAKE ME AFRAID. Here again we must be aware that the hostile attitude to Tobiah is part of the Nehemiah tradition. Tobiah himself would, we may assume, have seen his own actions as equally patriotic and there is nothing to suggest that he was not a loyal worshipper of Yahweh. As in other moments of Old Testament history, the application of loyal faith to a political situation is by no means a simple matter. We can well appreciate that there were those in Nehemiah's time who viewed his building of the city wall and his separatist tendencies (cf. ch.13) with suspicion. A true faith is not necessarily to be preserved by such means; and the means themselves may well contain the seeds of other ills.

THE RESTORED COMMUNITY

7.1-72

1. The dedication of the wall is dealt with only at a later point (12.27ff.). Here the theme of protection is taken a little further, with the note that, after the completion of walls and gates, there were appointed GATEKEEPERS. The mention of SINGERS and LEVITES here is probably due to a later copyist who supposed the reference to be to temple gatekeepers; neither singers nor Levites have any concern with the city gates (but cf. on 13.22).

2. The appointment of officers over the city is another aspect of security; HANANI MY BROTHER was mentioned in 1.2; HANANIAH THE GOVERNOR OF THE CASTLE (citadel) is marked out as both a loyal subject of the Persian king, an important factor and one which suggests the closeness of the link between Nehemiah's activity and Persian policy, and also a GOD-FEARING man, important for the confidence which he will engender in the community.

3. In one reading, the opening of the text is understood to refer to Nehemiah in the first person; but the text may be read as a third-person form, in which case it is possible that the instructions now given are issued by Hananiah. The text of the verse is not clear. It is evident that in the particular situation the gates were to be opened late and closed early as an extra precaution; but the second part of this statement is very obscurely worded, and the RSV rendering is not really very appropriate. A reference to shutting before sunset would be expected, and some commentators have emended the text to obtain this. The guarding of the city is also presented as a responsibility of some of the inhabitants, presumably those whose houses abutted on the wall or (cf. ch.3) formed part of the wall.

4. A new theme is introduced here which will be taken further in ch.11. The population of the city is too small for its size, and this must mean weakness in time of danger. The last clause of the verse may, as translated, similarly reflect the smallness of the population; an alternative rendering would give 'no (new) families had yet been established', since the word for 'house' can also mean 'family unit'.

5. The verse appears as a development of this theme of population, but should more probably be regarded as providing the introduction to the list which follows. Its concern seems to be rather that of the control of membership of the true people.

6-72. The list itself corresponds to Ezra 2 and has been examined there (cf. pp.217ff). The Hebrew text lacks the material of v.68, presumably by inadvertence in copying. Only in vv.70-72 does there appear some substantial difference, the text here being considerably fuller than that in Ezra 2. The origin of the list is uncertain. Its use here shows a concern with status and membership, as is particularly clear in vv.61-65.

After this, the story of Nehemiah is broken off, to be resumed only in ch.11-13 (see pp.309ff.).

THE WORK OF EZRA – II

Nehemiah **8-10**

THE READING OF THE LAW

7.73-**8.**18

The narrative which resumes at this point is clearly part of the story of Ezra, told here, as in Ezra 7 and 10, in the third person. In I Esdras, this passage, though extending only to the middle of 8.13, follows immediately on the foreign-marriage action of Ezra 10 (I Esd. 9.37-55), but as we have seen (p.250f.), a more probable sequel is to be made from Ezra 8 so far as chronology is concerned. By reading the narratives in this order, the commission of Ezra to bring the law to Judah (Ezra 7) is fulfilled at the next convenient date, THE FIRST DAY OF THE SEVENTH MONTH (8.2), the first day, that is, of the new year reckoned as beginning in the autumn.

7.73. This link verse, which appears also at the end of Ezra 2 (v.70), is quite evidently not in order. It really needs a reference, as there, to Jerusalem and its environs as the dwelling-place of the first persons listed, while the remainder live in the towns outside. But the precise relationship of this verse to what follows remains somewhat uncertain, as we have seen in the discussion of Ezra 2 (cf. p.221). Some degree of harmonizing of the texts and of mutual influence appears likely.

8.1-2. The real narrative begins with the assembly of ALL THE PEOPLE in a public SQUARE in the city; it is an assembly which includes BOTH MEN AND WOMEN AND ALL WHO COULD HEAR WITH UNDERSTANDING, an expression which suggests the bringing into the reading of the younger members of the community who are now of an age to accept the obligations of

full membership (for this, cf. the comparable statements in
Deut. 31.10-13). There is clearly some relation between what
is here described and the injunction laid down in Deut. 31.
There the reading of the law is to take place every seven years
at the autumnal feast, the date of which is not specified,
though in I Kings 8 it was evidently held in the seventh month
as the later legislation of Lev. 23.33ff. laid down (cf. v.14
here). There is some evidence in later Samaritan thought for
the law being associated with new year, it being believed
that the law dated from creation and that creation began on
the first day of the spring new year. It seems possible to see
some reflection of such thought in this passage. It is evident
that there was a quite wide range of ideas connected with the
law, developing so as to bring it into association with the
great religious festivals, though in the event in Judaism the giving of the law came to be associated with the feast of weeks
(Pentecost). In this account of the reading of the law, there
are clear signs of particular liturgical practice.

1. EZRA THE SCRIBE is told TO BRING THE BOOK OF THE LAW.
(The plural THEY TOLD probably does not refer to the assembly,
but is an impersonal plural equivalent to a passive. No interest
is shown in who did the instructing. THE ASSEMBLY consists of
those who should be there (see above).

3. The reading takes place from dawn to midday. The people
are responsive.

4. Ezra is ON A WOODEN PULPIT which had been made (the
same construction as in v.1) FOR THE PURPOSE – or alternatively
'for the word', i.e. for the divine word and its exposition. The
pulpit, literally 'tower', is presumably a platform, perhaps not
unlike that envisaged in II Chron. 6.13 (see note on p.112),
though a different word is used here. He is supported – and
this suggests a fairly large construction – by six men on his
right and seven on his left (in v.7 there are thirteen Levites,
but the various ancient versions of this text provide variously
here twelve – the most obvious number – thirteen or four-

teen; there may have been some conflating of lists).

5. Ezra's formal opening of THE BOOK (actually, of course, a scroll) was seen by the whole assembly and ALL THE PEOPLE STOOD to hear the word of God (cf. Judg. 3.20).

6-8. Ezra pronounces a blessing of the name of Yahweh; the people respond with the affirmation AMEN, stressing their endorsement of what is being said as true and sure, and they lift their hands in the characteristic ancient posture of prayer, before prostrating themselves before God. While the people remain stationed as they are, the Levites interpret.

The relationship between these formal procedures and those of later synagogue practice is sufficient to suggest that here we have a model from which the later forms developed. But the degree of formality strongly suggests that there is here a reflection of an already existing pattern, and the appearance of a pattern in the narrative of Josiah's reform (particularly clearly in the older form in II Kings 22) and indications of a form in Deut. 31.10-13 suggest that we have in this passage one indication of a development already under way in which older practices of worship, including the reading of law and the acceptance of covenant obligation, are being adapted to newer needs. We cannot write a history of the development of Israel's worship, but here and there we can pinpoint moments in that history.

The interpretative activity of the Levites indicated here is not expressed in such a way as to enable us to say with precision what they did. Our knowledge of legal material, particularly in Deuteronomy and the Holiness Code in Lev. 17-26, strongly suggests that the interpretation implied in v.7 is that kind of expounding of the meaning of the law which makes possible its application to new situations. For one of the evident needs of a community which claims to live by obedience to divine command is to know how older injunctions, which perhaps no longer correspond to current reality, are to be understood. An example which has occurred in the Nehemiah material is that of the holy war; we saw how, in ch.4, the principles of that ancient religious practice, governed by certain laws, could be seen to be relevant to a different situation. Deuteronomy in particular has a whole range of interpreted laws of this kind.

8. clearly The sense of the word rendered in this way is not certain. It may simply mean 'distinctly', but this would seem to be too trivial a meaning. It may denote 'separating it into sections', i.e. dividing it up into units which could be understood and expounded. It could imply exposition or commentary. It could denote translation into another language which, in this context, could only be Aramaic, the diplomatic language of the western imperial area, used for communication, as we have seen, in Ezra 4-6 and 7, and also in the Elephantine letters, and gradually to become the vernacular of Palestine. But how far was such translation necessary in the time of Ezra? Traditionally the origin of the Aramaic translations, the *targums*, is traced back to Ezra, but this is likely to derive in part at least from one possible understanding of this passage. It is tantalizing to be so uncertain, though the emphasis on interpretation appears the most probable.

9-12. The response to the law-reading is now seen. In v.9 the mention of NEHEMIAH, WHO WAS THE GOVERNOR, is a harmonizing note (cf. also 10.1; 12.36). Nehemiah's name does not appear in I Esdras, and the title THE GOVERNOR does not appear in the Greek translation. Here is the result of scribal activity, drawing together the activity of two leaders whose work does not overlap in time. It is Ezra alone who is the subject of the verb in this sentence and the next, and even the mention of THE LEVITES WHO TAUGHT THE PEOPLE is probably an expansion. We learn that the people's response is in mourning and weeping (cf. Josiah's response to the law in II Chron. 34.19). This suggests that some part of what was read was severe warning and injunction, though we must remember that weeping as a ritual form is part of an expression of deep emotion in worship. But the summons of Ezra is to rejoicing, to a day of feasting, a recognition that the hearing of the law is not to lead to sadness but to joy. The law as a source of joy

is the theme of Pss. 1; 19; 119; and such an emphasis on rejoicing is also characteristic of Deuteronomy (e.g. 12.12) and
of the Chronicler's frequent descriptions of religious festivity
(e.g. Ezra 6.22).

13-18. A further stage in the celebration follows. At this point
it is THE HEADS OF FATHERS' HOUSES who assemble for further
study of the law. We may recall that it was the duty of a man
to instruct his sons in the law (cf. Deut. 6.4ff., 20ff.). This is
the occasion for undertaking a renewed celebration of the
autumnal feast of BOOTHS (tabernacles), and the discovery of
this in the law (the allusion is most obviously to Lev. 23.33ff.)
leads to the summoning of the people to a feast in Jerusalem,
on the rooftops, in the temple courts, and in open squares
(v.16). The opening of v.15 may be better slightly emended
to read: 'and when they heard this, they proclaimed ...' The
celebration is undertaken by THOSE WHO HAD RETURNED FROM
THE CAPTIVITY, a clear allusion to those who had come with
Ezra and to the community understood, as the Chronicler
understands it, as that which has gone through the experience
of exile. It is perhaps this which explains the reference to the
time of Joshua (the text has the alternative spelling JESHUA),
for the return from captivity, understood as a second exodus
(cf. Ezra 1), makes it appropriate that there should be a religious celebration comparable to those belonging to the moment
of entry into the promised land. The statement of v.17 should
not be taken literally, but should be seen as making this theological point. Such a claim to the restoration of ancient practice is also made, and is to be similarly understood, in the
narratives of the reforms of Hezekiah (II Chron. 30.26) and
Josiah (II Kings 23.22; II Chron. 35.18). Centralized celebration of the feast, instead of the ancient celebration in the vine-
yards, for this was in origin a vintage festival, appears to be
more ancient than the time of Ezra (cf. Deut. 16.15), so that
centralization is not itself a new element. But the united celebration of the feast may be seen as drawing together the
community, and its connecting here with the reading of the
law may suggest that an older seven-year reading (as in Deut.

31.10-13) is now being given annual sanction. But this is not actually stated. If the date laid down in Lev. 23 is being followed – and no day is indicated – then the celebration would be from the fifteenth till the twenty-second of the month, and this would link neatly with the date given in 9.1. The SOLEMN ASSEMBLY ON THE EIGHTH DAY (v.18) recalls the dedication of Solomon's temple (II Chron. 7.9).

It is appropriate here to ask what law-book is intended in this narrative. The commission to Ezra in Ezra 7.25f. to impose the law does, in fact, already raise this question. And the answer must be that there is insufficient evidence for us to determine it. A comparable problem exists for the law-book read at the reform of Josiah, though there the author's intention, whatever the historical basis for it, is evidently to point to Deuteronomy. The fact that in the writings of the Chronicler we may trace very considerable influence of Deuteronomy suggests that this may well be part of what Ezra had. But the closeness of the link also with the law-material in the Holiness Code and the Priestly Work (the later strata now incorporated in the first four books of the Old Testament) suggests that Ezra brought with him something much nearer to the Pentateuch, the five books attributed traditionally to Moses, the Law as it came to be specifically known to Judaism. One of the arguments for this is the possession of this same collection, though with some variants, by the Samaritan religious community. Since the viewpoints of the Priestly laws and of Deuteronomy are not identical, it is possible that we should see in the work of Ezra and in the presentation of the history by the Chronicler an attempt at drawing together different strands of thought, an endeavour at unifying and consolidating the life of the community. But we must here remember that we see Ezra essentially only through the eyes of the Chronicler, who may have read back what he believed to be right.

THE CONFESSION OF FAITH

9.1-37

The major part of this chapter consists of a prayer or psalm (vv.6-37) which draws together a great many themes from the past and from the contemporary situation; it could be considered a kind of sermonic summarizing of the Chronicler's work. It is preceded by an account of a religious celebration on the occasion of a fast. This is dated (v.1) to THE TWENTY-FOURTH DAY OF THIS MONTH, and since the month is not specified, it would appear that it therefore follows closely on the narrative of ch.8 and that the fast took place only a couple of days after the completion of the feast of booths.

It cannot be denied that this is quite possible. It has been observed that ch.8 passes over in silence the great Day of Atonement held on the tenth day of the seventh month (so Lev. 23.26, and also Lev. 16.29 at the end of the long account of the nature of the ritual for that day). But the precise dating of annual celebrations appears to be later than their origin, and in this instance the date in Lev. 16.29 can be regarded as later than the account which precedes; the normal order would be to state the date of the celebration and then specify its detail, as is done in Lev. 23. It is therefore possible that in the time of Ezra, no final fixing of the date had been undertaken, and that it could be held at a convenient date, in this instance the twenty-fourth. But there is in fact no obvious reason for making such an identification at all. A fast could be proclaimed on an appropriate day if there was need (cf. Joel 2.15), and Zech. 8.19 refers to fasts celebrated in the fourth, fifth, seventh and tenth months of the year.

The question then arises whether the narrative of 9.1-5 belongs immediately with ch.8 or is quite separate, and since it refers to separation from FOREIGNERS (v.2), its relationship to Ezra 9-10 must also be considered. Various suggestions have been made for relating these; but it must be admitted that no entirely satisfactory order can be found. When we observe, however, that v.3 refers to a ceremonial reading of THE LAW and an act of confession and worship, we may wonder whether we are in fact dealing with a quite separate incident or even with an alternative statement of the acceptance of the law brought by Ezra. Ezra himself is not mentioned; we are thus confronted with a situation a little like that in Neh. 3, where the account of the building of the wall makes no reference to Nehemiah. Was there, alongside the well-attested Ezra tradition concerning the bringing and acceptance of the law, an alternative in which he was not mentioned? Has the Chronicler joined these different elements together, assuming them to be parts of one sequence?

1-2. An act of penitence and mourning, a deliberate separation from foreigners – to be understood as the counterpart of the repudiation of foreign worship – and a confession of sin mark the occasion.

3. A ceremony in which three hours are devoted to law-reading and three hours to confession and worship is indicated.

4-5. The act of praise is further specified with a twofold list of LEVITES in which the names do not exactly coincide (suggesting that various source materials have been used). Some of the names overlap ch.8; some overlap ch.10. Verse 4 indicates a great shout, a cry to God; v.5 has a call to praise, which should probably end at the end of the first sentence (EVERLASTING TO EVERLASTING). THE STAIRS mentioned in v.4 may in fact be simply another way of referring to a platform such as is mentioned in 8.4.

To this is loosely linked the long prayer which is best regarded as beginning at v.5*b*: BLESSED BE THY GLORIOUS NAME; the words AND EZRA SAID, which are not in the Hebrew text but only in the Greek, should, if they are supplied at all, be placed before this opening. The attribution to Ezra is not necessary; without it, the prayer is made to follow on as part of the worship of the Levites of v.5. But it is not surprising that such an attribution has been made, in view of the tendency to gather material around great figures. The complaint at the end (vv.36f.) has been thought to be unsuitable for Ezra who, as a loyal subject of the Persian empire, would hardly complain in this way of his people's condition. But Ezra – and the Chronicler – may have been political quietists and still have been sensitive to the contemporary situation.

It is not always easy to decide where we have poetry and where rhythmic prose in Hebrew, especially so in a passage such as this where there are so many allusions to other biblical material. The Jerusalem Bible sets the passage out as poetry; RSV and NEB follow older practice and regard it as prose. We should probably treat it as a rhythmic, liturgical prose, in which poetic language is continually breaking through. Its nearest parallels are to be seen in the great historical psalms, those such as 78; 105; 106, which offer a survey of Israel's history with comment on its meaning. It is also close to statements of faith such as those to be found in Josh. 24, or Judith 5.6-21 (in the month of an Ammonite enemy), or Stephen's speech in Acts 7. The extent of allusion to other biblical material is such that long lists of cross-references can be built up (as for example in the commentaries of Myers and Rudolph). In many ways the thought is closest to Deuteronomy and the writings of the Deuteronomic school, but this we have seen often to be the case in the Chronicler, who was deeply influenced by his predecessors in interpreting his people's history. It is a prayer based upon a rich and appreciative handling of Israel's traditions, and upon an interpretation of those traditions as relevant to the needs of a contemporary situation.

(5b) 6. These verses set the tone in an act of praise to the one God, the creator and controller of all, acknowledged by the very HOST OF HEAVEN.

7-8. This leads immediately into the call of ABRAM and his renaming, his being found faithful and the promise of the land.

9-15. These verses cover the period of affliction in Egypt, the crossing of the Sea and the SIGNS AND WONDERS of deliverance.

The PILLAR OF CLOUD and the PILLAR OF FIRE guide the people. The law is given from SINAI, and the people are given BREAD and WATER in the wilderness on their way to possess the land promised to them.

16. The tone changes to that of disobedience.

17-18. From the wilderness traditions there are picked out those which emphasize the lack of faith of the people – their desire TO RETURN TO THEIR BONDAGE IN EGYPT (the text has 'bondage in their rebellion'), the golden CALF; but these are interwoven with the assurance of the mercy of God.

19-25. This theme is developed again in allusions to guidance in the wilderness, to MANNA and WATER again, to the provision of every need, to the possession of the land, with a whole series of allusions to the presentation of the conquest as it is set out in the opening chapters of Deuteronomy.

26. The theme of disobedience recurs, expressed in the rejection of the law and the killing of the PROPHETS.

27-31. Allusion is made to the pattern of disaster, repentance and deliverance which is exemplified particularly in the narratives in Judges, and then more generally to the whole period of the monarchy, with its repeated pattern, very much as this appears in the Chronicler's own accounts, of faith and unbelief, warning and stubbornness. The people, when they repented, were heard by God FROM HEAVEN (v.28, a phrase reminiscent of the prayer of Solomon); they were repeatedly warned by the working of God's SPIRIT THROUGH THY PROPHETS (v.30, cf. II Chron. 36.15f.). Finally, they were given over INTO THE HAND OF THE PEOPLES OF THE LANDS, in the judgment of the exile (v.30). But even this did not mark the end of God's GREAT MERCIES (v.31).

In all the sections of the prayer up to this point, we may see allusions to a wide range of older material. It is clear that these allusions are not by any means limited to what has already appeared in the Chronicler's work, and in fact the appearance of references both to the patriarchal period and to the Exodus and wilderness periods introduces areas of Old Testament thought conspicuously absent from the Chronicler's presentation. For this reason many commentators have regarded the whole prayer as a later addition to the work, and one which cannot represent the outlook of the Chronicler himself. It is more probable that we should see here the taking over of already existing material, comparable to psalms which provide similar coverage of the history, and that we should recognize also that it is not only here that the Chronicler expects his readers to know more of the religious background than he actually relates. To the extent that he is writing a commentary on his people's history, he assumes that they are already familiar with it, and at a number of points we have observed that he alludes to narratives not included or makes such abbreviated references as not to be wholly intelligible unless we know the fuller narratives found elsewhere. In some cases cryptic references remain obscure because it so happens that we do not have the fuller material in our Old Testament. It is quite impossible to suppose that the Chronicler, familiar with the great wealth of material in the Pentateuch – whether he knew it more or less as we have it or in a somewhat divergent form – was not familiar with the Exodus traditions. His very reason for not dilating on these may well have been that such interpretations were already available and familiar to his contemporaries. His concern was both with giving a larger perspective and with showing the significance of certain major themes. And when we look at the last verses of the prayer, we may see a concern with the contemporary situation which is significant for his understanding of his people's need. This suggests that the present form of the prayer owes a good deal to contemporary interpretation.

32. Now therefore Here is the real nub of the prayer. As in letter forms, the introductory greeting leads up to the point where the substance of the message is reached (e.g. Ezra 4.11f.). So here, the praise of God and the recording of his actions in relation to his people are the occasion for the statement of

contemporary need. It is an appeal to God not to regard as
LITTLE ... ALL THE HARDSHIP THAT HAS COME UPON US ...
UNTIL THIS DAY.

33-35. The community has suffered much. That the suffering
was justly imposed is acknowledged, for that is of the nature
of God, and the people and its leaders have been guilty of
disobedience.

36-37. But – and here we reach the contemporary situation –
WE ARE SLAVES THIS DAY; IN THE LAND THAT THOU GAVEST TO
OUR FATHERS ... WE ARE SLAVES. The blessings which derive
from this promised land go to alien rulers who exercise absolute and arbitrary power: WE ARE IN GREAT DISTRESS.

The prayer opened with the reminder of the divine promise
of the land to Abraham; it closes with the picture of that land
occupied by a subject people, a slave people, which does not
enjoy the kind of blessing which clearly lay within God's intentions for his people.

There is revealed here – as already earlier in the prayer of
Ezra in Ezra 9 (cf. esp. v.9) – evidence of the sensitivity of the
Chronicler to the delicate contemporary situation. The whole
sweep of his presentation from the exile to Ezra is dominated
by his confidence that Persian rulers, moved by God himself
(cf. most clearly Ezra 1.1), have worked for the good of the
Jewish community. They have authorized the return more than
once; they have supported the rebuilding of the temple, enjoined the imposition of the law. The narrative of Nehemiah
provides a parallel to this, and its place in the Chronicler's
work is clearly justified not least by its awareness of a similar
benevolence on the part of a Persian ruler. But the fact
remains that it is a subject people for whom all this is done.
They are 'slaves' (RSV correctly renders the text thus at Neh.
9.36, though curiously the same word is rendered 'bondmen'
in Ezra 9.9). The word carries immediate overtones of the
position of Israel in Egypt. It is a reminder that a hope of
renewed divine action is rooted in Israel's thought. The
Chronicler is one of those who sees hope precisely there, and
he finds a clear successor in the author of the book of Daniel,

for whom hope lies not in the military action of the Maccabaean family but in the reality of divine intervention (esp.
Dan. 11). To the Chronicler and his contemporaries, Persian
rule, benevolent though it might be in some of its aspects, was
nevertheless alien rule. The people of God must wait for God
to act; but it was also aware that its present slave condition
was a direct contradiction of that divine promise of the enjoy-
ment of the land which formed so central an element in its
long religious tradition.

THE COVENANT

9.38–10.39

The major problem for the understanding of this chapter*
is that of its relationship to the Ezra and Nehemiah material.
As it stands, it is clearly intended to be linked to the preceding
chapters 8-9, the opening words BECAUSE OF ALL THIS providing
a neat sequel to the distress of 9.37. It thus purports to be the
record of an agreement entered into by the community as a
result of Ezra's reading of the law. Two features of the section,
however, point to a link rather with Nehemiah: on the one
hand, the name of Nehemiah appears in 10.1 whereas Ezra is
not mentioned; on the other hand, the undertakings of vv.28-
39 have a number of points of correspondence with Neh. 13.
But a closer examination of the material suggests that the
matter is not so simple. While it is possible that the Chronicler,
or perhaps a later editor, may have transferred a Nehemiah
section to provide the climax to Ezra's work, it seems more
likely that in fact the Chronicler has here made use of independent material which appeared apt to his understanding
of Ezra. The list of names in vv.1-27 looks very much like
other examples of inserted lists (e.g. Ezra 8.1-14 and Ezra 2),
a procedure which is characteristic of the Chronicler's work.
The absence of Ezra's name applies equally to ch.9, and this

---

* The Hebrew text divides more conveniently so as to treat this
section as ch.10. The verse numbering in the Hebrew is therefore
one higher in each case.

suggests that here too we have other matter, not originally connected with Ezra's work, now drawn into the account given of him. The connections with Neh. 13 are only partial, and while the three main points of correspondence – the sabbath, foreign marriages, the wood offering – are interesting, there is much else here which is not covered by that chapter. The comments on ch.13 itself will suggest too that the material there, so different in nature from the remainder of the Nehemiah narratives, needs to be carefully scrutinized, for it may be that here we have evidence of a growth in the Nehemiah tradition dependent on just the kind of material which appears also in this chapter.

The most satisfying hypothesis is that the Chronicler has here, in bringing his account of Ezra to a close, made use of other material, not originally connected; and that the Nehemiah narratives of ch.13 depend on the same or similar matter. But it must be recognized that this is not a matter in which proof is possible.

9.38. a firm covenant The word actually used is not the normal word for covenant, but a word meaning 'something sure' (used again in 11.23 for a 'settled provision'). We may note that it is sealed by PRINCES, LEVITES and PRIESTS, and in the natural sequel in 10.28 the rest of the people adhere to the agreement by the taking of an oath.

10.1-27. The list of names does not follow this order, but lists NEHEMIAH THE GOVERNOR followed by one ZEDEKIAH who has been identified with Zadok the scribe who appears in 13.13; THE PRIESTS, named largely by family names (vv.2-8, corresponding closely with 12.1-7, which links them with the time of Zerubbabel); THE LEVITES (vv.9-13, with some overlaps with chs.8,9 and 12); and lastly THE CHIEFS OF THE PEOPLE (vv.14-27, with links to Ezra 2, Neh. 7 and also some to Neh. 3). This would seem to suggest an archival list belonging to some other situation.

28-29. There is next a description, though without any detail, of some kind of ceremony of taking an OATH, an undertaking to obey the law in accordance with the particular terms of the covenant. We may note those involved in the oath as being the people, religious officials of various kinds, AND ALL WHO HAVE SEPARATED THEMSELVES FROM THE PEOPLES OF THE LANDS, an expression immediately reminiscent of Ezra 6.21, showing a linkage with the thought found there in relation to the re-dedication of the temple. The phrase ALL WHO HAVE KNOWLEDGE AND UNDERSTANDING suggests a link with Neh. 8.2, part of the Ezra law-reading narrative.

30. From here on, the statements are made in the first person plural, suggesting the actual terms (perhaps beginning in the middle of the previous verse, where a truncated opening to the document might be detected: '... TO OBSERVE AND DO ...') The first undertaking is the rejection of marriages with foreigners (cf. 13.23-27 and also Ezra 9-10, though the latter is concerned with a different aspect of the problem, the dissolution of existing marriages of this kind).

31. Linked with the foreign marriage question is one aspect OF SABBATH observance (cf. Neh. 13.15ff.), extended here to cover any HOLY DAY, and to this is added THE SEVENTH YEAR observance of leaving the land fallow (cf. Exod. 23.10f.; Lev. 25.1-7) and the foregoing of EVERY DEBT (cf. Deut. 15.1-11).

32-33. No law governing the annual support by one THIRD PART OF A SHEKEL for the worship of the temple appears in the Old Testament; later practice knows of a half-shekel temple tax (cf. Matt. 17.24-27), and Exod. 30.11f. appears to envisage a once-for-all payment of this amount, though it may reflect a traditional explanation of the origin of the tax. This tax is designed to support the whole running of the regular ceremonial, and probably also repair work, covered here in the phrase ALL THE WORK OF THE HOUSE OF OUR GOD.

34. the wood offering This matter (cf. 13.31) is not covered by Old Testament legislation; the verse is perhaps out of place, or even a later addition to the passage, since the sequel to v.33 appears to be in v.35.

35-37a. first fruits Various aspects including the redemption of THE FIRST BORN OF OUR SONS and the offering of FIRSTLINGS OF OUR HERDS AND OF OUR FLOCKS (alluded to briefly in 13.10, 31; cf. Exod. 22.29f.; 23.19) are dealt with here.

37b-39a. This is again perhaps a later addition, giving more detailed points concerning the handling of TITHES (cf. 13.5, 12) and the ways in which these are used for the support of priests and Levites.

39b. We will not neglect the house of our God This clause (cf. 13.11) underlines the nature of the obligations here stated. Obedience is expressed primarily in the maintenance of the worship of God in the temple. The whole theme of restoration after the exile, linked back into the stress laid in I and II Chron. on the planning and building of the temple, centres on the right ordering of the temple and the right support of its worship. The centre of the community's life rests here (cf. also Hag. 1).

If, as seems not improbable, this is where the Chronicler's work really ended, then we may see his answer to the distress uttered in 9.37 in his belief that a faithful worshipping community will in the end be in the way to receive divine blessing and protection.

THE WORK OF NEHEMIAH – II

Nehemiah **11-13**

THE POPULATING OF JERUSALEM

11.1-36

1. The narrative of 7.4 is resumed again here, though only the first two verses of the chapter are on the subject of the repopulating of Jerusalem. With the context of 7.1-3 in mind, we may see that the concern is evidently with the security of city and people, and so here we find the LEADERS living in JERUSALEM (the wording could imply that they 'came to live' in the city), and THE REST OF THE PEOPLE CAST LOTS so that one in ten came to the capital, a sort of tithe of the whole population.

2. This implies that some volunteered to go to Jerusalem, but although it may mark a distinction between those compelled to go because the lot was drawn for them and those who chose to go, it is more probable that no such difference is intended. Those upon whom divine choice has fallen – and the lot was believed to be so controlled – can quite properly be considered as those who accept willingly what God has decreed and are BLESSED for this particular status. The narrative is not concerned with the social problems which such a removal might make.

Incorporated in this is an idea which we may detect in earlier thought. In Amos 5.3; 6.9, the figure of a tenth is used in a proverbial manner with reference to judgment. This seems to be reapplied in Isa. 6.13 with a possible reference to Israel, the north, with ten tribes, contrasted with Judah, the south, with one tribe (on one kind of understanding of the symbol in I Kings 11.31f.). Here a further extension appears to be

309

made: JERUSALEM THE HOLY CITY is a tenth of Judah. The concept of the HOLY CITY may be traced in earlier passages, such as Isa. 48.2.

3-19. The remainder of the chapter contains archival material, with a heading in v.3 covering the inhabitants of both JERU-SALEM and JUDAH. Then lists are given for JERUSALEM, closely related to the list in I Chron. 9 (cf. the notes on pp.43ff). We may note the absence here of any mention of Ephraim and Manasseh in v.4, perhaps accidental, but perhaps reflecting a more exclusive attitude). Judahites and Benjaminites come first, and then PRIESTS, LEVITES and GATEKEEPERS.

21-24. These verses form a short supplement with some additional notes about particular groups and their position. Verse 23 includes an interesting indication of royal (i.e. Persian) PROVISION FOR THE SINGERS.

20. This is the heading for vv.25-36, which concern the inhabitants of JUDAH and provide some important topographical information about the area of the province, though it is by no means certain that this applies to the period of Nehemiah.

The chapter, taking as its starting point the populating of Jerusalem and hence the question of security, goes on to show a wider concern with the community of Judah as a whole, and with that idea of the occupation of the land which is an important element in post-exilic thought.

DEDICATION AND REFORM

12.1-13.3

Three quite distinct sections may be seen in this passage: an important priestly list in 12.1-26; the account of the dedication of the city wall in 12.27-43; summarizing statements of reform in 12.44-13.1.

12.1-26. The first is quite evidently a late addition to the work, its position perhaps prompted by the lists of ch.11. It offers summarizing information concerning the priesthood of the post-exilic period: vv.1-9 PRIESTS and LEVITES of the time of ZERUBBABEL and JESHUA, to which has been appended in vv. 10-11 a genealogy tracing the line of high priests to JADDUA. The chronology is not fully clear, but more evidence appears in a further note on the high priests in v.22, which traces them to the reign of DARIUS THE PERSIAN. We note JESHUA in the period of the rebuilding of the temple; ELIASHIB in the period of Nehemiah, with JOIAKIM conveniently fitting into the seventy years between. The position of JOIADA would bring us in all probability to about 430-420, and JONATHAN (or JO-HANAN) to the end of the century, fitting with Elephantine and with Ezra. His son JADDUA is associated by Josephus with the time of Alexander the Great, Josephus claiming that Jaddua died at about the same time as Alexander; since he could have been very elderly, the chronology is not impossible. Josephus' information about this period is, however, very confused and Jaddua may belong a little earlier. The DARIUS of v.22 could be Darius II (423-404), but that is rather too early; or Darius III (336-331), which fits well with Josephus' information. If we place the Chronicler about 350, then he could have known Jaddua as high priest. Verses 12-21 list priestly families in the time of JOIAKIM, son of Jeshua, and this is supplemented by levitical lists which appear to cover a longer period (vv.22-26). According to the end of this section (v.26), the lists cover the period of JOIAKIM, NEHEMIAH and EZRA; but this looks rather like a resumé designed to suggest that a complete coverage of the period is given – which it evidently is not.

27-43. The second section brings us back to the Nehemiah narrative, and it breaks into the first-person form again for vv.31-43. The context of this is in reality the completion of the wall in 6.15, but the narrator has placed the celebration of dedication as the climax of Nehemiah's work, properly seeing that all else may be regarded as subordinate to this one moment of his achievement. Verses 27-30 may represent a later supple-ment to the narrative, laying the kind of stress on the SINGERS which is more characteristic of the Chronicler's work than of

the Nehemiah narrative. It contains also certain pieces of
archival information in v.29 which link it in some measure
with the lists. It would not be impossible to see this short
section as containing an alternative version of the ceremonial,
which appears to be complete with the ritual of purification
of v.30.

The account in vv.31ff. portrays a great processional ritual.
Two processions are formed, the one followed by HOSHAIAH
AND HALF OF THE PRINCES OF JUDAH (v.32), the other by Nehemiah and the other HALF OF THE OFFICIALS (v.40). Each procession has its list of priests and musicians (vv.33-36 and vv.
41-42), though these are quite differently ordered. The first
procession goes TO THE RIGHT, i.e. southwards along the wall,
and then appears to take a cut through the city BY THE STAIRS
OF THE CITY OF DAVID (v.37) – perhaps the wall-route would be
too steep – to reach THE WATER GATE ON THE EAST; the second
goes TO THE LEFT, i.e. northwards, and a list of points is given,
until eventually the processions meet in the temple (v.40). A
harmonizing note quite inappropriately places EZRA THE SCRIBE
at the head of the first procession (v.36 end), but this is due
to the combining of the Ezra and Nehemiah narratives. The
culmination is in a celebration of rejoicing in the temple. The
repeated emphasis on rejoicing is characteristic of religious
ceremony on such an occasion, and the climax is in the statement that THE JOY OF JERUSALEM WAS HEARD AFAR OFF (v.43),
the counterpart to 6.16, in which the building of the wall
brings awe on the surrounding nations (cf. also Ezra 3.13). It
is not just in the vicinity that this is heard, but by implication
among the surrounding nations.

At this point (v.43) the narrative of Nehemiah comes to a
first conclusion, to be followed in 13.ff. by an account of the
second period of his governorship. All that has been related
belongs only to less than a year of activity, except for the
broader indications in ch.5. But the author of the account has
appropriately concentrated on the most significant moment of
Nehemiah's work, referring to subsequent events only in relation to this building of the wall, the establishment of security
for the people.

The third section contains two loosely linked passages, 12.44-47 and 13.1-3. The introductory ON THAT DAY in each case suggests that the particular reforms mentioned were carried through on the day of the dedication of the wall. But the expression is often used as a loose chronological link, and we may see here a stage in the elaboration of the Nehemiah narrative.

12.44-47. Nothing in the material so far points to Nehemiah as a religious reformer; but here we find attributed to him the organizing of priestly support, the duties of SINGERS and GATEKEEPERS, linked back with the foundation work of DAVID AND ASAPH or DAVID and SOLOMON. It is clear from 12.47 that in reality we have here a summarizing statement about the wider post-exilic period, with a reference to ZERUBBABEL and NEHEMIAH. Here is an idealization of these two leaders, providing a comment on the period as a whole.

13.1-3. A similar process may be observed here, where we somewhat surprisingly find a reading of the law. Nehemiah is not mentioned, though the context suggests a reference to him. The law passage in question is evidently Deut. 23.3ff., slightly modified and interpreted as an injunction to avoid foreign marriages, where originally it is concerned with right of membership of the community. It seems possible that there is here a transfer to Nehemiah of the law-reading tradition belonging in reality to Ezra, or, as perhaps also in 12.44-47, an extension of his functions in such a way as to suggest that he has in some respects a royal status; this appears in some measure in the 'remember' passages (cf. p.285), in his rebuilding activity, for this is often claimed of kings, and here in the upholding of law and in the organization of worship according to the Davidic pattern. The figure of Nehemiah is beginning already to grow, as we may see it growing further in the later material of II Macc. 1.

It is possible that we should see the last verses of ch.13 (vv.30-31) as intended to offer a concluding comment on this. If so, we may wonder whether an original final 'remember me, O my God, for good' has been there expanded with a specific allusion to the removal of foreign elements and the provision of proper duties and wood offering and first fruits as examples of religious reform. The last part of the Nehemiah narrative appears to have been a point at which considerable later expansion has been undertaken.

NEHEMIAH'S SECOND GOVERNORSHIP

13.4-31

A consideration of this section immediately brings to light the frequency in it of the 'Remember' passages (vv.14, 22, 29, 31) by contrast with their rarity in the remainder of the Nehemiah material (only 5.19; 6.14). We have just noted the possibility that the last of these (and the accompanying verse 30) may belong to the ending of the Nehemiah material at 13.3. The use of the repeated pattern three times in the passages concerned with the second stage of Nehemiah's activity may reflect a different handling of the material, a fitting of three separate elements of the tradition into the existing form, with a modified use of this comment now appearing virtually as a refrain. The very loose chronological linkages (vv.4, 15, 23) may represent an attempt at co-ordinating the three sections into what purports to be a coherent account of the second term of governorship. But it is not inconceivable that some part of this material belongs in reality to other moments of his activity, since only the first unit, and here only vv.4-9, is precisely linked to that part of his career. We may also observe some indications of the growth of the Nehemiah tradition, as we have already seen this in 12.44-13.3.

4-9. The occasion of the first part of the first section is provided by the chronological note in v.4: NOW BEFORE THIS, a note which is quite imprecise, but can be regarded as pointing to something which developed during Nehemiah's absence referred to in v.6. But we are not told to what the THIS refers, since it would hardly seem to link back to 13.1-3, and we must probably assume that there was a different original connection.

The particular problem concerns the TOBIAH whose activity
has been drawn out in some passages in chs.1-6 and particularly
in 6.17-19; indeed we might link this passage to those verses
and wonder whether the record of difficulties with Tobiah
there actually belongs to the later stages of Nehemiah's activity.
A specific example of Tobiah's 'connections' with Jerusalem
(cf. 7.18) is here given, though the exact nature of the link
with ELIASHIB is not made clear. Nor do we know who ELIASHIB
was. We might quite properly suppose that since in 13.28
'Eliashib the high priest' is mentioned, this must be another
man of the same name, and this would seem to be confirmed
by the description of his office as OVER THE CHAMBERS OF THE
HOUSE OF OUR GOD. But if we recognize that 13.28 stands in
a passage quite independent of 13.4-9, the first part of the
argument is not valid; the high priest is not invariably given
his full title. Furthermore, we do not know enough about the
priestly offices to say dogmatically that the office here described is a minor one; we could understand it to mean that
Eliashib, in virtue of his office as (high) priest, had ultimate
control of the disposal of temple rooms. At all events, the
situation revealed is one in which the hostility of Nehemiah
to Tobiah is quite evidently not shared by others who have
status in the community. The particular evil which incenses
Nehemiah so greatly appears to be the allocation to secular
use of a room intended for sacral purposes, connected with
various materials for worship and TITHES for levitical support.
In its present context, following on 13.1-3 which refers to
Ammonites and Moabites, the reader, recalling that Tobiah
is called 'the Ammonite slave' (2.10), may suppose that Tobiah
was himself an Ammonite and unacceptable in the temple.
But this is an unwarranted assumption. Tobiah's name, as we
have seen (p.272), suggests that he was a loyal Yahwist. What
appears here is an attitude in sacral matters in which Nehemiah's strictness is contrasted with a greater laxity even among
the priests. Secular use of the room is condemned, the belong-
ings of Tobiah are thrown out, and the room is quite properly
cleansed so that it may be restored to its proper purpose (vv.
8f.). That personal animus against Tobiah was also involved

may be the case, but we are not invited to consider that.

This incident is associated with a second period of governor-ship (vv.6f.). Here (cf. 5.14) we are informed that after a twelve-year period, presumably the fixed term of 2.6, Nehe-miah, back in Persia for an undefined period, is granted a new term of office in Jerusalem. We are not told that he asked for a further term because he had heard of abuses in Jerusalem; indeed the text implies that he found the Tobiah situation only when he arrived. It is more probable that a normal procedure was being followed. Arsames, Persian satrap in Egypt, was absent for three years from 410 to 407; Nehemiah may have been absent for a similar period. At all events he must have returned before the death of Artaxerxes in 424. The point of this narrative is to stress that the governor, by virtue of his authority from the king, has the right to order cultic matters; in this, he is clearly seen as a true successor to the kings of Israel and Judah, though we may observe in the Old Testament narratives some differences of view about the extent of the royal prerogative.

10-13. Now comes a second, comparable example. RSV adds an ALSO to the text, implying an immediate link which may or may not be intended. Perhaps we should rather treat these verses as a related theme, placed here because of the similar content, and perhaps belonging to another situation. This passage concerns what is vividly described in Nehemiah's rhetorical question: WHY IS THE HOUSE OF GOD FORSAKEN? (v.11; cf. 10.39, where the same word is translated 'neglect'). To fail to undertake the proper practices – here the provision of THE PORTIONS OF THE LEVITES (v.10), and, perhaps a second element, the payment and proper care of the tithes (vv.12f.) – is to neglect worship and hence God's house. The LEVITES and SINGERS have been forced to go back to their family pro-perties (v.10) because lack of support prevents their remaining in Jerusalem to perform their duties. This is now properly ordered, with reliable officials in charge (v.13).

14. The two passages together are then provided with a com-ment, in which a prayer for the remembering of THIS is paral-

leled by one that God WIPE NOT OUT MY GOOD DEEDS, i.e.
should not erase their record from his book (cf. Mal. 3.16).
We may note how much fuller a formula is used here than
in the comparable 5.19.

15-22. The second section of the chapter (vv.15-22*a* with its
comment in v.22*b*) again appears to contain two elements.
There is a loose link in the words IN THOSE DAYS in v.15 (cf. on
12.44; 13.1). Verses 15-18 are concerned with work of various
kinds ON THE SABBATH – treading grapes, carrying corn and
other produce, buying and selling. It is first men of Judah who
are involved, and then Tyrian merchants who live IN THE CITY,
engaged in the fish trade (did they perhaps live near the Fish
Gate? cf. 3.3). We see here a problem which inevitably affects
a community which has certain legal or religious requirements
which differ from those of its neighbours. Entirely separate
life makes obedience possible, but this is not practicable.
Where there is any intermingling or contact of groups, difficulties must arise. The breaking of the SABBATH by men of
Judah is one thing. To impose the sabbath law on the non-
Jewish population is another and may well create ill-feeling.
The precise application of such a law is not necessarily a
simple matter to resolve. Here the first stage of action is in an
appeal to the leadership, with a substantial warning of the
consequences, a warning which in its terms is closely reminiscent of that of Ezra in Ezra 9.14; 10.10. We may also see a
relationship to prophetic material, notably Jer. 17.19-27 (often
thought to be later than Jeremiah) and Ezek. 20.12-24. The
sabbath as a prime requirement of faithfulness in Judaism
becomes clearer in post-exilic times, though the basis of the
religious practice is very much older.

Verses 19-22 present a second stage of action, and may be
seen as in some degree a counterpart to 7.1-3; the latter passage, in context, refers to security for the city. But the shutting
of the gates may also be understood in terms of separation.
So it is here, where an attempt at excluding alien influence is
made by the shutting of the city gates before dusk on the
sabbath – the sabbath begins at sunset – and the driving away

of foreign merchants who lodge just outside, perhaps in the hope of tempting Jewish people out to buy and sell. The guarding of the gates is first (v.19) put in the hands of Nehemiah's personal bodyguard, and second (v.22a) in the hands of the Levites. We may perhaps assume that although the Levites would not normally be concerned with the city gates but only with those of the temple (cf. 7.1), the sacral duty of preserving the sabbath would make such an extension of duty proper. Verse 22b elaborates the remembrance form into a fuller prayer for divine favour and forgiveness.

The third section of the chapter also contains two separate elements, vv.23-27 and v.28, with the prayer comment in v.29.

23. Again there is the loose chronological link: IN THOSE DAYS. The first part deals with the effects of inter-marriage, here specified as with WOMEN OF ASHDOD, AMMON AND MOAB.

24. Since the text refers only to the LANGUAGE OF ASHDOD – the rather cryptic BUT THE LANGUAGE OF EACH PEOPLE being in all probability an attempt at harmonization – AMMON and MOAB may be intrusive under the influence of vv.1-3. The national and religious fervour of Nehemiah appears here expressed in a concern for the preservation of the language of Judah, Judahite, a term which may be presumed to indicate the particular form of what we call Hebrew which was spoken in Judah itself (cf. II Chron. 32.18). The mother of the family naturally teaches her children her own language, in this case Ashdodite. Evidence for the use of Aramaic in this period may indicate that Ashdodite was a local form of Aramaic and therefore considerably different from Judahite; or it may be that Ashdodite, from its connections with the Philistines, preserved something of the language mixture which resulted from alien settlers who adopted much of local custom and no doubt of language, but would also have vocabulary and idiom of their own. (The Old Testament preserves at least one clearly Philistine word, *sōren*, for the ruler of a Philistine city [cf. I Sam. 5.8], a word probably connected with the Greek *tyrannos*, ruler.) Such a desire as that of Nehemiah to preserve his native language may be seen in other situations of national upsurge – clearly in the time of Bar Cochba (AD 132-135), probably also in the second century BC under the Maccabees, and in the use of the old Hebrew script for sacred writings in Qumran texts, sometimes for the text, more often for the divine name alone. More modern parallels may also be seen (e.g. in Greece and in Israel) for the revival of an ancient language being linked with national development.

25-27. Nehemiah is described as taking violent action against the culprits and as imposing an oath (cf. 10.28f.). He underlines the point by the example of SOLOMON, using the account which we know from I Kings 11.1ff., a part of the story of Solomon which the Chronicler passes over, though he would know that his readers were aware of it. The argument is that if Solomon, the great king and the BELOVED of God (using a different word but perhaps reminiscent of the naming of Solomon as Jedidiah with just that meaning in II Sam. 12.25), could be led astray by FOREIGN WOMEN, what hope was there of ordinary people avoiding apostasy?

28. This is a special case, concerning a grandson of ELIASHIB, here specifically indicated as HIGH PRIEST. That he had married a daughter of SANBALLAT, governor of Samaria, the arch-opponent of Nehemiah, was clearly sufficient reason for Nehemiah to be suspicious of him and turn him out. This particular detail may well belong to an earlier period of his activity. We may recall (cf. p.272) that there is no valid reason for supposing Sanballat to be anything other than a Yahwist, in view of his naming of his sons with Yahweh-compounds. But by placing the incident here, the compiler of this section is certainly implying that Sanballat was a foreigner with whom a marriage bond, particularly within the high-priestly house, must be regarded as improper (cf. the comments on Ezra 9-10 on pp.261ff.).

29. This comment is concerned, like 6.14, entirely with the negative side of what God is asked to remember. Probably the end of this verse has been overloaded with its reference to

THE PRIESTHOOD AND THE LEVITES, and we should read simply
DEFILED THE PRIESTHOOD AND THE COVENANT, an allusion to
Num. 25.12f., which expounds the nature of the priestly
covenant.

30-31. The story of Nehemiah is now rounded off with what
can be seen as a comment on vv.23-27(28), but more appropriately as a comment on 12.44-13.3. The final prayer is that
the memory of Nehemiah will be preserved; it rests with God
to maintain the memory of a good man. A comparison may be
made with Wisdom of Solomon 3-4, and especially 4.1:

> Better than this is childlessness with virtue, for in the
> memory of virtue is immortality, because it is known both
> by God and by men.